# Bureaucrats and Ministers
# in Contemporary Japanese Government

Copyright © 1986 by the Regents of the University of California
ISBN 0-912966-84-x
Library of Congress Catalog Card Number 85-82273
Printed in the United States of America

INSTITUTE OF EAST ASIAN STUDIES
UNIVERSITY OF CALIFORNIA • BERKELEY
CENTER FOR JAPANESE STUDIES

# Bureaucrats and Ministers in Contemporary Japanese Government

YUNG H. PARK

A publication of the
Institute of East Asian Studies
University of California
Berkeley, California 94720

The Japan Research Monograph series is one of several publications series sponsored by the Institute of East Asian Studies in conjunction with its three constituent units—the Center for Chinese Studies, the Center for Japanese Studies, and the Center for Korean Studies. The others include the China Research Monograph series, whose first title appeared in 1967, the Korea Research Monograph series, and the Research Papers and Policy Studies series. The Institute sponsors also a Faculty Reprint series.

Correspondence may be sent to:
Ms. Joanne Sandstrom, Editor
Institute of East Asian Studies
University of California
Berkeley, California 94720

# Contents

# Preface

This monograph has grown out of a chapter written for a book on the relationship between the ruling Liberal-Democratic party and the governmental bureaucracy. In the course of doing research about these two key institutions of Japanese politics, I came to the conclusion that many of the popular generalizations regarding the cabinet minister and his relations with the agency he heads are gross exaggerations or untested assumptions, overlooking the complexity and extent of what he can to and what he does as an agency chief who is also a popularly elected diet-man of the semipermanent majority party. The popular generalizations are typically drawn from cases of "weak" ministers—supposedly incompetent, inexperienced, and ill-informed politicians, controlled or ignored by assertive, experienced, informed, and policy-initiating bureaucrats. Although "do-nothing" ministers (*banshoku daijin*) have certainly existed and continue to haunt some agencies, many contemporary ministers simply do not fit into the types depicted in the prevailing generalizations.

In these beliefs I am not alone. Muramatsu Michio of Kyoto University argues in his ground-breaking study of Japan's postwar bureaucracy that the contemporary minister's role in agency policy-making is much larger than commonly assumed. He attributes this to a variety of factors, including the minister's personnel power, policy expertise, and political leadership, and the support he has from his cabinet and the majority party.[3] In his 1969 study of the Liberal-Democrats, Nathaniel Thayer stated that although Japan's officialdom had had its share of "chapeau ministers" (figurehead ministers), the key members of any given cabinet, who were "at the heart of the government," were seldom chapeau ministers. They were more likely to be "muscle man ministers."[4] These generalizations, in my estimation, have far greater relevancy today than before. This monograph examines the various factors that have led me to this conclusion about the contemporary

---

[3] Muramatsu Michio, *Sengo nihon no kanryōsei* [The bureaucratic system in postwar Japan] (Tokyo: Tokyo keizai shinpōsha, 1982), p. 194.

[4] Nathaniel Thayer, *How the Conservatives Rule Japan* (Princeton: Princeton University Press, 1969), p. 206.

Japanese minister.

Much of the information contained in this book comes from interviews and informal conversations with nearly two hundred individuals in Japan who at the time of interviewing were, directly or indirectly, involved in and well informed about the various topics and institutions covered in this study. They include

1. Former cabinet ministers;
2. Former parliamentary vice-ministers;
3. Liberal-Democratic party dietmen (both upper-house and lower-house) and their aides;
4. New-Liberal Club (*Shinjiyū kurabu*) dietmen;
5. Members of the staff of LDP organs, including the Policy Affairs Research Council;
6. Members of the staff of Diet upper-house and lower-house committees;
7. Members of the research-reference staff of the National Diet Library; and the late Okabe Shirō who, then deputy director of the National Diet Library, taught me much about Japanese bureaucracy (a former bureau director of the Administrative Management Agency, Mr. Okabe was a foremost authority on Japanese bureaucracy);
8. Career officials (former and incumbent, ranging from administrative vice-ministers to section officials) of central ministries, including Home Affairs, Education, Finance, Foreign Affairs, Health and Welfare, International Trade and Industry, Posts and Telecommunications, Construction, Agriculture-Forestry-Fisheries, and the Cabinet Secretariat;
9. Members of "advisory commissions" (*shingikai*) attached to central ministries;
10. Officials of prefectural governments;
11. Chairmen and staff members of interest groups;
12. Political and social correspondents (former and incumbent) assigned to ministries, the LDP headquarters, and the Diet;
13. Scholars of politics, economics, and education, many of whom served as members of government advisory commissions;
14. Members of governmental research institutes (e.g., the National Institute for Educational Research, affiliated with the Ministry of Education).

Many of the individuals in categories 6, 7, 13, and 14 were former officials of central ministries.

Many interviewed individuals requested anonymity. In many cases the assurance of confidentiality to my sources was necessary to secure their cooperation. Even those who agreed to be identified and quoted in my published accounts requested anonymity on topics that they considered to be sensitive. The "conversations" took place in informal settings with my colleagues, acquaintances, and friends in Japan, who do not or would not want to be identified in my published writings. Although, to protect their anonymity, I do not disclose many of my sources, I wish to express my sincere gratitude to all interviewed individuals, colleagues, and friends who, highly successful in their professions and extremely busy, took time out to see me and enlighten me on many aspects of Japanese bureaucracy and politics. Because the bureaucracy and its interactions with the government party remain largely unexplored and published primary source materials are scarce, my efforts to learn about these pivotal institutions of Japanese politics would have made little progress without the generous support of these individuals in Japan.

Most of the interviews were conducted, and the conversations took place, during my several visits to Japan between 1978 and 1982, including two extended residences. I was supported, financially and otherwise, by a variety of institutions and individuals. They include the California State University Office of International Programs, which permitted me to stay in Japan as director of the California State University's Japan Program, 1978–80; Waseda University, where the California program is situated and I was a visiting professor of Japanese politics, 1978–80; the United States–Japan Friendship Commission, whose grant made available through Waseda University covered much of the expenses incurred in 1978–80; Kyūshū National University (*Kyūshū Daigaku*) Faculty of Law, which extended most generous support to me while I was a visiting research scholar there in 1982; Meiji University Graduate School of Politics and Economics, which in 1980 kindly invited me to share my thoughts on Japanese bureaucracy with its faculty and students and later published my presentation in its monograph series; the Japan Society of Educational Sociology (*Nihon kyōiku shakai gakkai*), which invited me to try out some of my ideas on one of the central ministries (the Ministry of Education) at its 1981 international symposium on Japanese education politics; and Humboldt State University, which generously provided me with sabbatical leaves and grants that enabled me to visit Japan on numerous occasions. I also wish to express my gratitude to the University of California (Berkeley) Center for Japanese Studies, which has given me opportunities to share my research findings with and learn from distinguished members of the center's Faculty Seminar on Contemporary Japan. Many others in Japan and the United States have given me support of various kinds over the years. They include Kibbey M. Horne, Chalmers Johnson, Alvin D. Coox, Uchida Mitsuru, Hashimoto Akira, Arai Ikuo, Soma Masao, Taki Yyoshie, Kimura Shūzō, Maki Masami, Ichikawa Shōgo, Yoko-o Takehide, Umakoshi Tōru, Yoshitake Hiroki, Genjida Shigeyoshi, Katō Eiichi, Muramatsu Michio, Kuroha Ryōichi, Yagi Jun, and Kawanaka Ichigaku. My greatest debt goes to my family (Chikako, Jason, Jennifer, and Emmy) for putting up with me all these years. My special thanks go to Morinaga Katsuji, my father-in-law and formerly a Ministry of Justice official, who has helped me in various ways. Finally, I wish to thank Anne Griffiths for her outstanding editing of the manuscript and Joanne Sandstrom and her competent staff at the Institute of East Asian Studies for seeing it through the labors of production.

# Abbreviations

| | |
|---|---|
| AMA | Administrative Management Agency (*Gyōsei kanrichō*) |
| AVM | Administrative vice-minister (*Jimu jikan*) |
| BESE | Bureau of Elementary-Secondary Education (*Shotōchūtōkyoku*) |
| ED | Education Division (*Bunkyō bukai*) |
| EPA | Economic Planning Agency (*Keizai kikakuchō*) |
| ICES | Investigative Committee on the Educational System (*Bunkyō seido chōsakai*) |
| JAL | Japan Air Lines (*Nihon kōkū*) |
| JMA | Japan Medical Association (*Nihon ishikai*) |
| JNR | Japan National Railway (*Nihon kokuyū tetsudō*) |
| JTU | Japan Teachers Union (*Nikkyōso*) |
| LDP | Liberal-Democratic party (*Jiyūminshutō*) |
| MAFF | Ministry of Agriculture, Forestry, and Fisheries (*Nōrin suisanshō*) |
| MFA | Ministry of Foreign Affairs (*Gaimushō*) |
| MHA | Ministry of Home Affairs (*Jichishō*) |
| MHW | Ministry of Health and Welfare (*Kōseishō*) |
| MITI | Ministry of International Trade and Industry (*Tsūshō sangyōshō*) |
| MOC | Ministry of Construction (*Kensetsushō*) |
| MOE | Ministry of Education (*Mombushō*) |
| MOF | Ministry of Finance (*Ōkurashō*) |
| MOJ | Ministry of Justice (*Hōmushō*) |
| MOT | Ministry of Transport (*Un'yushō*) |
| MPT | Ministry of Posts and Telecommunications (*Yūseishō*) |

NAPSSI            National Association of Public School Superin-
                  tendents of Instruction (*Zenkoku kōritsu gakkō
                  kyōtōkai*)
PARC              Policy Affairs Research Council (*Seimu chōsakai*)
PVM               Parliamentary vice-minister (*Seimu jikan*)
SDA               Self-Defense Agency (*Bōeichō*)
SMEA              Small and Medium-Sized Enterprise Agency
                  (*Chūshō kigyō-chō*)

# I

# Introduction

The major administrative units of the Japanese government under the present constitution are ministries (*shō*) and state agencies (*chō*).[1] A ministry is headed by a minister (*daijin*), and a state agency by a director general (*chōkan*). Formally, however, both are referred to as "state minister" (*kokumu daijin*). Appointed by the prime minister, these state ministers make up the Japanese cabinet, which is entrusted with the state's executive power and responsible to the Diet. According to the Law of the National Administrative Organization (*Kokka gyōsei soshikihō*) and the Law for the National Public Personnel System (*Kokka kōmuinhō*), the minister has broad powers over agency policy-making, policy implementation, expenditures, and personnel. As the legal and administrative chief of his agency, he manages and supervises its officials and their administration of laws and other policies, submits bills and government ordinances (*seirei*) to the cabinet for approval, and issues ministry ordinances (*shōrei*), public notices, (*kokuji*), and communications (*tsūtatsu*). He is the chief decision-maker of the agency, and his approval is required for all agency policies and actions. He is also given the power to appoint and remove agency officials, although he is expected to abide by a merit principle in his personnel decisions, and his high-level appointments (bureau directors and higher) require cabinet concurrence. In short, he is the policy-making and administrative head of his agency.[2]

---

[1] A cabinet-level state agency should not be confused with an agency, also known as *chō*, created within a ministry and headed by a career official rather than a cabinet minister. A specialized office of the ministry, this agency is functionally treated as one of the ministry bureaus and is thus under the administrative direction of the ministry's chief executive, the minister.

[2] These formal powers of the agency chief are given in *Kokka gyōsei soshikihō* [National administrative organization law], Articles 10–16, and *Kokka kōmuinho* [National public personnel law], Article 55.

These are, of course, the legal powers given to the minister. Between this formal prescription and the actuality there is a considerable gap, for in reality he is not able to exercise these powers in toto. Even "formalistic" studies of Japanese politics recognize this discrepancy. The view that has gained wide currency among students of Japanese politics, however, has it that the reality of ministerial powers is the complete opposite of formal principles. Thus, most studies of contemporary Japanese policy-making and bureaucracy tend to treat the minister as an insignificant appendage worthy of no serious consideration. He is depicted as a figurehead who has no substantive powers over the agency he heads. His role is passive and reactive, confined to legitimizing decisions made by the agency's career officials and, at best, to efforts to secure funding for agency programs if he has political muscles of any importance. He assumes the cabinet post ill informed and inexperienced in agency affairs. Perpetually driven by his electoral and partisan imperatives, he has no time to develop even a modicum of policy specialization and is thus helplessly dependent upon his subordinates for information and guidance.

Any minister attempting to deviate from the well-prescribed reactive roles to the detriment of agency interests (as determined by career officials) is quickly dubbed persona non grata and is effectively checked by the bureaucrats. As one scholar put it, "Bureaucrats are capable of punishing a maverick minister or, for that matter, any LDP MP who would incur their ire."[3] Hence it is not surprising that the administrative vice-minister (AVM), the agency's highest career official and the minister's chief deputy, is often portrayed as "No. 1 in real power."[4] In short, the cabinet minister is a powerless transient who simply wears the hat of the ministry for a short period. In the words of one Japanese observer, "An average cabinet minister is little more than the nominal head of his ministry, even when he is endowed with appropriate educational and career credentials."[5]

The generalizations that place the minister in a reactive, subordinate position vis-à-vis the career officials have been abetted by several assumptions. One such assumption is based on the mechanics of Japanese organizational decision making that puts higher officials at the

---

[3] Taketsugu Tsurutani, *Political Change in Japan* (New York: David McKay, 1977), p. 106.

[4] Richard Halloran, "No. 2 Men in Tokyo Ministries Are No. 1 in Real Power," *New York Times,* December 27, 1973.

[5] Tsurutani, *Political Change,* p. 106.

disposal of their subordinates, and the concept of *gekokujō* (rule of senior by junior officials) in which lower officials (*zokkan*), armed with "the tyrannical power of written words," initiate all policy proposals (*ringisho*). When policy proposals reach the higher echelons via all the intermediate levels, the top officials have no choice but to concur with the documents and bless them with legitimacy. "Should the higher executive ignore the protocol of *ringisei* (policy proposal circulation system) and try to assume leadership in this decision making process," according to a prominent Japanese scholar of bureaucracy, "he would be certain to antagonize his associates and create disturbances in the office. There are two alternatives for such a higher executive: either accept exclusion from the office, or accept the conventional methods of *ringisei.*"[6]

This perspective of organizational decision making, as advanced by Tsuji Kiyoaki, has deeply permeated Japanese and American scholarship on Japanese organizations, including governmental ministries. In his 1949 essay, Maruyama Masao portrayed Japan's wartime decision making as one in which lower officials presented their superiors with "the plots" as faits accomplis, which "came to represent the supreme policy of the nation." This phenomenon of *gekokujō* "paradoxically became more and more pronounced as the antidemocratic, authoritarian ideology, centered on the military, began to make headway on all fronts."[7] Robert J. C. Butow, in his book *Tōjō and the Coming of the War,* also expounded on what he called the "puppet politics" of prewar Japan. In his own words:

> The Japan of which General Hideki Tōjō became premier was operated by remote control. It was a country in which puppet politics had reached a high state of development, to the detriment of the national welfare. The ranking members of the military services were the robots of their subordinates—the so-called *chūken shōkō,* the nucleus group, which was active "at the center" and which was composed largely of field-grade officers. They, in turn, were influenced by younger elements within the services at large.[8]

---

[6] Tsuji Kiyoaki, "Decision-making in the Japanese Government: A Study of Ringisei," in *Political Development in Modern Japan,* ed. Robert E. Ward (Princeton: Princeton University Press, 1968), pp. 457–475; and by the same author in Japanese, "Nihon ni okeru seisaku kettei katei" [Process of decision making in Japan], *Shisō,* no. 487 (January 1965), pp. 28–37. See also Nobutaka Ike, *Japanese Politics,* 2d ed. (New York: Alfred A. Knopf, 1972), pp. 7274.

[7] Maruyama Masao, *Thought and Behavior in Modern Japanese Politics* (London: Oxford University Press, 1963), pp. 109–110.

[8] Robert J. C. Butow, *Tōjō and the Coming of the War* (Stanford: Stanford University

Writing about today's ministry policy-making, Nobutaka Ike also has echoed the notion of *gekokujō* by arguing that, contrary to the conventional charts on Japanese organizations suggesting the downward flow of authority, the actual decision-making power is held by low-level officials. In a variation of Tsjui's *ringisei* model, Hosoya Chihiro, a leading student of Japanese foreign policy-making, has identified middle-level officials as the locus of decision making in the foreign-policy agencies, not only in prewar but also in postwar Japan. These officials "took the initiative in making plans and drafted the relevant documents — *ringisho* — by themselves. In this fashion, the flow of influence proceeded from the middle, rather than from the bottom, to the top."[9]

Standing at the apex of this *gekokujō*-based structure is an extremely busy politician who is woefully ill prepared for the office. Inasmuch as the criteria for selecting cabinet officials place much stress upon interfactional balance and seniority, experience and expertise are not always the foremost considerations in ministerial assignments. Take the 1981–82 Suzuki cabinet for illustration. Although many dietmen were given portfolios in their areas of expertise and experience, others were appointed to posts for which they had little professional training. The post of foreign minister went to Sakurauchi Yoshio, a veteran dietman with an extensive background in economic and foreign policy; the Health and Welfare post, to Morishita Motoharu, whose Diet experience included chairmanship of the Social and Labor Affairs Committee; the Economic Planning Agency directorship, to Kōmoto Toshio, a recognized LDP expert in economic policy; and the Agriculture portfolio, to Tazawa Kichirō, an agrobusinessman and former managing director of a prefectural cooperative association (*Nōkyō*). At the same time, Sakata Michita, a veteran dietman versed in education and health-welfare policy, was given the Justice post, and Ogawa Heiji, a businessman-turned-legislator with major experience in fiscal affairs and taxation, was appointed to the Ministry of Education.

The contemporary minister is an elected dietman and a member of the majority party. He also belongs to a variety of intraparty groups, the

  [9] Ike, *Japanese Politics,* pp. 72–73; Hosoya Chihiro, "Characteristics of the Foreign Policy Decision-making System in Japan," *World Politics* 26, no. 3 (April 1974): 360–563. For a recent *gekokujō*-based account by a MITI official of prewar and postwar Japanese policy-making, see Doi Masao, *Gekokujō: sanbōhonbu to gendai seiji* [Rule of seniors by juniors: the General Staff Office and contemporary politics] (Tokyo: Nihon kōgyō shimbunsha, 1982).

foremost of which is his faction. The political and legislative role he is expected to perform has myriad claims on his time and energy, and as the widely held notion of "ministerial impotence" goes, he simply has neither time nor energy to effectively perform his role as agency chief. He spends hours in Diet hearings and cabinet, party, and factional meetings. Boning up on answers to possible questions from the critical opposition in the Diet consumes a great deal of his time. Poor legislative performance—a disgrace to his agency, the cabinet, and the constituency—is also highly frowned upon by his party. Repeated poor showings will invite not only chidings by the prime minister but also a warning from the party's Executive Board (*Sōmukai*), a "watchdog agency" over cabinet members.[10] A poor Diet record may even keep him from obtaining another ministerial post or any major party post. Moreover, he has to perform an infinite variety of duties to nurse his constituency and its major interests, such as weekly visits to his district and meetings with interest group representatives.

The typical Japanese minister's term of office is lamentably short, and this brevity is widely cited as a major reason for his weakness in the agency. Because of frequent cabinet shuffles, a minister seldom stays in office more than twelve months, hardly enough time to get acquainted with agency personnel and workings, not to mention initiating and pushing through a major policy program.[11] Thus, the conservative bureaucrats are much tempted to withhold agency secrets and policy issues from an activist minister who might interfere with agency affairs. Moreover, the minister is viewed as unable to exercise his appointment power over agency personnel. It has been widely asserted that personnel decision making is one key prerogative jealously guarded by the career bureaucrats, never shared with any "outsiders." Hence, many have argued that the minister never manages to penetrate the thick curtain separating him from the rest of the agency.

Contemporary policy issues are increasingly complex and require trained and specialized personnel to deal with them. This situation vastly enhances the minister's dependence on the bureaucrats for information and technical details and for bill drafting. Without a staff of his own, the Japanese minister is far more dependent upon the bureaucrats than his American and French counterparts, who are aided in their policy-making roles by their personal staff of experts and advisers—a

---

[10] Interview with Murakawa Ichirō, senior staff member of the LDP Policy Affairs Research Council, August 23, 1976.

[11] Interview with Kaifu Toshiki, April 27, 1979. Kaifu is a former education minister.

counteradministration, so to speak. The Minister's Secretariat (*Daijin kanbō*), encompassing several staff organs composed of career officials, like other offices of the ministry, is the staff office for the ministry rather than for the minister. According to a recent survey of eight central ministries, a majority of the officials interviewed cited "technical" and "legal" difficulties as the two most effective arguments against the minister's policy proposals.[12] In technical and legal expertise the minister is markedly deficient and needs bureaucratic help the most. In initiating a new policy, therefore, a major hurdle he has to overcome is to deal with legal and technical problems raised by officials of the ministry and other agencies (e.g., the Cabinet Bureau of Legislation). He must also anticipate and deal with clientele groups' reactions. Funding has to be secured, which is by no means an easy undertaking. LDP approval must be sought if the proposal originated outside the party. All these things must be completed within the short time available to him. It is no wonder that, as a former bureau director put it, "a minister can accomplish, at most, one thing during his tenure."[13]

In his policy-making role, the minister is also restrained by what Morton Halperin calls "the essence of the organization"—the definition that the organization's career officials give to its purposes and scope of activities. It is a key determinant of organizational decision making. Policy proposals generated within the organization are likely to be in accord with the organizational essence; those inconsistent with the organizational essence, imposed from outside (e.g., by the prime minister or an LDP organ), will be resisted, even vigorously.[14] In the Ministry of Education (MOE), considered a "conservative agency," ministry officials tend to define their organizational mission more narrowly than MITI (Ministry of International Trade and Industry) bureaucrats, who in the words of a former MITI AVM, have "a large appetite for new policies."[15] They are reluctant to take on additional functions or activities incidental to their ministerial mission, prompting many interviewed LDP dietmen and even MOE officials to remark that the agency is deeply afflicted—much more so than many other agencies—with the so-called

---

[12] Muramatsu Michio, *Sengo Nihon no kanryōsei*, p. 195.

[13] Interview with Miyaji Shigeru, president of Fukuyama University, March 10, 1980. Miyaji headed several bureaus in the Ministry of Education in the 1960s.

[14] Morton Halperin, "The Presidency and the Bureaucracy," in *The System*, ed. Charles Peters and James Fallows (New York: Praeger, 1976), pp. 9–22.

[15] Yoshihisa Ojimi, "Government Ministry: The Case of the Ministry of International Trade and Industry," in *Modern Japanese Organization and Decision-making*, ed. Ezra Vogel (Berkeley: University of California Press, 1975), p. 104.

*kotonakare shugi* (don't-rock-the-boat mentality).[16]

Reasons for this are easily found. Education policy, given its long-lasting impact upon society as a whole, requires prudence on the part of policymakers. Moreover, the contemporary Japanese education polity is polarized and ridden with deep ideological conflicts, far more so than any other domestic-policy system. This conflictual character dates back to the 1950s when the conservative party launched the controversial "reverse course" program and the efforts to weaken the vehemently antigovernment Japan Teachers Union (JTU). Today, any major education policy issue of a nonincremental nature invariably provokes a serious confrontation with such vociferous groups as the JTU and the Association of National Universities (*Kokuritsu daigaku kyōkai*). Understandably, therefore, the career-conscious MOE official shuns a confrontation during which, in case of mishap, he is likely to be made the scapegoat or pay dearly.

Then there is the organization's "policy current" or "policy direction" (*seisaku no nagare*) (a former central bureaucrat likens it to the "movement of a gigantic ship"),[17] which also has a powerful conservatizing influence upon agency policy-making. Just as the Ministry of Foreign Affairs (MFA) was influenced in its China policy of the 1960s by its postwar policy *nagare* of cooperating with the United States, so the MOE, whose postwar policy current centered on "setting up and consolidating the 6–3–3 school system," has tended to be cool to proposals calling for restructuring of the educational system.[18] Kaifu Toshiki, a former education minister, noted: "The education minister must conform to the *nagare* of education policy. If every minister rejects the *nagare* and wants to do things his way, there will be nothing but confusion in the education policy system."[19] A former MOE bureau director put it differently in his comments on Ōdachi Shigeo, an activist minister of

---

[16] This view is shared by those who have worked with MOE officials. For example, take Asari Keita, a noted stage director. After serving on an MOE advisory council, he said: "The press portrays bureaucrats as evil. This is the impression we get from the newspapers, to say the least.... The bureaucrats are not evil; rather, they are timid. Are they timid about everything? They are so toward things that they are not used to or that are widely considered impossible to achieve." *Asahi shimbun,* June 1 and 2, 1974 (hereafter *Asahi*).

[17] Imamura Taketoshi, "Kyōiku gyōsei zakkan" [Thoughts on educational administration], *Kyōiku iinkai geppō,* no. 333 (May 1978), p. 10.

[18] Interview with Iwama Eitarō, former administrative vice-minister of education, February 29, 1980.

[19] Interview with Kaifu Toshiki, April 27, 1979. Kaifu served as deputy chief of the Cabinet Secretariat and chairman of the LDP Diet Strategy Committee before assuming the Education portfolio (1976–77).

education of the early 1950s whose accomplishments included the passage of the controversial 1954 twin laws limiting teachers' political activity: "In attaining his policy objectives...he was aided by the fact of
Japan being in a transitional period. He was a minister during a turbulent era (*ran no jidai*). Nowadays, ministers are serving the peaceful
Japan and do not have much to do, for things are run rather routinely.
After all, a hero comes into being during a turbulent era."[20]

Admittedly, many of the aforementioned factors governing the
minister's relations with the bureaucracy are real; they are significant
checks upon his powers and policy-making role. Other supposed limitations, however, are gross exaggerations, untested assumptions, or conclusions drawn from highly selective, atypical cases. Also, the restraints on
the minister are more effective on certain types of minister than on others. In other words, they are by no means universal, for they can be and
are overcome by assertive, competent, and experienced ministers who
perceive themselves as activist leaders determined to achieve their policy
goals.

In short, the interpretations that allow the minister only a minor
role in agency decision making apply largely to weak ministers; they do
not take into account the powerful ministers who have reigned in not
only such partisanized agencies as the MOE but also such bureaucratic
giants as the Ministry of Finance (MOF) and MITI. Thus, valid generalizations about the contemporary Japanese minister must include state-
ments about activist ministers. The Japanese minister should then appear less diminutive and impotent than he does in much of the contemporary literature.[21]

This study takes issue with the popular characterization of the
Japanese minister as what Bruce W. Headey calls a "minimalist"—a
figurehead who, manipulated and controlled by the career officials, only
goes through the motions of administrative leadership. Undoubtedly,
postwar Japan has seen many minimalist ministers come and go, but the
contemporary cabinet minister and his role cannot be explained solely by
the minimalist notion. He performs a far more powerful and complex
role than is widely assumed in the so-called bureaucratic dominance
thesis (although any conceptualization that highlights only what Headey

---

[20] Interview with Miyaji Shigeru, March 10, 1980.

[21] Muramatsu Michio of Kyoto University is one of the very few Japanese political
scientists who argue that the powers of the contemporary Japanese minister have been un-
derestimated. Muramatsu takes issue with "the notion widely held by [Japanese] political
scientists that all policy decisions of every ministry are bureaucratic products and that the
minister is powerless." See his *Sengo Nihon no kanryōsei*, p. 194.

refers to as the "policy initiating" role would be an exaggeration of his powers and abilities.)[22] For this reason, any study of agency policy-making, whether a general or a case study, that leaves out the role and place held by the agency minister or ministers will be unable to unravel the full complexities of policy-making.

The present study is limited in its aim and scope and makes no pretense to be a comprehensive treatment of the topic. Many questions regarding the contemporary minister remain unanswered. It is hoped, however, that this monograph will contribute to expanding our knowledge of the cabinet minister, one of the most underrated institutions of the contemporary Japanese political system.

---

[22] For Headey's typology of British cabinet ministers, see his "A Typology of Ministers: Implications for Minister–Civil Servant Relations in Britain," in *The Mandarins of Western Europe: The Political Role of Top Civil Servants,* ed. Mattei Dogan (New York: John Wiley, 1975), pp. 63–86.

# II

# Contemporary Bureaucracy: A Haven for *Gekokujō?*

*Ringisei* is one of the most misunderstood features of Japanese organization; it has engendered many myths and erroneous assumptions. As a limitation upon the higher echelons of bureaucracy, it is not only exaggerated but also grossly misunderstood by Tsuji and others who fail to take into account a variety of important factors that bolster the superiors' powers in the politics of agency decision making. Thus, the notion of *gekokujō* or *zokkan seiji* (rule by lower officials), based on the concept of *ringisei,* is an inadequate, if not misleading, portrayal of the power structure of contemporary Japanese bureaucratic organizations. All interviewed officials and former cabinet members reject much of the Tsuji argument, although it has a large following among the Japanese academicians interviewed. From the interview responses and other sources, several basic and interrelated shortcomings of the *ringisei*-based notion of *gekokujō* can be identified.

Perhaps the most glaring weakness inherent in the *gekokujō* argument is that it ignores one key development of post-1955 Japanese politics—the centralization of power within the policy-making units of bureaucracy. This phenomenon has affected not only such traditionally authoritarian agencies as the MOE but also MITI, noted for its intraorganizational democracy. The conventional model of organizational decision making in Japan, especially as it applies to government bureaucracy, views the division (*ka*) and its subunits—sections (*kakari*) and teams (*han*)—as the foremost organs responsible for initiating and drafting agency policy. The division is seen as the hub or linchpin of activity in its area of specialization.

The late Okabe Shirō, a former bureau director in the Administrative Management Agency (AMA) and a leading authority on public administration, characterized the division as "the key unit responsible for working out details (*gutaika*) of ministry policy and measures." It is "at the division level that even policy proposals initiated by the AVM or bureau director strike root."[1] Hashiguchi Osamu, one of the celebrated MOF graduates, concurs with Okabe, stressing the central role performed by division chiefs (*kachō*) in agency decision making. In his own words, "Agency policy in the MOF... is largely determined at the division chief level." As head of this key policy-making unit, the division chief enjoys numerous advantages over his superiors. As Hashiguchi puts it:

> Up-to-date information and data are submitted to him first. It is only natural that the first person to obtain information is the one to make the most of it. He is the first to screen policy drafts and compositions prepared by the division's deputy chiefs (*kachō hosa*). Hence the division chief's job is bound to be enjoyable. He is the one to determine whether or not his information should be shared with his superiors—bureau director and deputy director. Thus, it would not be too difficult for him to monopolize the information and keep his superiors in the dark if he wanted to be sinister.[2]

Hashiguchi's observation is shared by former MAFF official Takeuchi Naokazu, who adds:

> The bureau director is all alone, but the division chief has his own troops—members of the division. When supported by them, he is absolutely powerful. In view of the system under which the bureau director can instruct his bureau staff solely through the division chiefs, the only way for the superior to have his views communicated [to the staff] is to replace the division chief [who is not cooperative].[3]

To endow the division chief with a near-absolute power, as Hashiguchi and Takeuchi do, however, not only overstates the middle-level official's power but also underestimates the policy role of his superiors (bureau directors and even the AVM), which has steadily grown over the years and especially after 1955, when the conservatives merged to form the LDP. Notice what the bureaucrat-turned-dietman Kakizawa Kōji said about MITI, which he called "the home of the rule of seniors by juniors" (*gekokujō no honba*): "Hardly heard of late are the loud, authoritative voices of junior officials." This is a dramatic contrast to the earlier agency tradition that allowed "the outspoken junior officials unhesitatingly to stand up to anyone and even their bureau director."[4]

---

[1] Okabe Shirō, *Gyōsei kanri* [Administrative management] (Tokyo: Yūhikaku, 1970), p. 154.

[2] Hashiguchi Osamu, *Shinzaisei jijō* [New financial situation] (Tokyo: Saimuru shuppankai, 1977), p. 224.

[3] Takeuchi Naokazu, *Konna kanryō wa yameteshimae* [Bureaucrats of this type should quit] (Tokyo: Nisshin hōdō shuppanbu, 1978), p. 145.

[4] Kakizawa Kōji, "Taikenteki gendai kanryōron" [An empirical view of contemporary

Yasujima Hisashi, former MOE bureau director and now an aide to the emperor, also noted that the powers of MOE division chiefs and their deputies "had undergone a major change over the years." As he put it:

> When I was a young deputy division chief in the early 1950s, I thought I was a big shot, and my immediate superior, the division chief, had much discretionary power. Starting in the mid-1950s..., however, the division chief and his assistants have become increasingly restricted in what they can do and cannot do, and consequently the bureau director's responsibilities have expanded considerably.[5]

This observation was endorsed by another former ranking MOE official, Iwama Eitarō, who in his comparisons between the earlier years of his career and the 1970s went as far as to say that "nowadays, not only in big matters but also even in small matters, bureau directors and deputy directors (*shingikan*) must get involved."[6]

What has caused this development of greater high-level participation in agency policy-making? At least two major contributory factors can be identified. One is the growth in the scope and complexity of bureaucratic activities that Japan has experienced in postwar years, as many other competitive societies have. This growth has mitigated the traditional autonomy of intraagency units (e.g., divisions) in Japan by creating what Francis Rourke calls "an irresistible need for coordination of effort that can only be achieved by vesting authority over decision making in the higher ranks of authority." This need was given an additional impetus as Japan entered the era of growing budgetary constrictions in the 1970s, for the subordinate units, left to themselves, "cannot escape duplication of effort or the pursuit of contradictory objectives," as Rourke notes. Duplication was something that no agency could afford because of the increasing budgetary limitations the MOF placed on

---

bureaucrats], *Chūō kōron* 91, no. 10 (October 1976): 268. Kusayanagi Daizō, a veteran journalist who has long specialized in governmental ministries, offers similar impressions of MITI in his *Kanryō ōkokuron* [A study of the bureaucratic kingdom] (Tokyo: Bungei shunjū, 1975), pp. 252–277. For insiders' accounts of the powerful role of high-level officials, see Saitō Taijun, *Bunkyō gyōsei ni miru seisaku keisei katei no kenkyū* [A study of policy-making as seen in educational administration] (Tokyo: Gyōsei, 1984), pp. 34–35. Saitō is a high-ranking (deputy bureau director–level) MOE official. See also discussions by Matsushita Yasuo, a former MOF AVM, in Nihon keizai shimbunsha, ed., *Jimintō seichōkai* [The LDP Policy Affairs Research Council] (Tokyo: Nihon keizai shimbunsha, 1983), pp. 182–183.

[5] Interview with Yasujima Hisashi, February 29, 1980. Yasujima headed many MOE bureaus, including the Elementary-Secondary Education Bureau, before his appointment to the post of director of the MOE's Cultural Agency (*Bunkachō*), his last MOE post.

[6] Interview with Iwama Eitarō, February 29, 1980.

governmental spending.[7]

Another important factor, far more significant than the previous one, that has contributed to elevating decision-making power to the higher echelons is the decline of bureaucratic power vis-à-vis other sectors of Japanese politics, and especially the "political authorities" (the LDP, its policy-making organs, and its dietmen in the government such as the prime minister and cabinet ministers) who have consecutively ruled the nation for nearly thirty-six years. This has lead to the "politicization" and "partisanization" of higher officials and their role as principal intermediaries between the bureaucracy and the political sectors. In the increasingly pluralistic polity, an agency policy, to be authorized and implemented, must be acceptable to the key sectors of politics, and especially the party in power and its representatives in government. An agency decision not taking into account the party's inputs and anticipated reactions will simply not "fly" with the party and its policy organs. For this reason, all agencies maintain various mechanisms of active communication with the party. In the career bureaucracy, the pivotal role in party-agency interactions is assumed by bureau directors and, less frequently, by the AVM.

Several interviewed officials, including one affiliated with the powerful MOF Budget Bureau, characterized the high-level contingent of bureau directors, deputy directors (*shingikan*), and the AVM as the most politicized, partisanized segment of the agency's career bureaucracy. A number of factors account for this. Ever since their days as division chiefs, and even as deputy division chiefs in the case of a major staff division (e.g., general affairs, personnel, and budget-accounting, the three top divisions of the Minister's Secretariat), they have been in constant contact with key members of their corresponding (PARC) division. Thus, they are intimately familiar with the party dietmen's basic orientations and their views on major policy issues. Moreover, they are the ones who regularly see the party's two representatives in the agency—the minister and the parliamentary vice-minister (*seimu jikan*; PVM). From these interactions with the political authorities, the higher officials acquire a great deal of "political knowledge" and thus are in the best position among the career officials to answer key political questions such as Where does the minister stand on the issue under consideration? Will he support the agency position in cabinet, party, and Diet meetings? If not,

---

[7] For discussions by Rourke of the relationship between the need for policy coordination and centralization of decision making, see his *Bureaucracy, Politics, and Public Policy,* 2d ed. (Boston: Little, Brown, 1976), pp. 129 and 144.

can he be persuaded into going along with the agency position? Will the party committees and factions endorse and support the agency bill if it is brought up in the Diet now? Is the agency's draft bill sufficiently reflective of party views? How would the Diet and the opposition parties react to it? What will be the reactions of the public and the press? What about the clientele groups? What about the traditional foes and critics of the agency (e.g., the Japan Teachers union for the MOE)? Furthermore, "the higher officials are markedly sympathetic and amenable to party views," as an MOF division chief put it, "although their juniors are quite legalistic and *tatemae* (principle)-oriented on many policy issues." He went on to note:

> The junior officials tend to look at a policy proposal not only in terms of its acceptability to their superiors but also from legalistic and budgetary perspectives. The first question the higher officials raise, however, is political; it pertains to the extent to which the proposed bill endorses and supports party interests.

This pro-LDP orientation of the higher officials, notwithstanding their vigorous public denial of it, is understandable because their political fortunes are intimately linked with those of the conservative party. "If the Socialists were to come to power now," as an interviewed LDP dietman put it, "they [higher officials] would be the first to have to go." The higher officials' pro-LDP orientation is also a function of their long association with the party dietmen, who are more involved in high-level agency personnel decisions than in lower appointments. As former MOF bureau director Imai Kazuo observed, an official's partisanization is directly proportional to his post. The higher he moves up, the more partisanized he gets.[8]

An interviewed dietman noted, and others agreed, that "the bureau director is the only responsible and authoritative official speaking for his bureau on matters within its jurisdiction; division chiefs cannot speak for their bureau with authority. Even on matters under their jurisdiction they cannot speak definitively without first checking with their bureau director. So we don't want to waste our time with lowly officials." According to a former MOE bureau director interviewed, however, the sit-

---

[8] *Imai Kazuo-shi danwa sokkiroku* [Stenographic records of interviews with Mr. Imai Kazuo], no. 14 (June 18, 1975), p. 166. This *danwa sokkiroku* was published as part of the ongoing oral history project under the sponsorship of *Naiseishi kenkyūkai* (Research Committee of Domestic History), Tokyo. These published interviews are available at leading Japanese university libraries including the Library of Kyūshū University Law Faculty whose copies I used.

uation was quite different in the early 1950s. As he put it:

> When I was division chief in the 1950s, I often represented my agen-
> cy in dealing with the party organs and dietmen, but nowadays, if a
> division chief showed up at a party meeting slated to take up a
> measure of some importance, they would scream: "Go and get your
> bureau director. We need him." Thus, no bureau director would
> dare to send his division chief as his proxy to a party meeting. I
> think this trend started in the second half of the 1950s, after the
> LDP was formed.

Not only in the partisanized MOE but also in other agencies, the
typical pattern is for the appropriate bureau director to represent his
agency at PARC meetings, although he is usually accompanied by his
courtiers, including division chiefs and even deputy division chiefs.
Again, it is the bureau director, not the division chief, who is responsible
for efforts to persuade the party and its minister on the merits of a proposed agency policy.

The representational and intermediary role expected of the bureau
director is taken very seriously by all interviewed bureau chiefs; they all
consider it to be the foremost of the roles they perform. The "political"
role requires familiarity with not only the contents and implications of a
proposed policy but also the basic orientations and pulses of all divisions
they are responsible for. Hence, it has placed enormous burdens on the
contemporary bureau directors, whose predecessors of the 1950s "had
quite a comfortable bureaucratic life," as an official put it. He went on
to observe:

> The present-day bureau director is expected to know everything go-
> ing on in his bureau and divisions. In the meetings [with the ap-
> propriate PARC division], he is expected to respond in one way or
> another to party questions, requests, and suggestions. Before he can
> say, "Yes, we can do it," he should be familiar with what goes on in
> the offices under his jurisdiction—their abilities and limitations. If
> he keeps saying, "Well, I have to check with my people on that," or
> "At this point, I don't know enough to make any judgment on that
> issue," he will be marked as an incompetent superior (*jōshi*), who
> does not keep tabs on his subordinates and does not do his home-
> work. If he repeatedly goes against the commitments made to the
> party because he later finds that for some reasons the division in
> charge cannot carry them out, he will still be considered incom-
> petent.

Even when he is accompanied by his aides from the appropriate divisions, he "cannot always turn to them for answers [to questions from the
dietmen], unable to handle them on his own." If he did this, he "would

look very bad compared to another bureau director who has answers to all the questions raised and can make commitments that he later lives up to." Not only will this competent director be remembered for future promotions but also he will be held in greater confidence by the party. He will be known as "an official with good connections with the party" (*tō tono paipu ga futoi hito*).

The combination of expanded jurisdiction and heightened accountability imposed on bureau directors has had centralizing and hierarchical influences on the organizational culture of the bureaucracy. Higher officials are expected to hold a tight rein on the activities of their subordinates, and lower officials are required to keep their superiors informed of every major development within their administrative units. There can be no major surprises for the bureau director as he testifies before Diet and LDP committees and confers with the minister. As one MOE official put it, "The growing policy involvement of the LDP has caused a closer bottom-to-top communication in our agency." This pattern is not confined to the MOE and other highly partisanized agencies; it is noticeable even in such agencies as MITI, noted for the independence of its spirited junior officials.[9] It is not surprising, therefore, that although the Japanese polity as a whole has become markedly competitive and pluralistic, its governmental bureaucracy has increasingly taken on the characteristics of what Victor Thompson calls "monistic organizations."[10]

Because of the monocratization that has gradually permeated his agency, the bureau director finds his division chiefs cooperative, although some "do not readily give in to their superiors, as in the case of the rule-oriented officials of the Taxation Agency [of the MOF]."[11] In dealing with his immediate subordinates, he is aided by a variety of factors—not only his own experience, expertise, authority, and personnel power, but also the politicization and partisanization of the middle-level officials themselves, albeit not to the degree that has affected bureau directors and AVMs. Upon becoming deputy chief in a major division,

---

[9] Kusayanagi, *Kanryō ōkokuron,* pp. 252–277.

[10] For Thompson's monistic organization, see his *Modern Organization,* 2d ed. (Alabama: University of Alabama Press, 1977), pp. 73–77. Unlike Thompson's "monistic" formulation (Max Weber called it "monocratic" organization), which conceptualizes organization entirely in terms of hierarchy, the contemporary Japanese bureaucracy is of course based on interactions of hierarchy and specialization. The basis of the bureau director's power includes not only his authority but also his knowledge and expertise that come from his service of more than thirty consecutive years in the same agency.

[11] Interview with a deputy division chief of the Taxation Agency, the Ministry of Finance, February 13, 1970.

a career official starts accompanying his bureau director to party and Diet meetings, as previously noted. When he becomes chief of a key division, he becomes an important advisory member or resource person of the bureau director's contingent at all party and Diet gatherings. Here his major interactions with influential members of the relevant PARC division occur; at this stage of his career his politicization commences. As a former MOF ranking official put it, "Nowadays, even chiefs of principal divisions have to wag their tails to the party to some extent." This is inevitable because "in reality," in the official's words, "the party intervenes in personnel decisions involving not only bureau directors but also senior division chiefs. He goes on to say:

> Party intervention in [ministry] personnel matters is an inevitable consequence of the contacts between the party and major division chiefs. A key point of interactions is party-agency breakfast sessions [where relevant division chiefs must be present, along with their bureau directors]. The party's personnel power has gradually corrupted government officials. I am not denying that there are some officials with strong backbones, but on the whole, the officials have become progressively weak.[12]

As widely acknowledged by interviewed officials, therefore, the contemporary division chief is far less likely than his predecessors of the 1950s to "buck" his superiors' policy directives honoring their commitments to the party. He usually complies with them—has a policy document drafted by his deputy in line with a directive and sends it up for approval by his superiors, including the minister and the PARC division.

The eminence of the higher officials in contemporary bureaucratic policy-making rests not only on their experience and expertise and the increasingly centralized setting of their agency but also on the powerful role hierarchy plays in agency policy-making.

Deeply imbued in numerous studies of policy-making is the notion that it is a "rational" process in which authority and hierarchy assume no major role; it is seen as an act among reasonably equal actors who are carefully guided by objective data in their groping for solutions to given problems. Because, in Tsuji's scheme, the lower officials who initiate and prepare all *ringi* documents have data and skill necessary to bill drafting, they really dominate policy-making. This concept is well echoed in the celebrated articulation by the MOF bureaucrat-turned-dietman Kondō Tetsuo: "The MOF is the embodiment of logic."[13]

---

[12] *Imai Kazuo-shi danwa sokkiroku,* no. 15 (November 5, 1975), p. 124; no. 14 (June 18, 1975), p. 93; and no. 15, p. 166.

[13] Cited in Kusayangai, *Kanryō ōkokuron,* p. 323.

In reality, however, decision making cannot always be explained in terms of the so-called rational calculation model. It is also what a Japanese scholar calls "an intuitive (*chokkanteki*) process."[14] It is affected by such non-rational factors as bravery, honor, or pride, as stingingly brought home in Tōjō Hideki's famous exhortation to Konoe Fumimaro, "Sometimes a man will find it necessary to jump from the veranda of Kiyomizu Temple, with his eyes closed, into the ravine below."[15]

Moreover, Kondō needs to be reminded that the MOF's logic, however brilliant it may be, can be and is often suppressed by the requirements of authority and hierarchy. As any MOF budget officer should know, the facts and logic laboriously worked out by budget examiners can be and are often struck down by a simple stroke of the Budget Bureau director's pen. As Victor Thompson has noted, "Modern bureaucracy attempts to fit specialization into the older hierarchical framework." Hence, agency policy-making is by no means dominated by skilled bureaucrats; they are often subordinated to the commands of hierarchical superiors who, without equal technical competence, have authority—"the right to decide."[16] In other words, agency policy-making is politics among actors of unequal ranks.[17] Because of the "inequality of power inherent in hierarchy," in the words of Francis Rourke, "the views of highly placed individuals carry immense weight, not because of the persuasiveness of their arguments, but simply because of the exalted status from which they speak. Subordinates may have to go along with policy decisions reached at higher levels even when they know that their superiors are wrong."[18]

In all ministries of Japan, intraagency socialization places strong emphasis on the overriding importance of hierarchy, seniority, and deference to superiors to a degree not found in other democracies. "It is true," as Nobutaka Ike has observed, "that all bureaucracies are hierarchically organized; but one gets the impression that the sense of

---

[14] Interview with Yoko-o Takehide, April 15, 1980. A former professor of comparative education at Hiroshima University, Yoko-o is deputy director of the National Institute for Educational Research, the Ministry of Education.

[15] Translated from the text cited in Butow, *Tōjō*, p. 267.

[16] Thompson, *Modern Organization*, p. 6.

[17] This orientation was conspicuous in the comments made by many interviewed former ministers, including Okuno Seisuke, Hasegawa Takashi, Kaifu Toshiki, and Naitō Takasaburō. For discussions by scholars, see Muramatsu, *Sengo Nihon*, pp. 193–197, and Rourke, *Bureaucracy*, pp. 131–132.

[18] Rourke, *Bureaucracy*, p. 131.

hierarchy is particularly acute in the Japanese instance."[19] Commenting on the bureaucracy of MITI, noted for its intraagency egalitarianism, Chalmers Johnson was prompted to note, "This age grading *(nenkō joretsu)* and 'respect for seniority' *(nenji sonchō)* among bureaucrats influences everything they do, not just their activities in a ministry."[20] Former MOF bureau director Imai Kazuo relates how a lower official who covered his office desk with his personal green tablecloth—a standard governmental issue to higher officials—became a subject of much discussion and later had to take it back home. Imai also recalls how an official was transferred because his child, who was in the same class in school as his superior's child, had performed better scholastically.[21] When Ōba Tetsuo, then president of All-Nippon Airways, appeared as a witness before a Diet committee investigating the Lockheed scandal in 1976, "he shook with barely controlled anger under questioning." The explanation, according to the press, was that the dietman interrogating Ōba was his former junior in the Ministry of Transportation (MOT), and "he was overcome by the impudence of a junior questioning a senior."[22]

These cultural and organizational traits significantly affect agency policy-making, as recalled by former MOE bureau director Imamura Taketoshi. In a poignant commentary on his life in the bureaucracy, Imamura characterizes the typical superior as "making unreasonable demands on his subordinates" and, "without shared experiences, making differing assessments of a situation." He notes, "Man is an emotional animal; the more ill informed his superior is, the more he is given to bullying" his subordinates. He goes on to say:

> "Being a subordinate" is not fun either. There are superiors of all types. You can resist an unlawful order by citing evidence to the contrary, but orders are seldom illegal. You are bound to feel from time to time that an order, though legal, could stand on better judgment. Of course, you may speak out, but it is not as easy as it may seem.
>
> You are worried that if you express your thoughts your superior may think, "This young punk is putting himself on an equal footing with me," and upbraid you. On the other hand, if you keep your thoughts to yourself, you are frustrated. It is difficult to calculate the

[19] Ike, *Japanese Politics,* p. 150.

[20] Chalmers Johnson, *MITI and the Japanese Miracle* (Stanford: Stanford University Press, 1982), p. 59.

[21] Imai Kazuo, *Kanryō sono seitai to uchimaku* [Bureaucrats: their mode of life and behind-the-scenes activities] (Tokyo: Yomiuri shimbunsha, 1953), pp. 57–61.

[22] Johnson, *MITI,* p. 59.

advantages and disadvantages inherent in the methods for stating your views.

When I disagreed with my superiors, I quietly complied with him in five out of ten cases, and in four cases I expressed my views. Only in one case did I argue vigorously against [my superior], set my own course, and nearly succeed in faithfully following it, but I would not say it was a great success.[23]

In short, hierarchy is a powerful force that propels organizational policy-making toward the views firmly held by the superiors; it becomes a greater force when data available to the policymakers is inconclusive. Expertise and knowledge are allowed their full potentials in an egalitarian setting and when they are not questioned.[24]

This centralized, politicized, and hierarchical milieu of bureaucracy governs the politics of agency decision making on important and controversial policy issues. Over minor, routine policy matters, the democratic, dispersed process that Tsuji calls *ringisei* prevails. In other words, the "tyranny of written words" supposedly allowed to lower officials under *ringisei* applies only to minor, routine policy matters, which "occupy well over 90 percent of bureaucratic decisions" and for which prior approval by higher officials is hardly necessary.[25] As far as big matters are concerned, as former MOE AVM Kobayashi Yukio put it: "A *ringisho* is prepared by a division only after careful consultations with its bureau director. During the consultations he may give his approval or instructions as to how the proposal on hand should be prepared or modified." His go signal must be given before anything can happen. "Thus, a *ringisho* is a written version of what transpires between the bureau director and the division. Hence it is not necessarily synonymous with the ideas originally entertained by the division."[26] Moreover, before the bureau director can give his blessings to the division's proposal, he must consult with and seek approval from his superiors—the AVM and, especially, the minister. He must take similar consultative and clearance steps with

[23] Imamura, "Kyōiku gyōsei zakkan," pp. 8–9.

[24] For discussion of how hierarchy can be undermined by expertise and knowledge, see Rourke, *Bureaucracy,* pp. 128'*n129.

[25] Interviews with Kida Hiroshi, April 15, 1980, and Naitō Takasaburō, April 8, 1980. A former MOE AVM, Kida is director of the National Institute for Educational Research. A former LDP upper-house dietman, Naitō served in the MOE as AVM and minister.

[26] Interview with Kobayashi Yukio, February 18, 1980. For first-hand accounts of agency policy-making that run counter to Tsuji's *ringisei,* see *Jimintō seichōkai,* pp. 180–185. See also Ōkita Saburō, *Nihon kanryō jijō* [The reality of Japanese bureaucracy] (Tokyo: TBS Buritanika, 1984), pp. 161–170. These pages contain a useful analysis by Tanimura Hiroshi, a former MOF AVM.

the ministry's PARC counterpart. If he anticipates a major problem from the minister and the LDP, he will veto the proposal from below unless he is prepared to fight for it.

The factors mentioned above that place higher officials in a powerful position vis-à-vis their subordinates in agency policy-making also apply, mutatis mutandis, to relations between the higher officials and their dietman-minister, who stands at the apex of the centralized, politicized structure of hierarchy. In the agency he is the authorizer and legitimator of all agency policy decisions and actions, including personnel decisions. As the party's primary representative in the agency, he also takes part in the party's legitimation of agency policy, although elaborate consultations that the bill-drafting officials carry on with their PARC counterparts also constitute a major part of the party's legitimation process. Contrary to popular impressions, the minister plays a significant part in agency personnel decision making. He is far more experienced in his governing role than commonly assumed; he may even have relevant experience and expertise in the affairs of the agency he heads. These notions are elaborated in subsequent chapters.

The shortened chain of vertical intraagency communication mentioned above, made possible by higher officials' vigorous and often forced participation in agency policy-making, allows the activist minister to deal with fewer subordinates in getting his ideas legislated and implemented. In other words, he can go directly to the partisanized higher officials, whereas under a more dispersed system of policy-making he would have to deal with not only higher executives but also middle-level officials.

This notion clearly runs counter to the basic premise of Tsuji's notion of *zokkan seiji*: because a higher official could not assume the role of leader and decision-maker, he could only send his policy idea "as a mere proposal or item for future reference to the appropriate low-ranking administrator. Even if this lowest administrator accepted and acted upon it, he still had to wait a long time until the *ringisho* concerning that policy reached him."[27]

Even in policy-making situations where the minister performs the reactive role of approving and legitimating initiatives from below, the proposals prepared by the divisions in today's bureaucracy are far more likely to be in tune with the minister's views. This is so for a variety of reasons. Because of the upward move of the agency's decision-making power discussed above, the bureau director is active in divisional policy-

---

[27] Tsuji, "Decision-making," p. 463.

planning and bill drafting. In other words, these divisional activities occur under the close supervision of bureau directors who, closer to the minister and better informed of his views than division chiefs, can better anticipate his likely reactions to policy proposals. Moreover, they are more sensitive and responsive than their subordinates to the dietman-minister because they are more politicized and partisanized. Thus, when his proposed policy ideas or inputs are perceived to be in agreement with the ministry's PARC counterpart, they will command special consideration by the higher officials. On the other hand, the minister who is neither supported by nor in tune with the potentates of the appropriate PARC division will find it very difficult, unless he is independently powerful (e.g., a faction leader or a minister strongly backed by the prime minister), to effectively use the opportunities and powers bestowed upon the contemporary minister. This theme is further examined in a later chapter.

In all contemporary ministries, not only the heavily partisanized agencies but also traditionally assertive agencies, the necessary paperwork—the preparation and circulation of *ringisho*—on important or politically sensitive matters, and especially those requiring LDP, cabinet, and Diet approval, commences *only* after the proposed policy has been cleared with the minister. "If he says no," as former MOE AVM and minister Naitō Takasaburō put it, "nothing happens."[28] According to a former MITI bureau director, "As far as big matters are concerned, though not small items, it is absolutely impossible for the administrative officials to make decisions and act at their own discretion without the participation of the minister, a politician."[29] Commenting on the central role assumed by the minister of finance on "important items" requiring "political judgments" (e.g., whethr or not public bonds should be issued, and if so, what type), a former MOF AVM noted: "Political judgments...are not handled through a bottom-up proposal; they are dealt with on the basis of words from above."[30] In the words of former MOE AVM Kida Hiroshi: "Big decisions involving which direction we should go, left or right, depend primarily on the views and inclinations of the incumbent minister. Thus, we have to know where he stands before we proceed any further."[31] In short, in major policy matters, *ringi-*

---

[28] Naitō Takasaburō, "Toranomon yowa" [Chatting in Toranomon], no. 12, in *Nihon kyōiku shimbun*, July 21, 1980.

[29] "Kanryō wa naze jidai ni okureruka?" [Why do bureaucrats fall behind the times?], an interview with Hayashi Shintarō in *Ekonomisuto* 55, no. 31 (July 26, 1977): 55.

[30] Ōkita, *Nihon kanryō jijō*, pp. 170–171.

[31] Interview with Kida Hiroshi, April 15, 1980. Kida's views are shared by his MOF counterpart Tanimura Horishi. See Ōkita, *Nihon kanryō jijō*, pp. 170–171.

*sei,* which appears to be an embodiment of intraorganizational democracy, merely formalizes decisions previously made via informal and hierarchical channels.

Ojimi Yoshihisa, a former MITI AVM, gives us a glimpse of his agency and of the place the minister holds in it. As far as formal decision making is concerned, the ministry conference (*shōgi*) is the most important organ, for it is here that "most matters of importance, especially in general areas such as the budget and laws, are decided." The meeting, presided over by the AVM, is seldom attended by the minister. However, though absent from the meeting, the minister maintains "constant contact" with his AVM. "Because the vice-minister meets the minister every day, he is fully informed of the intentions of the minister and often receives directives from the minister." Without much difficulty the AVM can anticipate the minister's most likely reactions. Though lower officials are given "a great deal of authority" over routine items, important matters "cannot be settled without discussion with the cabinet minister." Subordinates "give their opinions freely and generously, but there are no cases where the actions of the subordinates do not reflect the intentions of their superiors."[32] In other words, what Carl F. Friedrich calls "the rule of anticipated reactions" or what the Japanese refer to as *jishu kisei* (self-imposed control) is a key regulator of superior-inferior relations.[33]

The assertive minister is not naive enough to assume that *jishu kisei* will always ensure his undisputed status in the agency. He finds it necessary to resort to his formal powers from time to time. One such tool is his veto power, which is exercised over policy recommendations from below that fail to properly reflect his views. Araki Masuo, an active MOE minister of 1960–63, "always had a pen in his hand when going over documents from below."[34] Okuno Seisuke, another assertive minister of education, 1972–74, also carefully scrutinized policy proposals.[35] Several interviewed MOE officials of the 1950s and 1960s remembered Nadao Hirokichi, a soft-spoken, four-term minister of education,

---

[32] Ojimi, "Government Ministry," pp. 102–106.

[33] Carl F. Friedrich, "Public Policy and the Nature of Administrative Responsibility," *Public Policy* 1 (1940): 3–24. See also his book, *Man and His Government* (New York: McGraw-Hill, 1963), pp. 199–215. I am grateful to Professor Soma Masao, then of Kyūshū National University, for his discussion of the importance of *jishu kisei* in Japanese organizations while I was a visiting scholar at the university's law faculty, February–August, 1982.

[34] Interview with Shinozawa Kōhei, May 7, 1980.

[35] Interview with Iwama Eitarō, February 29, 1980.

as a tough, assertive minister, not hesitant to contradict higher officials of the agency. An MOE official recalled several incidents in which the minister forcibly overruled a consensus among career officials on issues of school curricular policy. These and other similar incidents convinced the interviewed MOE official that "Nadao was a man of strong will and leadership."[36]

The following account by Tanaka Kakuei of a 1957 Ministry of Posts and Telecommunications (MPT) decision to grant licenses to VHF television stations illustrates what can happen to a *ringi* document incongruent with the minister's views. Note that the MPT post was the first cabinet assignment for Tanaka, who, a junior member of the Satō faction, was then only thirty-nine years old—a good deal younger than most division chiefs—and knew little about agency affairs.

> I immediately summoned Asano, chief of the Documents Division, and told him: "The MPT offices in charge are opposed [to the application for VHF television operating licenses], but I am prepared to approve it. What steps should I take?" His answer was clear and simple: "The minister's decision has the force of a law."
>
> I sent for AVM Ono as Asano was departing. Ono came promptly. I told him: "The officials handling electric waves have sent up this document rejecting an overall licensing of VHF stations. I need your views. I feel that the time has come for us to make this momentous decision for the future of Japan's telecommunication, and that now is a good time to put an end to the disorderly system prevailing throughout the country...."
>
> The calm Ono responded in a clear-cut manner, "As you please, sir." I then marked with a red pen a big X on the covering page [of the *ringi* document], already all red with rouge from the seals of the officials involved: section officers, division chief, and bureau director. I then asked Ono to replace the cover page with a new one showing "This Item Approved."
>
> In less than five minutes, the AVM, who had gone into his office, came back with the document indicating on its cover "The Attached Item Approved." It carried his signature only. Without hesitation I stamped my seal on it. To this date I simply don't know whether or not he subsequently had his bureau and division chiefs sign the new document.[37]

---

[36] Interview with Hirata Kizō, March 10, 1980. Hirata, now a professor of education at Hiroshima University, was a curricular specialist in the MOE Bureau of Elementary-Secondary Education.

[37] Quoted in Manabe Shigeki, Chiba Hitoshi, and Nakayama Masaru, "Abaku Kakuei ōkoku: yūseishō no ranmyaku" [Kakuei's kingdom exposed: the disorder of the Ministry of

Many ministers, not only in weak agencies but also in such powerful ones as the MOF, have perceived their role in more than reactive terms. They have assumed an initiating role in policy-making, and their efforts more often than not have resulted in legislative success. Because of the LDP's growing role in policy-making, it is only logical that, as a recent commentary on Japanese bureaucracy put it, "the cases in which the minister assumes the role of directing his subordinates on the key points of a new policy have grown in number.[38] Muramatsu Michio of Kyoto University wrote, "If the minister vigorously pushes for adoption of his policy idea, he, as a general rule, succeeds." The former MITI AVM Ojimi also has noted that "the policies desired by the minister usually pass."[39]

The minister's initiative may be prompted by his long-held personal convictions; he may be acting on behalf of powerful interest groups; he may be promoting his factional or party policy. In any case, the pattern of policy-making in a case of ministerial initiation conforms to *ato ringi*, in which the minister sends his policy directive to his subordinates for elaboration into a *ringi* document for his final approval. Naitō Takasaburō, chief of the MOE's Accounting-Budget Division in the mid-1950s, recalls what the minister's directive means to agency officials: "Education Minister Matsumura [Kenzō] summoned me. He carefully explained the five principal programs of his administration, including promotion of social and private school education—the areas hitherto denied major budgetary support. He then instructed me to generously increase budgetary allocations for these programs." Naitō later recalled that he was not only able to get intraagency consensus for the minister's programs (hence, priority items for the agency) but also to secure the necessary funding from the MOF.[40]

The partisanized agencies involved in the "reverse programs" of the 1950s, such as the MOE, had liberal shares of initiating ministers, who put a premium on their party policy of correcting the "excesses" of the SCAP (Supreme Commander, Allied Powers) programs.[41] "I am a faithful servant of the government party," a claim widely attributed to MOE minister Kiyose Ichirō (1955–56), was by no means out of touch

Posts and Telecommunications], *Gendai* 14, no. 2 (February 1980): 218–219.

[38] Kyōikusha, ed. *Kanryō* [Bureaucracy] (Tokyo: Kyōikusha, 1980), p. 111. This volume was prepared by a group of informed observers that included a senior LDP Policy Affairs Research Council staff member.

[39] Muramatsu, *Sengo Nihon*, p. 196; Ojimi, "Government Ministry," p. 106.

[40] Naitō, "Toranomon yowa," no. 15, in *Nihon kyōiku shimbun*, August 11, 1980.

[41] Interview with Naitō Takasaburō, May 8, 1980.

with the realities. Ōdachi Shigeo, another powerful MOE minister, often dealt directly with division chiefs and even lower officials, bypassing the higher echelons, as illustrated in the preparation of the 1954 laws on teachers' political neutrality. Saitō Sei, then chief of the division responsible for drafting the bills, recalled: "The minister ordered me to prepare measures necessary to insuring education's political neutrality.... We had to prepare several drafts and submit them to the minister before we finally learned his true intentions and wishes."[42] To be sure, the decade of the 1950s was a "turbulent era" (*ransei*) in which policy processes were far from stabilized and opportunities were abundant for ministerial initiatives. Although *ran* no longer characterizes Japan, its contemporary political system operates in a setting vastly supportive of the minister's assertiveness and power in agency decision making; there are too many reported cases of activist ministers for us to unreservedly accept the widely held concept of "impotent ministership."

---

[42] Saitō Sei, "Kyōiku no seijiteki chūritsu no tameni" [For the purpose of attaining the political neutrality of education], *Kyōiku iinkai geppō* 200 (April 1967): 68.

# III

# Ministers: Specialization, Partisanization, and Politicization

Contemporary cabinet ministers, except for a very few notable cases, are members of the Diet, the national legislative body constitutionally endowed with the supreme decision-making authority of the state. More important, they are veteran members of the majority party that has ruled the nation ever since 1948. They are conscious of not only their party's unrivaled status in the polity but also their own position of authority vis-à-vis their agency subordinates.[1] Not only are they given to the belief that agency policy-making is politics among actors of unequal ranks, but also, increasingly, they are equipped with a key tool for governing—relevant experience and expertise—when they assume their ministerial posts.

---

[1] This attitude was manifested in the comments by interviewed former ministers and even parliamentary vice-ministers. They include Hasegawa Takashi (labor minister), Okuno Seisuke (education minister), Naitō Takasaburō (education minister), Karasawa Shunjirō (parliamentary vice-minister of education), Mori Yoshirō (deputy chief of the Cabinet Secretariat), and Nishioka Takeo (parliamentary vice-minister of education). For discussions by veteran political reporters of the bureaucrats' changing attitude toward LDP cabinet ministers from one of assertiveness to that of deference, see Andō Hiroshi et al., "Kanryō to seiji" [Bureaucracy and politics], *Sekai,* no. 411 (February 1980), pp. 75–76. LDP dietmen's domineering attitude toward bureaucrats is typified in such utterances as "The AVM and the director of the Minister's Secretariat who refuse to go along with us should be fired" (*kubi ni shiro*) and "You fool! Don't you realize how strongly I am stressing the importance of natural resources? I'll have you fired" (*Omae no kubi nanka tobashiteyaru*). The former remark by an irate LDP dietman was directed at top MOE officials. See *Asahi,* June 3, 1969. The latter fiery chiding by a prominent LDP dietman was hurled at an MOF Taxation Bureau director. For this and other similar chidings by the LDP and its dietmen directed at MOF officials, see Moriyama Takashi, "Ōkurashō Shuzeikyoku nanatsu no daizai" [Seven big crimes of the Finance Ministry's taxation bureau], *Bungei shunjū* 61, no. 5 (May 1983): 289–291.

This observation obviously does not square with the notion that the minister is a timorous amateur ill equipped to deal with agency personnel and policy matters. In this notion of the "amateurish minister," he is depicted as too occupied with his electoral, political, and Diet duties to devote any serious and sustained attention to substantive policy matters, not only before but even after assuming his cabinet post. A concomitant notion is the popular assumption of "bureaucratic expertise and information," in which career officials are viewed as policy specialists armed with the kind of experience and expertise that can only come from sustained and concentrated attention to policy issues. A principal problem inherent in these assumptions is that they overstate the bureaucrats' knowledge and expertise[2] and overlook the contemporary minister's multifarious activities (party, Diet, bureaucratic, and electoral) that combine to make him a dietman of experience, informed and even specialized in policy areas often including those under the ministry's jurisdiction.

In the words of Hashiguchi Osamu, a former MOF Budget Bureau director and later the AVM of the National Land Agency (*Kokudochō*): "The number of LDP dietmen who have served as ministers and parliamentary vice-ministers has increased during the long reign of the LDP government. Moreover, the functions of the LDP PARC have grown stronger. These developments are responsible for the accumulation of vast administrative knowledge and experience in the hands of the politicians." Hashiguchi goes on to note that "these specialist dietmen, affiliated with particular policy groups (*zoku*)," are "better informed about some policy issues and their evolution than bureaucrats who are rotated annually or every two years."[3] The zoku members, usually

---

[2] Several interviewed officials and published accounts by former officials confirm this point. A former MOE official now a professor of education noted that as far as legal data (laws and regulations) are concerned the bureaucrats are well endowed. "As for other data much needed in policy-making, they are awfully deficient." A former MAFF official observed that "the frequency of transfers" is "bound to produce officials not proficient in their jobs. Most career officials are nothing more than a bunch of amateurs, notwithstanding their [permanent] career status." See Takeuchi, *Konna kanryō*, p. 41.

[3] Hashiguchi, *Shinzaisei jijō*, p. 196. See also Shioguchi Kiichi, "Tenkanki no kanryō" [Bureaucracy at the turning point], in *Naikaku to kanryō* [Cabinet and bureaucracy], a supplement of *Hōgaku seminā*, March 1979, pp. 142–145. In the words of this *Asahi shimbun* analyst, "All dietmen are divided into such groups as *Kōkūku zoku* (aviation dietmen), *Un'yuzoku* (transportation dietmen), and *Nōgyōzoku* (agriculture dietmen), which, involved in particulars of administration and having stronger ties with governmental agencies, are playing a growing role [in public policy-making]." For discussion of *Bōeizoku* (defense dietmen), see Shimazaki Seigo, "Hirogaru 'bōeizoku' giin" [The expanding "Tribe of Defense Dietmen"], *Sekai*, no. 422 (January 1981), pp. 159–164. For analyses of *Bunkyōzoku* (edu-

affiliated with the appropriate PARC divisions (*bukai*) and investigative committees (*chōsakai*), can roughly be compared to the congressional members of what Ernest S. Griffith refers to as the "whirlpool" found in each of the American policy subsystems—transportation subsystem, agricultural-policy subsystem, and so forth. Just as the American whirlpools or "complexes" are triangular structures consisting of congressional, executive (departmental), and interest group elements, so the pivotal sectors of the Japanese policy subsystems are the triadic groupings of LDP zoku and bureaucratic and interest group actors.[4] Just as a veteran congressman (e.g., Russell Long of the Senate Finance Committee) acquires expertise and experience in a specific policy area through his extended committee activities, so an LDP dietman undergoes a process of policy specialization through his activities in Diet committees and, especially, in PARC divisions, which are organized in parallel to government ministries and perform oversight functions à la Communist Party Secretariat departments in Communist polities. Although under the American system of separated powers the legislators cannot concurrently hold congressional and executive posts, the Japanese parliamentary system allows members of the majority party to assume executive responsibilities as cabinet ministers and parliamentary vice-ministers, thus affording them added opportunities to get acquainted with the affairs and policy issues of the agencies in which they serve.

Hashiguchi's assessment of the contemporary LDP dietmen's experience and expertise is shared by other bureaucratic sources. A senior Economic Planning Agency (EPA) division chief commented: "Because they have handled policies of all kinds for the thirty years after the war, the politicians have gradually acquired bureaucratic know-how and are intimately familiar with even minute policy details. These specialists intervene not only in generalities but also in technical specifics." The same

---

cation dietmen), see Yung Park, *Jimintō to kyōiku kanryō* [The Liberal-Democratic party and the education bureaucracy] (Tokyo: Meiji daigaku gakujutsu kōryū iinkai, 1980); and Habara Kiyomasa, "Jimintō bunkyōzoku no jitsuryoku" [Power of the LDP tribe of education dietmen], *Sekai*, no. 444 (November 1982), pp. 65–71. For an enlightening description of the importance attached to policy specialization and expertise by members of the Tanaka faction, see Tawara Kōtarō, "Naze ima 'Tanaka' nanoka?" [Why "Tanaka" now?], *Bungei shunjū* 59, no. 9 (August 1981): 92–106. Perhaps the best comprehensive treatment of LDP zoku is found in *Jimintō seichōkai* [LDP Policy Affairs Research Council] (Tokyo: Nihon keizai shimbunsha, 1983). Also useful is Nakamura Akira and Takeshita Yuzuru, eds., *Nihon no seisaku katei* [Policy process in Japan] (Tokyo: Azusa shuppansha, 1984), pp. 38–63.

[4] For Griffith's discussion of policy whirlpools, see his *Congress: Its Contemporary Role,* 4th ed. (New York: New York University Press, 1967), pp. 55 and 144–151.

EPA official went on to observe: "We hear that Hitler, who knew much about diametric measurements of [German] machine-gun barrels, severely chided his General Staff officers for not knowing them. We often encounter similar incidents nowadays [in our dealings with LDP dietmen]."[5] A MITI division chief spoke in a similar vein about the veteran LDP dietmen "who have fully mastered their subjects by their continuous attention. In fact, there are many areas in which bureaucrats, subject to constant rotations, are poorly informed."[6] A former MOE bureau director echoed this, saying: "Politicians are now specialized professionals. They have acquired skills and expertise. In fact, LDP education policy veterans consider MOE division chiefs to be young tenderfoots (*shinmai*)."[7] A senior MOF division chief noted that "the party dietmen are continually in charge of the same policy area" and are thus familiar with MOF precedents in budget making. "When they say, 'With your predecessors this was the policy,' we cannot do less than that."[8]

The growing expertise of the LDP parliamentary contingent has not only impressed the bureaucrats who have had to deal with them on a continuous basis but also has affected others in touch with them. For illustration, let us take Miyazaki Teru, a *zaikai* (big business) member of the Second Ad Hoc Commission on Administrative Reform (*Dainiji rinji gyōsei chōsakai,* or in short, *Daini rinchō*) created in 1981. He recalls the commission's meetings with LDP dietmen to assess the justifications for the existing programs:

> We were bombarded with counterarguments on nearly all issues before us. On all policy programs, whether involving the "Solitary Islands" (*Ritō*) or the "Special Rules on Regions" (*Chiiki tokurei*), the PARC dietmen turned out to be those personally involved in the making of the laws in question. They argued that we, ill informed of the circumstances under which the laws were passed, were not really qualified to discuss their validity. We thought they were right.[9]

Watanabe Yasuo, a leading scholar of Japanese bureaucracy who once described party-bureaucracy relations primarily in terms of bureaucratic expertise, also sees the legislators' specialization as a principal develop-

---

[5] The transcripts of interviews with this economic official and others are found in "Ima keizai kanryōwa nanio kangaeteiruka?" [What is on the minds of economic bureaucrats nowadays?], *Shūkan tōyō keizai,* April 26–May 3, 1980, pp. 42–50.

[6] Ibid.

[7] Interview with Miyaji Shigeru, March 10, 1980.

[8] "Ima keizai kanryō wa nanio kangaeteiruka?" p. 45.

[9] Miyazaki Teru, "Kigyō katsuryoku to seifu no yakuwari" [Business vitality and government's role], *Keidanren geppō,* 29, no. 10 (October 1981): 2.

ment of postwar Japanese politics. As he puts it:

> The number of the *nisei* and *sansei* dietmen has grown; so has that
> of the dietmen who have been elected many times. Given their ex-
> perience [prolonged exposure to policy problems], it is inevitable that
> they become specialists and veterans in policy administration. The
> conventional perspective views the legislators as policy novices and
> the administrators as policy experts, but in reality there are now
> many legislators who have a better command of administration than
> the administrators themselves, who are rotated once every two
> years.[10]

All LDP dietmen are subjected to the intraparty, intra-Diet process
of socialization and training in which policy specialization assumes a
prominent part. As they go through this process, an overwhelming majority of the legislators are significantly aided by their pre-Diet experiences. Former bureaucrats (approximately one-third of LDP dietmen
come from this background) embark upon their political careers with experience of at least twenty-five years in a central ministry. Their
knowledge, expertise, and bureaucratic know-how are substantial advantages that aid them in their efforts to diversify their policy specialization
and interests to meet their expanding electoral and political needs. In
addition, the recent Diet has experienced steady streams of *nisei* and
*sansei* dietmen, socialized in not only the political skills but also the policy concerns of their seniors prior to their entry into electoral politics.
There is also a sizable group of politicians who enter the Diet after a
long apprenticeship as aides and secretaries to LDP dietmen. And some
move up into the national legislature from political careers at the subnational (prefectural and municipal) levels where, as in national politics,
the elected representatives have increasingly assumed an activist role in
policy-making. According to a recent study compiled by an affiliate of
the Ministry of Home Affairs, major positive changes in prefectural as-
semblymen include their growing penchant for policy specialization and
the attendant emphasis on their supervisory role vis-à-vis the administration in their areas of specialization.[11]

---

[10] Watanabe, "Toshi ni okeru chihō gikai to giin no yakuwari" [Local assemblies and
the role of legislators], *Jichi kenshū,* no. 275 (March 1983), p. 11. For Watanabe's earlier
view stressing the notion of bureaucratic dominance, see his "Rinchō to seitō" [The temporary administrative reform commission and political parties], in *Gyōsei kaikaku no
suishin to teikō* [Promotion of and resistance to administrative reform], no. 5 of *Nenpō
gyōsei kenkyū* [Annual of studies in public administration] (Tokyo: Keisō shobō, 1966), pp.
103–123.

[11] Watanabe Yasuo, "Toshi ni okeru chihō gikai," p. 11. This report was prepared by
*Chihō jichi kenkyū shiryō sentā* [The Research and Data Center for Local Autonomy], Tokyo.

Most of today's LDP national legislators come from these four major pre-Diet backgrounds. Whether of these backgrounds or not, all LDP dietmen go through the process of intraparty, legislative socialization, which in its earlier stages is quite uniform and institutionalized.[12] After the initial stages, however, this process takes on a great deal of diversity, allowing them several different patterns of upward mobility.

In their freshman year the dietmen are all assigned to Diet standing committees and the corresponding PARC divisions. Typically, they join a few additional PARC divisions and investigative committees, whose meetings they attend. Here in the party and legislative committees they spend most of their morning and afternoon hours several days a week; here they are exposed to and get acquainted with ministry policy measures that come to them for party and legislative approval.

Particularly important are their PARC divisional activities, for the divisions play a major part not only in the party's legitimation of ministry policy but also in its development and formulation, as previously noted. The dietmen also take part in policy seminars and public hearings, sponsored by PARC divisions, where specialists (both practitioners and academics) and interest group representatives are invited to lecture and make presentations. In the Education Division, between March 25 and May 11, 1982, the division and its subcommittees held no fewer than

---

[12] Most of the information used in this section comes from interviews with LDP dietmen and staff members including Mori Yoshirō, Isibashi Kazuya, Tanikawa Kazuo, Karasawa Shunjirō, Okuno Seisuke, Kaifu Toshiki, and Murakawa Ichirō. Kōno Yōhei, a key member of the so-called LDP Young Turks before he left the party to form the New Liberal Club, calls the initial part of this process "a life in the lower strata" (*shitazumi no seikatsu*) during which a great deal of hard work and study is done. Under the contemporary system, unlike the early postwar years, LDP dietmen must go through this process, which rewards accumulated experience and seniority and militates against lateral entries into the party, a pattern of recruitment quite prevalent in the 1950s. See Kōno Yōhei, *Jimintō no kindaika* [Modernization of the LDP], *Getsuyōkai repōto* [Reports of the Monday Club], no. 507 (Tokyo: Kokumin seiji kenkyūkai, 1970), pp. 17–18. I am most grateful to him for granting me a highly instructive interview on September 7, 1977. Useful information on the process of intraparty and intra-Diet socialization is found in "Bū-chan no seiji dōjō" [Bū-chan's political arena], 9th installment, transcript of Itō Masaya's interview with Kaifu Toshiki, in *Chūō kōron* 98, no. 14 (December 1983): 178–186; and "Seimu jikan sedai wa shuchōsuru" [Assertions by the generation of parliamentary vice-ministers], a panel discussion by Aichi Kazuo, Kawara Tsutomu, and Noda Takeshi, *Chūō kōron* 97, no. 1 (January 1982): 96–103. LDP Dietman Shirokawa Katsuhiko gives a good account of his daily policy-related activities in "Jimintō daigishi no nichijō katsudō" [Daily activities of a Liberal-Democratic party dietman], in *Nihon no seitō* [Japanese political parties], a special expanded issue (no. 35) of *Jurisuto* (Tokyo: Yūhikaku, 1984), pp. 102–107.

seventeen meetings, most of which were study sessions and public hearings devoted to specific policy issues.[13]

Similar activities undertaken by PARC investigative committees and, especially, ad hoc committees (*tokubetsu chōsakai*) have also contributed to the dietmen's policy expertise and specialization. These committees are found in every conceivable area of public policy, such as education, health insurance, transportation, foreign trade, national defense, and anti-monopoly. True, many of the investigative committees are largely dormant and carry on few activities of any importance. As Education Minister Mori Yoshirō put it, "Membership on these committees merely extends the list of formal titles (*katagaki*) a dietman holds."[14]

However, many functioning committees, through multifarious activities, measurably aid the members' policy expertise. The Investigative Committee on the Educational System (*Bunkyō seido chōsakai*), created in 1966 to succeed the Education Investigative Committee (*Bunkyō chōsakai*), is one such. Between September 1966 and November 1968 (the peak of the 1968–69 campus disturbance), the committee had no fewer than thirty-two sessions, most of which were policy hearings where a variety of education-policy experts and lobbyists spoke on major policy issues of higher education.[15] The committee membership included all of the surviving former education ministers as well as education policy dietmen who later rose to become MOE PVM or minister.

Another example of activist PARC committees is the Special Investigative Committee on Anti-Monopoly Law (*Dokkinhō ni kansuru tokubetsu chōsakai*) created in January 1983 to study problem areas of the controversial law. In 1983 alone, the committee met seventeen times, with a majority of sessions given to presentations by specialists, who included academics, corporate executives, interest group representatives, consumers, and government officials. The committee hearings culminated in the dispatch of an investigative team to the United States

---

[13] For analysis of the intraparty process of policy specialization that education dietmen go through, see Yung Park, "Kyōiku gyōsei ni okeru jimintō to mombushō" [The Liberal-Democratic party and the Ministry of Education in educational administration], in *Nihon kyōiku no rikigaku* [Dynamics of Japan's education], ed. Shimbori Michiya and Aoi Kazuo (Tokyo: Yūshindo, 1983), pp. 49–78.

[14] Interview with Mori Yoshirō, September 21, 1981. Former deputy chief of the Cabinet Secretariat and chairman of the LDP PARC Education Division, Mori is former education minister.

[15] For committee proceedings for September-November 1968, see Jiyūminshutō, *Kokumin no tameno daigaku* [Higher education for the people] (Tokyo: Jiyūminshutō shuppankyoku, 1968).

and Western European nations. Naturally, the final report prepared by
the visiting team (which was chaired by Dietman Saitō Eisaburō, an
academic–turned–LDP specialist in anti-monopoly) was shared with
other members of the PARC investigative committee.[16] Participation in
PARC committee activities such as these is an important part of the
dietmen's educational process.

This pattern of participation in PARC activities continues even
after the dietmen have attained considerable seniority. All interviewed
LDP sources (e. g., dietmen and their aides) confided that the dietmen
take their legislative and, especially, PARC assignments very seriously
because of the growing importance their party and factions attach to the
quality of their performance in considering their future assignments and
promotions. Those deemed delinquent in these activities are often excluded from serious consideration for important party, Diet, and governmental duties. In other words, it takes more than seniority to be seriously considered for important posts, including cabinet appointments.

In their second terms, many lower-house dietmen are made deputy
chiefs of the PARC divisions they first joined. As such, they assist their
division chairmen, coordinate divisional activities with the higher
officials of their counterpart ministries, and sound out the senior
members (*zoku*) of the division on major policy issues. In their third
terms, the dietmen are given governmental appointments as parliamentary vice-ministers, frequently but not always of the ministries relevant to
their PARC divisional experiences. Because of the importance of policy
specialization to their upward mobility and constituency building, many
dietmen prefer and obtain their first governmental posts in the agencies
corresponding to their PARC duties.

Though typically one year in duration, the PVM post is an important training ground for junior dietmen.[17] It affords its occupant new or
additional opportunities to become familiar with agency affairs and
operations. Through his activities as an intermediary between the agency and the political sectors (the Diet, the party and its constituencies,
and the factions) he develops an intimate insight into the patterns of
party-ministry interactions as well as the policy issues coordinated with

---

[16] For analysis of the committee's activities by its staff director, see Kishida Fumitake,
"Kaigai jūyō senshinkoku no dokusen kinshi seisaku no dōkō" [Trends in the anti-
monopoly policies of select advanced nations], *Keidanren geppō* 32, no. 1 (January 1984):
pp. 58–64.

[17] The following account is based largely on interviews with several former PVMs and
published accounts. Interviewed dietmen include Kōno Yōhei, Tanigawa Kazuo, and
Nishioka Takeo.

the party and its influentials. Always coming from a party faction different from the minister's, the PVM is also a major link between the agency and his faction. If he is from the appropriate PARC division (for example, the Education Division in the case of the MOE), he is already familiar with agency affairs and much of what he does as the PVM.

Contrary to the widely accepted notion that the PVM is "the vermiform appendix" (*mōchō*) of a ministry,[18] the contemporary PVM is by no means a useless entity. In the words of former MOE bureau director Miyaji Shigeru, "Major [agency] policy programs are unthinkable without the active intervention of the minister and the parliamentary vice-minister. The MOE listens to them." Former MOE PVM Nishioka Takeo (1970–71), asked if he had been the MOE's *mōchō,* emphatically responded: "No. Not at all. In fact, I wrote some [agency] bills myself."[19] Commenting on his generation of PVMs, Nishioka had this to say:

> In terms of average age, our group is the youngest of all PVMs. Previously, the newly appointed PVM, busy giving reports on his new assignment to his constituents, could not be found in his ministry office. Unable to wait to get his signature, agency officials had to bypass him in their circulation of documents. That's why he was known as the vermiform appendix. This is no longer the case with our group of PVMs, who are all young and assertive in their ministries. During my tenure as the MOE PVM, I never went to my election district except on Sundays. I always showed up in the agency to work.[20]

Upon completing their first governmental assignments, the dietmen return to party and Diet duties. Typically, they affiliate or reaffiliate with the PARC divisions and investigative committees corresponding to their ministry posts and participate in divisional activities, which include not only acting on ministry policy proposals but also hearings and seminars on policy issues of current interest. Although some former PVMs choose procedure-related Diet and party assignments (e.g., committees working on Diet operations), many, and especially "policy-oriented dietmen" (*seisakutsū*), are appointed chiefs of the appropriate PARC divisions. They are also given concurrent assignments on the corresponding Diet committees as "executive members" (*riji*).

---

18 *Asahi,* February 23, 1967.

19 Interview with Miyaji Shigeru, March 10, 1980. Interview with Nishioka Takeo, February 19, 1980.

20 Quoted in Toyoda Kōji, *Seishun kokkai gekijō* [The youthful theater of the Diet] (Tokyo: Bunka sōgō shuppansha, 1976), p. 134.

PARC divisional chairmanship is a key policy-making office. In the area of divisional jurisdiction, the chairman is one of the most powerful actors. Of course, he runs his division in close consultation with his elders, the *zoku* members and *gosanke* ("top three"), whose views must be carefully taken into account in making divisional decisions. As far as the ministry under the division's supervision is concerned, he is the first and, most likely, foremost party figure who must be persuaded in support of its major policy program. Without his blessings, no agency policy can get party authorization. Hence he plays a major role in agency policy and budgetary processes and even in agency personnel decisions. He is a principal medium through whom the party influences ministry decisions.

In the long process of intraparty socialization and upward mobility, the initial stages of which are outlined above, the dietmen place a premium on gaining wide recognition as members and elders (*gosanke*) of policy groups (*zoku*) vital to their factional and constituency needs. Policy specialization, a key ingredient of power, is "the name of the game" (*nerai*), as one interviewed LDP dietman put it. Getting involved in too many policy areas is taboo, for it has the obvious danger of spreading too thin. The road to recognized *zoku* status requires more than mere affiliation with the relevant PARC organs. It requires active participation, experience, and expertise in the appropriate policy areas.[21]

All LDP dietmen are increasingly cognizant that they need substantive policy specialization not only to command deference and response from the bureaucrats but also to obtain the benefits of interest group backing, which include votes and political funds. All groups seeking to influence major governmental policies, not only those requiring legislative approval but even those handled as ministry decrees and measures, increasingly turn to relevant *zoku* dietmen and, especially, *gosanke* for support.

This pattern of interest group operations, incongruent with the popular "bureaucratic ascendancy" thesis, is a principal development of postwar Japanese politics, not only with the policies administered by the so-called partisanized agencies but also in other areas. Just as education interest groups seek support from the LDP education policy *zoku* (*Bunkyōzoku*), so the transportation industry attempts to influence the party's transportation specialists (*Un'yuzoku*).[22]

---

[21] Much of the information used in this section comes from interviews with members of LDP education,labor, and local government policy *zoku*.

[22] For discussion of this development, see Utsumi Kenji, "Riken ni muragaru 'atsuryoku giin' no jittai" [All about "pressure dietmen" swarming around special interests], *Gendai*

Votes and monetary contributions are not the only benefits a diet-man draws from interest group backing. Party-group interactions also contribute to his informational resources and expertise, for groups are an important source of specialized information often not available to the bureaucracy. As Muramatsu Michio has concluded from his extensive surveys of interest group representatives, "Pressure groups share their information not only with the administrators but also a powerful political party, and in some cases the party becomes the sole beneficiary of group information."[23] The LDP is not only a powerful political party but also the only majority party continuously in power for nearly thirty-six years.

Other contexts are educational for LDP dietmen. Contacts with their constituencies (voters, local influentials, and interest groups) and their own local political machines give them continuous exposure to dominant constituency interests and issues, contributing to their expertise in these areas. Hence, it is not surprising that LDP dietmen from the districts where the JTU has strong local organizations are affiliated with the party's *Bunkyōzoku* and are widely considered experts on JTU matters, just as Senator Donald Riegle of Michigan is an "automobile policy" expert and Jesse Helms of North Carolina is a "tobacco-smoking policy" senator. Also important to the dietmen's educational process are a variety of factional meetings—"training institutes" (*kenshūkai*), "study meetings" (*kenkyūkai*), and seasonal and weekend "retreats" where invited policy experts share their findings and opinions with members of the faction.

Many LDP dietmen have also benefited from the educational activities sponsored by a multitude of so-called policy groups (*seisaku shudan*) that mushroomed in the second half of the 1970s.[24] Some policy groups have a long history and predate this period. Among them are such cross-factional, intraparty groupings as *Seirankai, Chiyodakai, Hirokawakai,* and *Ajia afurika mondai kenkyūkai* (Society for Study of Asian-African problems, or the so-called AA Group).

Composed largely of LDP dietmen, many recent policy groups are really nothing more than factional groupings. For example, the Institute for Policy Science (*Seisaku kagaku kenkyūjo*) is a new name given to the Nakasone faction previously known as *Shinsei dōshikai* (Association of

---

16, no. 8 (August 1982): 140–159. See also *Asahi,* June 12, 1982.

[23] Muramatsu Michio, "Seijiteki tagenshugi to gyōsei kanryōsei" [Political pluralism and the system of administrative bureaucracy] in *Naikaku to kanryō,* p. 125.

[24] For an excellent analysis of these groups by a *Mainichi* political reporter, see Inoue Yoshihisa, *Habatsu to seisaku shūdan* [Factions and policy groups] (Tokyo: Kyōikusha, 1979).

Comrades for New Policy Studies). Some groups were formed primarily to coordinate political and factional activities for "a post-LDP regime" or "a new intraparty leadership" of younger dietmen. Many came into being with a specific view to studying and exploring policy issues (both domestic and foreign policy) faced by "postindustrial Japan" or the politics of "post-LDP Japan."

These groups typically include in their memberships not only dietmen of various factions but also outside influentials such as *zaikai* leaders, former ranking bureaucrats, and academics. Hence, they provide an excellent forum for party-business-bureaucracy interactions and policy coordination. In their operations, they vary significantly. Some are rather inactive, occasionally getting together for exchange of ideas and social functions. Others, however, are very active, holding scheduled study-discussion sessions and even publishing newsletters for members. Naturally, these activities aid the members' educational experience and resource-building.

Because of the process of education and specialization that LDP dietmen undergo, a typical cabinet contains a contingent of veteran legislators "trained" in their areas of jurisdiction; never is a cabinet made up solely of policy amateurs new to their governing and policy-making roles. The portfolios assigned to the individual ministers, however, do not always match their policy backgrounds and specialization because other factors such as factional considerations (e.g., interfactional balance and intrafactional seniority) also enter into the politics of cabinet formation. Relevant policy specialization, however, is increasingly important—far more so than popularly assumed—and recognized by the prime minister and others participating in cabinet making.

The individual cabinet minister gains from assuming the portfolio in his area of specialization, for it further contributes to his specialization, a requirement increasingly critical to his support-building among the clientele groups. Thus, a dietman who has specialized in education policy will be very interested in the Education portfolio unless he wants to diversify his specialization for personal and electoral reasons. It is not coincidental that two of the four postwar MOE bureaucrats who entered national politics served as education minister and the third as the parliamentary vice-minister of education. Nor is it accident that a large majority of the dietmen with backgrounds in the business community and the economic agencies have held economy-related portfolios such as the MOF, MITI, and the EPA.

Often left out of contemporary discussions of Japanese cabinet ministers are the frequent cabinet changes and the small pool of LDP dietmen eligible for cabinet assignment, which have allowed a contingent of veteran dietmen to hold several different cabinet posts over the years and accumulate a great deal of bureaucratic experience. Fukunaga Kenji, first elected to the Diet in 1952, has held four cabinet posts. Takeshita Noboru, a dietman since 1958, has held three posts. Ogawa Heiji, in the lower house since 1949, has headed three ministries. Yamanaka Sadanori, in the Diet since 1953, has held four cabinet posts. Sakata Michita, elected consecutively since 1946, has held four ministerial portfolios. The list can easily be extended to demonstrate that there is a small elite of LDP dietmen repeatedly preferred for cabinet posts and that the widely held notion of "equal share," which supposedly governs the politics of cabinet formation, is not fully adhered to.

At least one-third of the LDP dietmen and most of the veteran legislators have held multiple cabinet posts; when not in government, they held Diet and party responsibilities that also required extensive dealings with the bureaucracy. Notwithstanding ample opportunities for repeated cabinet assignments, some LDP dietmen, even with a long tenure in the Diet, never get their second ministerial appointments. The reason is simple: factional balance and seniority are not the only factors governing cabinet assignments; merit is also a major determinant. A dietman judged incompetent in his first cabinet assignment is seldom given another portfolio. Incompetency is judged to include lack of leadership over his agency, inadequate homework, poor performance during Diet interpellations, an indifference to party considerations, among other things. On the other hand, competent dietmen are repeatedly appointed to cabinet posts. Most likely they get their first cabinet posts long before meeting the usual seniority requirement. Watananbe Michio, a seven-term dietman, has already held three posts, including the coveted MOF post. Kosaka Tokusaburō, a five-term legislator, has held three posts.

The LDP dietmen are often classified into two broad categories by their pre-Diet backgrounds: *kanryōha* (bureaucratic faction) and *tōjinha* (pure politician faction). The former consists of bureaucrats-turned-dietmen; the latter is composed of those coming from "party politics" backgrounds at the local and national levels. This bureaucratic–pure politics dichotomy has generated a variety of assumptions, many quite flattering to *kanryōha* dietmen but insulting to *tōjinha* politicians. According to one such assumption, *kanryōha* ministers, educated at elite national universities and trained in the central bureaucracy, are policy specialists equipped with the skills necessary for effective handling of the bureaucrats, but *tōjinha* dietmen, many schooled at less prestigious private institutions, are policy amateurs easily susceptible to bureaucratic control.[25]

Although correctly stating the advantages possessed by the bureaucrats-turned-dietmen, this notion grossly underestimates the effects that intraparty, intra-Diet socialization has on *tōjinha* dietmen. Veteran *tōjinha* dietmen, and especially *zoku* ministers, with extensive party, Diet, and executive experiences relevant to their agencies are formidable—often more so than *kanryōha* dietmen—from the bureaucrats' standpoint.

To illustrate these observations, let us take Sakata Michita, *tōjinha* education minister of 1968-71. Widely recognized as an elder statesman of the *Bunkyōzoku* (education dietmen), Sakata is a pure party politician. First elected to the lower house in 1946 after brief municipal government employment, he is one of the veteran members of the party, with no fewer than fifteen consecutive Diet terms. He was given his first cabinet appointment in 1959 in the Ministry of Health and Welfare (MHW), in which he had held part-time employment before he entered politics.

His early party and Diet assignments included the education committees, where he quickly proved to be an active and contributing member. Prior to his MOE appointment, he had chaired all the principal party (first the Liberal party and later the LDP) and Diet organs relating to education policy: the lower-house standing committee on education and the two LDP PARC committees on education—the Education Division (ED) and the Investigative Committee on the Educational System (ICES). In the 1950s and 1960s he was a chief architect of his party's anti-JTU strategy; as such, he is well acquainted with major issues of elementary-secondary education—the JTU's principal policy concern because of the union's heavy membership concentrations in these sectors of public education. Familiar with the plight of private institutions and their financing, he has also been a major LDP promoter of governmental aid to private education. In the 1960s he added higher education to his list of specializations, and in 1968, at the peak of the nationwide campus disturbances, he presided over the highly publicized,

---

[25] For typical arguments of this genre, see Watanabe Tsuneo, "Nihon seiji no nakano kanryō to seitō" [Bureaucracy and political parties in Japanese politics], *Tsukuru* 4, no. 1 (January 1974): 43-44; and Tanaka Zen'ichirō, *Jimintō taisei no seiji shidō* [Political leadership under the Liberal-Democratic party system] (Tokyo: Daiichi hōki, 1981), pp. 193-197. J. A. A. Stockwin echoes a popular view when he states that "the tradition of bureaucratic dominance is particularly strong, and is maintained by the recruitment of former senior civil servants into the LDP." See his *Japan: Divided Politics in a Growth Economy* (New York: W. W. Norton, 1975), p. 132.

LDP-sponsored hearings on problems of higher education, where specialists and representatives of major education groups presented their views on reform of higher education and interacted with members of the LDP *Bunkyōzoku*.[26] By 1968, before he assumed the Education portfolio, therefore, he had established his reputation as a senior member of the party's education-policy group, intimately familiar with MOE affairs and top personnel.[27]

The likes of Sakata, the specialist veteran dietman and "*zoku* minister," are found in not only the MOE but also many other agencies. Admittedly, not all ministers have relevant policy experience and specialization as extensive as the Sakata type, but many do. Even those without Sakata's extensive experience have considerable exposure to the policy matters of the ministries they are assigned to. They may have served as parliamentary vice-ministers in the ministries or chaired the ministries' corresponding divisions in the LDP PARC. The *zoku* minister is typically an activist minister who wields a great deal of influence in agency decision making. Agency bureaucrats defer to and even fear him not only because of his expertise and experience but also because, as a longtime member of the party *zoku,* he is well acquainted with the agency's operations, orientations, and key personnel. He is a member of the agency's overseeing group in the party. If he is of the Sakata type, he will have been a major participant in not only substantive policy decisions but also those concerning agency personnel. In short, he is not really an "outsider" to the agency.

Then there are bureaucrats-turned-ministers, nearly all of whom spent twenty to thirty years in the bureaucracy as career officials before entering elective politics. Most *kanryōha* dietmen return sooner or later to their parental agencies as ministers, although some do not. Familiar with agency affairs and personnel, these ministers often become the actual decision-makers and managers of the agencies. If inclined toward an

---

[26] Jiyūminshutō, *Kokumin no tameno daigaku.*

[27] All interviewed LDP dietmen unanimously viewed him as an elder statesman of the party *Bunkyōzoku.* In the words of Karasawa Shunjirō, a member of the *Bunkyōzoku,* "Sakata is a member of the education-policy group *gosanke*; in fact, he is the recognized leader of the education group." Interview with Karasawa, July 4, 1980. In health and welfare policy, the influential LDP dietmen comparable to Sakata Michita of the *Bunkyōzoku* include Saitō Kunikichi, Tanaka Masami, and Ozawa Tatsuo, all former ministers of health and welfare. These three are widely referred to as the *gosanke* of the LDP *Sharōzoku* (social and labor policy group). See Ashizaki Tōru, *Kōseishō zankoku monogatari* [The Ministry of Health and Welfare inside out] (Tokyo: Ēru shuppansha, 1981), pp. 159–161. Ashizaki is a correspondent covering the LDP and the MHW.

activist policy role, they are indeed in a powerful position to direct their subordinates to desired policy goals. Even in ministries other than their old parental agencies, the *kanryōha* ministers, because of their extensive bureaucratic experience and expertise, quickly acquire the basics of agency expertise and information necessary for their leadership role. Many emerge as powerful ministers.

Again turning to the MOE for illustration, let us take Okuno Seisuke, an education minister (1972–74) in the Tanaka cabinet. By all accounts, he was one of the most assertive ministers of education in recent years. When asked about the minister's role in the MOE, Okuno promptly responded, "Both in theory and reality, the education minister is the leader of his agency." Emphatically denying that the AVM is the real and efficient head of the agency, Okuno noted: "The AVM is the primary assistant to the minister on agency affairs. The minister is in charge of important policy and political matters; the AVM handles administrative matters (*jimutekina mondai*)."[28] A division chief under Okuno recalled: "Okuno was a minister of brilliant memory, with a serious interest in education. He solicited views from even division chiefs, including myself. He was a most assertive, powerful minister."[29] A former MOE AVM offered the following reminiscences of Okuno:

> He often took part in our ministry conferences, which his predecessors rarely attended. There were occasions when we thought of him as a nuisance, for he would want to get involved in even small policy matters. He made decisions for us; we didn't make any key decisions. In a sense this was good because we did not have to struggle with the onerous task of working out consensus among us.[30]

What was the basis of Okuno's commanding posture within the MOE? Though not a member of the Tanaka faction, he was close to the prime minister. He recognized education as a key agent of political socialization—a tool to impart traditional values to the youngsters. His interest in education was further bolstered by his conviction that education was used by the JTU to indoctrinate innocent youngsters in its revolutionary ideology.[31] He is one of the most successful Ministry of Home Affairs (MHA) graduates; he entered the prewar ministry (*Naimushō*) and held the AVM post in its postwar successor (*Jichishō*). As a *Naimushō* official, he served as chief of school education (*gakumu ka-*

---

28  Interview with Okuno Seisuke, April 23, 1979.
29  Interview with Shinozawa Kōhei, May 7, 1980.
30  Interview with a former MOE AVM who served under Okuno.
31  Interview with Okuno Seisuke, April 23, 1979.

*chō*) in a prefectural administration; in the *Jichishō* he was widely considered a fiscal expert on local government and compulsory education (an important subnational function).

Before his appointment to the MOE post, he was affiliated with the party organs on education. When he assumed the education post, therefore, he was by no means a stranger in education policy. Moreover, as a longtime bureaucrat of the MHA, whose prewar predecessor effectively controlled the MOE, Okuno was well acquainted with bureaucratic operations, strengths, and weaknesses. True, in view of the volume and the technical complexities of the policy issues a ministry must cope with, even the bureaucrat-turned-minister finds himself heavily dependent upon counsel of his agency subordinates. Okuno, however, was a fast learner and effectively used his subordinates as sources of information and technical details to consolidate his power over the agency.

Approximately one-third of the ministers in any given cabinet are former bureaucrats, and many, though not all, of the bureaucrats-turned-politicians belong to the Okuno type of assertive, competent ministers. Ōdachi Shigeo (1953–54), Nadao Hirokichi (1956–57, 1958, 1963–64, and 1967–68), and Araki Masuo (1960–63), all widely considered to be among the powerful ministers of education, were former bureaucrats.[32]

One of the popular generalizations concerning bureaucrats-turned-dietmen and their policy behavior is that even after their election to the Diet they retain close ties with the agencies that nurtured them. This is true. Some scholars go as far as to argue that former bureaucrats are "Trojan horses" (ministerial subversives) within the party who are committed to the maintenance and promotion of bureaucratic (more specifically, their parental agency's) interests. This argument has been extended to its logical conclusion that, because of the large number of these dietmen within the party and its policy-making organs, the party cannot escape its "degeneration" into a bureaucracy-controlled entity—a tool for the bureaucracy. When *kanryōha* dietmen return to their old agencies as PVMs or ministers, as many do—so goes the "bureaucratic dominance" argument—they continue to perform their familiar role of articulating and championing agency interests. When caught in a policy conflict between the agency and the party, therefore, they are more likely to side with the agency than with the party to which they now belong.

---

[32] Interestingly, Kennoki Toshihiro (1966–67) and Naitō Takasaburō (1978–79), when in the upper house, were often excluded from the category of powerful bureaucrats-turned-ministers of education, although both are graduates of the MOE bureaucracy.

Viewed within the context of *ringisei* and *gekokujō,* these ministers are cheerleaders rather than leaders for the agency; they are promoters rather than initiators of agency policy. In other words, the ministers are the bureaucracy's instrument for control of the party rather than the party's instruments for control of the bureaucracy.[33]

The notions of bureaucratic primacy and *kanryōha* ministers' supportive roles, however, merely point to the bases of bureaucratic-ministerial consonance and grossly overlook conflictual elements found in the relationship between the two actors. The foremost sources of such discordance stem from the extent of politicization and partisanization *kanryōha* ministers have been subjected to since their entry into elective politics. All *kanryō* dietmen experience, of course to varying degrees, perceptual and attitudinal changes attendant upon their role changes—departure from bureaucracy and subsequent election to their Diet seats.

Once in electoral politics as LDP dietmen, they acquire new sets of constituencies they must cater to—the election districts, powerful interest groups, the party, and the factions. Like any other organization, the LDP has its share of overzealous "new converts" among its dietmen of bureaucratic background—those who are far more political and partisan than their *tōjinha* colleagues and refuse to see the "logic" of bureaucratic policy arguments.[34] Moreover, *kanryōha* dietmen, like others in the party, must go through the prescribed stages of intraparty training and upward mobility, as described above, which significantly contribute to their politicization and partisanization. They constantly interact with their *tōjinha* colleagues in factional gatherings, Diet committee sessions, party meetings and caucuses, PARC divisional sessions and hearings, and on informal occasions. They share their policy experience and expertise with *tōjinha* members, thereby contributing to the party's ability to deal better with the bureaucracy. *Tōjinha* dietmen, in turn, help educate the former bureaucrats on the intricacies of realpolitik and the policy convictions widely shared by the party politicians not afflicted with the "bureaucratic mentality."

In intraparty and intrafactional upward mobility, the experience and expertise of *kanryōha* dietmen are often recognized, and thus they

---

[33] For typical arguments of this nature, see Tsurutani, *Political Change in Japan,* pp. 106–107; and Watanabe Tsuneo, "Nihon seiji," pp. 38–44. Ministers of this type are known as "OB (old boy) ministers," a stigma that *kanryōha* ministers do not want to get stuck with. See "Shinkeizai kakuryō jitsuryoku: Kaneko Ippei" [Power of new economic ministers: the case of Kaneko Ippei], *Chūō kōron* 94, no. 2 (February 1979): 50.

[34] Interview with Yasujima Hisashi, February 29, 1980.

are occasionally allowed to rise faster and appointed to cabinet posts sooner than their *tōjinha* colleagues. In recent years, able bureaucrats-turned-dietmen Gotōda Masaharu and Hatano Akira, Okuno Seikuke, Satō Ichirō, and Hatoyama Iichirō are among those who have bypassed the usual seniority-based route to cabinet portfolios. These, however, are more exceptions than the norm. In general, a dietman, even with impressive bureaucratic credentials, must wait a minimum of twelve years before he can be seriously considered for a cabinet appointment. True, many of the powerful veteran LDP dietmen who regularly assume major portfolios are former bureaucrats, but they left the bureaucracy long ago. Nakasone Yasuhiro, a *Naimushō* official, entered the Diet in 1947; Fukuda Takeo, a former MOF official, in 1952; Furui Yoshimi, a *Naimushō* AVM, in 1952; and Miyazawa Kiichi, a former MOF official, in 1953. Having left the bureaucracy and entered elective politics long ago, they have been subjected to politicizing, partisan influences that instill in them political values and policy outlooks often incongruent with those of the bureaucracy.[35]

In recent years, an important change in the traditional pattern of bureaucrats' entries into elective politics has occurred. Previous cases were mostly high-ranking officials, typically bureau directors and administrative vice-ministers, although some, such as the late Ōhira Masayoshi and Nakasone Yasuhiro, entered politics early in their bureaucratic careers. Having spent well over thirty years in the bureaucracy to reach the top levels, most of the bureaucrats-turned-dietmen were in their fifties when they first gained seats in the Diet.

Although this pattern continues, a growing number of middle-level officials—division chiefs and even assistant division chiefs—leave the administrative service to enter politics, rather than wait until the usual retirement age of mid-fifties. Naturally, an overwhelming majority of them run as LDP candidates; many backed by powerful LDP factions,

[35] Interview with Murakawa Ichirō, August 23, 1976. This point was widely confirmed by interviewed LDP dietmen. Even during the Taishō era, the so-called *kanryō no seitōka* (partisanization of bureaucrats) was in the making. As the political parties became increasingly active in the political process of Taishō Japan, retired bureaucrats joined the powerful parties. Not only did they become politicized and partisanized, but they also contributed to the parties' assumption of a larger role in policy-making. For useful studies of party-bureaucracy relations during this prewar democratic interlude, see Mitani Taiichirō, "Seitō naikakuki no jōken" [Conditions of the era of party cabinets], in *Kindai nihon kenkyū nyūmon* [Introduction to the study of modern Japan], ed. Nakamura Takahide and Itō Takashi (Tokyo: Tokyo daigaku shuppankai, 1979), pp. 68–86; and Daikakai, ed., *Naimushōshi* [A history of the Home Affairs Ministry], vol. 1 (Tokyo: Hara shobō, 1981), pp. 276–374 and 768–771.

succeed in winning Diet seats. Their motivation for early entry into politics is varied. Politically ambitious officials desire to get ahead in the highly seniority-conscious LDP. For some others, a political career is a reflection of their discontent with the bureaucracy's shrinking power and growing subservience to the party.[36] In age-conscious Japan, many bureau directors and AVMs, in their fifties and graduates of the prestigious Tokyo University Law Department, find it humiliating that they must often toil under "younglings" who, having entered the Diet in their twenties and thirties, have managed to attain cabinet posts in their forties. When Hashimoto Ryūtarō, a Keiō University graduate and son of a prominent LDP politician, headed the MHW at the age of forty, he was a good deal younger than even most of the division chiefs, who were largely products of the much more prestigious Tokyo Law Department.

The younger bureaucratic entrants into the parliamentary LDP, still in their forties or even thirties and with shorter tenures in the bureaucracy than their predecessors, will have undergone a politicization-partisanization process of at least twenty years when they reach their sixties. This pattern of early entry into elective politics, if continued (indications are it will be), is bound minimize bureaucratic influences within the governing party.

Naturally, politicization and partisanization affect the *kanryōha* dietmen to varying degrees, and hence they do not behave uniformly vis-à-vis their former agencies. At one extreme are those who are viewed by their agency *kōhai* (juniors) more as troublemakers than as allies. Highly politicized and intimately familiar with the agency operations and "secrets," these legislators perceive political and partisan interest articulation to be their foremost role. "Some of our seniors (*senpai*) in the Diet," as one interviewed official put it, "give us more trouble than others [of the ministry's counterpart in the PARC], notwithstanding their long ties with our agency. They know too much about us and the agency. We try to avoid them, usually to no avail." Then, there are *senpai* dietmen who are widely considered "*ōendan*" (cheerleaders) for their parental agencies. Always sought out by their *kōhai* bureaucrats for advice and support, these politicians take seriously their role of looking after the interests of their former agencies. Whether persona non grata

---

[36] For views voiced by Hamada Takujirō, a former MOF official who ran unsuccessfully in the 1979 Diet election, see Fujiwara Hirotatsu, "Ōkura ōchō nihon tōchi no karakuri" [The dynasty of the Ministry of Finance: the machinery for governing Japan], *Gendai* 14, no. 4 (April 1980): 58–59. For discussion of *shitazumi no seikatsu* based on experience and seniority, expected of all LDP dietmen (whether *kanryōha* or *tōjinha*), see Kōno, *Jimintō no kindaika*, p. 18.

or a dietman of the *ōendan* genre, a *senpai* dietman exercises considerable influence over his old agency, as long as he does not belong to a third and small group of inactive former bureaucrats who, as one interviewed official noted, does "not make demands on us and are usually men of low standing and without clout in the party. We seldom approach them to seek their support."

An MOF bureaucrat–turned–LDP dietman, interviewed by columnist Fujiwara Hirotatsu, candidly compared the two most celebrated graduates of his former agency—Fukuda Takeo and Ōhira Masayoshi—and their reputations during their tenures as prime minister. According to Fujiwara's informant, Ōhira was well liked in the agency but Fukuda was anything but the darling of the elite Finance bureaucrats. Fukuda was even feared. Ōhira, who left the MOF as a division-chief-level official, "delegated everything to the bureaucrats; he would only hear the final decisions made." Fukuda, former Budget Bureau director, who "knew too much about the internal workings" of the ministry, "intervened in agency decision making." He even "frequently phoned division chiefs."[37]

Ikeda Hayato, also an illustrious MOF product, resembled Fukuda in his dealings with his former agency. According to a former deputy director of the MOF Budget Bureau who had to contend with the politician Ikeda, he was the prototype of the overzealous new convert into partisan politics. First as finance minister and then as chairman of the Liberal party PARC, Ikeda was one of the hard-nosed party dietmen who "ganged up on" tightfisted MOF budget officials during the preparation of the 1952 budget, Japan's first postindependence budget. A key spokesman for party interests, Ikeda insisted on inclusion of the party's budgetary priorities in the budget.[38] Moreover, as prime minister, Ikeda successfully prodded the MOF's fiscal conservatives into "endorsing" the controversial National Income-Doubling Plan, which they had opposed when, in its embryonic form, it was first included in the LDP's 1956 Basic Guideline for Budgetary Compilation.[39] According to an informed contemporary observer: "Prime Minister Ikeda had a strong voice not only in the MOF's personnel matters but even over the future of retiring bureaucrats. This was a powerful weapon he used in pressuring MOF

---

[37] Cited in Fujiwara, "Ōkura ōchō," pp. 54–55.

[38] Mutō Kenjirō, "Mukai zōshō no yūdan" [Finance Minister Mukai's courageous decision], part 1, *Fainansu* 8, no. 10 (January 1973): 55–58.

[39] Daiichi Itō, "The Bureaucracy: Its Attitudes and Behavior," *The Developing Economies* 6, no. 4 (December 1968): 457–458.

bureaucrats into changing their minds" on the National Income-Doubling Plan.[40]

The parliamentary LDP of today abounds with the likes of Fukuda Takeo and Ikeda Hayato. Take Shiozaki Jun, a former MOF Taxation Bureau director and now a key member of the LDP "fiscal policy group" (*Zaiseizoku*), who in the view of the bureau is anything but its ally. As a bureau official put it: "Our attempts to correct the unfair taxation system are always frustrated by a group of LDP dietmen who are more concerned with their partisan interests. Spearheading this group is none other than our *senpai* Shiozaki."[41] When the likes of Shiozaki, knowing agency "secrets" as they do, start tearing apart the agency "logic" for a tax reform, their juniors in the Taxation Bureau are often hard-pressed for effective counterarguments. Take another former MOF official, Aizawa Hideyuki, who made his "fame" as Prime Minister Tanaka's "cooperative budget director" and was later promoted to AVM. A leading LDP fiscal expert, Aizawa has gained among his MOF *kōhai* the kind of "notoriety" that Shiozaki has acquired,[42] by his vitriolic attacks on the agency and the bureau that nurtured him. As he put it:

> More often than not, budgets prepared by bureaucrats are nothing more than "desk plans" out of touch with the realities. Moreover, they are inordinately influenced by the figures of the previous budget. As a result, progress by administrative means is often impossible. Take the case of social security programs. If we let the MOF have their way, we would be at a near standstill.[43]

Izurugi Michiyuki, also an MOF official before entering national politics as an LDP dietman, has also gained recognition as one of the "partisanized" legislators more feared than approached by MOF officials.[44]

[40] Kayano Mitsuo, "Keizaiha kanryō wa kapposuru" [Swaggering economic bureaucrats], *Chūō kōron* 76, no. 11 (November 1961): 266.

[41] Quoted in Takano Yasui and Ōkawa Kentarō, "Ōkurashō no hasan" [The bankruptcy of the MOF], *Bungei shunjū* 56, no. 12 (December 1978): 176–177.

[42] Ijichi Shigetaka, "Jichi kanryō no shin 'seijika jinmyaku' tankyū" [A study of Home Affairs bureaucrats' new "connections with politicians"], *Zaikai tenbō* 23, no. 1 (February 1, 1979): 83. According to reporters who have covered the Ministry of Home Affairs, Aizawa is a key member of the LDP *ōendan* (cheering group) for the MHA, which an interviewed MOF Budget Bureau official referred to as "our foremost rival." For discussion of Aizawa's articulate role for the MHA, see Ijichi Shigetaka, ed., *Jichishō zankoku monogatari* [The Ministry of Home Affairs inside out] (Tokyo: Ēru shuppansha, 1978), p. 198. Ijichi is a *Yomiuri shimbun* reporter who has covered the MHA.

[43] Quoted in Takano and Ōkawa, "Ōkurashō no hasan," p. 177.

[44] Yamamura Yoshiharu, *Ōkura kanryō no fukushū* [Revenge by Ministry of Finance bureaucrats] (Tokyo: Kōshobō, 1979), pp. 47–48.

Not only the MOF but also other ministries have had their shares of politicized and partisan critics among their graduates in the majority party. Take the MOE. Markedly nonpolitical in the postretirement career patterns of its officials, the postwar MOE has produced only four elected dietmen, who are understandably all members of the LDP. Two of them, Kennoki Toshihiro and Naitō Takasaburō, no longer active n party politics, followed remarkably similar tracks of upward mobility to attain the cabinet post for their parental agency. Both held the highest career post, the AVM, before entering elective politics as upper-house dietmen. Widely regarded as leading members of the party *Bunkyōzoku* during their active years, both were closely involved in party education policy-making. As longtime members of the *Bunkyōzoku,* both were affected by its mainstream thinking on various educational policy issues, although Naitō was far more "radical" than Kennoki on matters of educational reform and the Japan Teachers Union.

Education Minister Kennoki (1966–67), notwithstanding conservative MOE bureaucrats' misgivings, authorized the creation of the Central Council for Education (*Chūō kyōiku shingikai*) to undertake a comprehensive review of the postwar educational system and to propose, if necessary, ways to reform it. Also, Kennoki, in 1969, at the peak of the 1968–69 campus disturbances, authored a plan for reform of higher education that accommodated some of the ideas advocated by *Bunkyōzoku* elders, although the MOE's career officials viewed tampering with higher education as taboo. Kennoki was then chairman of a higher education subcommittee for the PARC Investigative Committee on the Educational System.[45]

Kennoki was more of an ally for his MOE *kōhai* than Naitō, however, for he often saw eye to eye with them on issues of education policy and sided with their positions. During the campus crisis of 1968–69, according to a well-informed source, Kennoki played a double role. Although advancing several reform suggestions, such as conversion of the prewar imperial universities (e.g., Tokyo University) into graduate centers, he stopped short of endorsing radical reform proposals popular in the conservative political and business sectors. The larger role he took upon himself was that of countering and moderating the so-called law and order members of the *Bunkyōzoku* who demanded a large-scale restructuring of the entire education system to prevent the recurrence of

---

[45] Sugawa Kiyoshi, "Daigaku mondai ni tsuyomaru seiji no atsuryoku" [Issues of higher education and growing political pressure], *Gendai kyōiku kagaku* 12, no. 4 (April 1969): 101. See also *Nihon keizai shimbun,* April 2, 1969.

campus disruptions. It stands to reason, therefore, that Kennoki was generally viewed by his *kōhai* as a valuable, albeit politicized, ally.

By contrast, Naitō was anything but a cheerleader for the MOE. A right-wing, anti-JTU hard-liner even from his bureaucratic days, Naitō was widely considered one of the principal troublemakers for the agency in the 1960s and early 1970s, during which he was an active *Bunkyōzoku* member. During the turbulent years of 1968–69, he was in the forefront of the intraparty movement pushing for "a fundamental reform of the education system" that his agency had spent most of its time and energy to develop and consolidate. It was he who privately counseled Prime Minister Satō that the education system required "a basic revision" in accordance with the suggestions of the party's education specialists.[46] A former MOE AVM and Naitō's *kōhai* commented on the Naitō of the 1960s: "Knowing much about education policy and how we work in the agency, he was actively involved in MOE affairs and policy-making. Luckily, we don't have many *Bunkyōzoku* members like him from our agency, for they can be and are quite annoying. They can well be compared to Shiozaki Jun," formerly of the MOF.

Politicization-partisanization is a major factor affecting *senpai-kōhai* relationships, but it is not the only factor. Interbureau and interfactional jealousy and conflict within the bureaucracy also play a major role, for they are reflected in the attitudes of agency graduates in the party. For the MOF Taxation Bureau, an MOF bureaucrat-turned-dietman nurtured by and loyal to the Budget Bureau is likely to be less sympathetic than its own graduates, just as a former MOE bureaucrat whose *hatake* (speciality) was elementary-secondary education can be less supportive of an MOE policy inspired by the Higher Education Bureau. This is not surprising in view of the traditional independence of bureaus and the intense rivalry and jurisdictional disputes among them, as portrayed in the popular adage *"Kyoku ari shō nashi"* (No ministry but bureaus).[47]

As noted above, there are *senpai* dietmen whom interviewed officials frequently refer to as "our *ōendan.*" How can we characterize their relations with, and their role vis-à-vis, the agency? Are they always relegated to the supportive and articulative role for the parental agency? The picture of the agency–*Ōendan senpai* relationship that emerges from

---

[46] *Mainichi shimbun,* August 15, 1968 (hereafter *Mainichi*).

[47] I am grateful to Kuroha Ryōchi, an editorial writer for the *Nihon keizai shimbun,* for enlightening me on this aspect of bureaucracy as it applied to the MOE, an agency he has reported on for nearly forty years.

interview responses negates the notion of "Trojan horse." In the most general terms, the relationship can be viewed as one of the two-way interactions in which *senpai* dietmen, though principal supporters of the ministry's interests, limit its freedom through their involvement—both direct and indirect—in agency affairs, including personnel matters.

Undoubtedly, it is through friendly *senpai* dietmen, among others, that that agency attempts to mobilize party and governmental (e.g., the MOF Budget Bureau) support for its policy programs, but no agency views its *senpai* dietmen as its extension in the party. The agency's *kōhai* officials know very well that their *senpai*'s support will be forthcoming only when he is convinced that a proposed agency policy is supportable and defensible within the party—that is, when it takes into account not only agency interests but also those of his party, faction, and constituency. Another factor, by no means marginal, affects the *kanryōha* dietman's policy posture. In general, he does not like to be accused by his party colleagues of placing his old agency's interests above those of his party and, especially, his faction.

The agency officials recognize these political considerations, which prompt them to be markedly receptive to their *senpai*'s policy suggestions and reservations in the early stages of agency policy-making. Therefore, when the agency bills and policy proposals so coordinated with their *senpai* dietmen and *zoku* members of the appropriate PARC division come before the division for formal legitimation, approval is a foregone conclusion. This situation has prompted many observers to conclude, of course mistakenly, that both the *kanryōha* and *tōjinha* members of the PARC organs are nothing more than yes-men for the bureaucracy. Party opposition to the ministry bills, if any, comes from the dietmen not included in the agency's mobilizational and *nemawashi* (laying the groundwork) processes.

There are other "prices" that an agency must pay for the helping hands from its influential *senpai* dietmen, as illustrated in the case of the MOT and its most illustrious graduate, Satō Eisaku. An influential "mainstream" dietman and later leader of his own faction, the former Transportation AVM was widely viewed as an effective mobilizer of party and government support for MOT programs. At the same time, as a source close to the MOT observed:

> The agency that has the prime minister among its former officials faces certain drawbacks as well. When the prime minister does something affecting all agencies [against their wishes], he often resorts to the technique of making his [parental] agency weep first and then seeking the cooperation of other ministries. In short, the

MOT must "tearfully perform the role of obliging" the prime minister.[48]

As the preceding discussions show, the widely held notion that the *senpai* dietman is merely the bureaucracy's tool in the party is far too simplistic, failing to take account of the political, partisan basis of his policy behavior. His politicization and partisanization, prompted by his electoral, legislative, partisan, and factional imperatives, is a key regulator of his policy behavior and attitude toward his parental agency.

We cannot be oblivious to this political side of *kanryōha* dietmen when we examine the policy behavior of the former agency official who has "come home" as minister. True, as the responsible officer of the agency, he is expected to speak for and articulate its interests. He certainly takes this organizational requirement seriously, for it affects his relationship with his agency subordinates. He is far more concerned with organizational needs and considerations than when he was a mere member of the appropriate party *zoku*. But it would be wrong to assume that he can brush aside his partisan, factional, and constituency requirements simply because he is one of the agency boys who have made it big in politics and come home to head the old ministry. As long as he is an elected dietman of the government party, he remains subjected to a multitude of considerations other than those of the agency that he was long affiliated with and now heads.

Thus, when caught in a serious conflict between party and agency priorities, his performance as agency head may fall far short of meeting organizational expectations in toto. Many ministers take their partisan and political identities and roles more seriously than agency priorities. As an interviewed dietman put it, "The bureaucrat-turned-minister is at times more sensitive to partisan needs and criticisms than his colleagues of pure politics background." His political socialization and role expectations aside, he does not want to be chided by his party colleagues for being too easy with his former agency and his *kōhai*. He has to prove to his party and faction that he stands above the "selfish" considerations of his agency.

---

[48] Kanryō kikō kenkyūkai, ed., *Un'yushō zankoku monogatari* [The Ministry of Transportation inside out] (Tokyo: Ēru shuppansha, 1979), pp. 39–40. The contributors to this volume were members of the MOT press corps.

# IV

# Ministers and Personnel Decisions

The contemporary minister's power to appoint and remove agency officials has helped bolster his role in agency policy-making. It has been widely argued that, notwithstanding his awesome formal authority, the minister has little actual power over agency personnel decisions, which are determined solely by factors internal to the agency. This view is echoed even by former bureaucrats, including Kakizawa Kōji, an MOF official-turned-dietman. As he put it, "The minister, with the exception of two or three cases, customarily does not exercise his formal appointment power," and "all officials, starting with the highest bureaucratic post of the AVM, are chosen consensually by the incumbent and retired officials of the agency."[1]

Data collected from a variety of interview and published sources, however, suggest patterns of personnel decision making considerably different from those Kakizawa observed. The politics of personnel decision making is complex, much more so than is commonly assumed, and is influenced by the powerful and often dominant roles of such extra-bureaucratic factors as the minister and his party. "Under the Japanese parliamentary system of government," as a former MOE PVM put it, "it is inevitable and proper that the party, through its PARC divisions and ministers, has a big voice over agency appointments, especially those involving the AVM and bureau directors, which are subject to cabinet understanding (*naikaku ryōkai*)."[2] Admittedly, the ministries vary a great deal in actors and patterns in pesonnel decision making. Decisional patterns and actors also vary in different posts. In spite of this variety

[1] Kakizawa Kōji, "Kokkai to kanryō: yosan hensei" [The Diet and the bureaucracy: formation of national budgets], an unpublished paper, pp. 3–4. I am grateful to Kimura Shūzō, formerly a senior researcher for the House of Councillors Committee for Foreign Affairs, for making a copy of the paper available to me.

[2] Interview with Ishibashi Kazuya, July 8, 1980. Ishibashi is an LDP dietman from Chiba Third District.

and the paucity of data on all agencies,[3] a few generalizations, at variance with the assumptions pointing to the dominance of intrabureaucratic factors in high-level personnel decisions, can be attempted.[4]

In general, it is true that the agency's personnel decision making is the responsibility of the career officials, including the AVM, director of the Minister's Secretariat (*kanbōchō*), bureau directors, and chief of the Personnel Division (*jinjika*). High-level appointments are made by the AVM and *kanbōchō* in consultation with bureau directors. Usually, the outgoing AVM picks his successor in close consultation with his predecessors. In making personnel decisions, the agency decision-makers are constrained by such traditional considerations as school education, types of civil service examinations passed, work performance, seniority, and established tracks of upward mobility.[5] Admittedly, in many cases the minister does not assume an active role; he performs the reactive role of legitimating the personnel recommendations made by the career officials.

As many interviewed officials and former ministers noted, however, although the career officials make personnel decisions by merit-related criteria and the minister often plays a reactive role, this does not necessarily mean bureaucratic dominance over the minister. As several interviewed dietmen stated, the LDP's long reign and close involvement in agency affairs over more than thirty-six years have largely negated the need for any major personnel changes in the bureaucracy. The intimacy and intensity of party-bureaucracy relations have helped socialize the bureaucrats in the basic values and policy priorities considered vital to

---

[3] Personnel decision making is one of the least explored areas of Japanese bureaucracy. Some useful information, however, can be gleaned from several publications including journalistic accounts. They include the *Zankoku monogatari* [Inside out] series on ministries, authored by reporters assigned to various ministries and published by Ēru shuppansha, Tokyo, since 1976. Also useful are the stenographic records of interviews (*danwa sokkiroku*) between prominent retired bureaucrats and members of the *Naiseishi kenkyūkai* (Research Committee of Domestic History). The interview records of Kennoki Toshihiro (former MOE AVM and minister), Suzuki Shun'ichi (former MHA AVM and now governor of the Tokyo metropolis), and Imai Kazuo (former MOF bureau director) are among the useful volumes of the series.

[4] Much of the information used here comes from interviews with LDP dietmen and their aides, Diet staff members, former and retired officials, and political and social affairs reporters.

[5] For discussion of the importance of these factors in personnel decision making at the prefectural government level, see Yung Park, "The Local Public Personnel System in Japan," *Asian Survey* 18, no. 6 (June 1978): 592–608. For much of the information pertaining to the role of these factors in ministry personnel decisions, I am grateful to many former and incumbent officials, including Katō Eiichi, Genjida Shigeyoshi, Kusaba Muneharu, Saitō Sei, Yoshitake Hiroki, Satō Teiichi, and Iwama Eitarō.

the party in power. In other words, partisanization of the bureaucracy has proceeded to such an extent that the basic bureaucratic values and policy priorities are now deemed tolerable and even acceptable to the part. On the whole, the party has confidence in intrabureaucratic socialization and "weeding out" processes and views the bureaucracy as a partisanized ally and even "tool." Thus, those who successfully undergo the bureaucracy's socialization and training processes—though these are by no means foolproof from the party's viewpoint—to reach the middle echelons (e.g., division chief) are far more likely to be acceptable to the party than not. The party and the party minister, therefore, can work with them, and the minister does not need to resort to his personnel authority and become active in agency personnel decisions. This is precisely what Karasawa Shunjirō, a former MOE PVM, implied when he commented on the agency he was familiar with: "There is no need for large-scale personnel changes in the MOE, but a Socialist victory at the polls would certainly be followed by a massive reshuffle targeted at higher officials."[6]

The Japanese experience of bureaucratic partisanization, as outlined above, may be compared to the process that affected the traditionally independent, assertive French bureaucracy during the long Gaullist reign.[7] There are, however, a couple of major differences between the two national cases. First, the LDP in Japan has been in power since 1948, considerably longer than the French rightist party, making it the longest reigning party among the competitive polities. Second, the Japanese party system, though multiparty in its numerical composition, is basically a one-party–dominant system in which the government party has held an unrivaled status; the Gaullist party, operating in a highly competitive multiparty setting, had to deal with serious challenges from other political parties. The long-term dominant status enjoyed by the LDP has contributed to making partisanization of the bureaucracy far more pervasive and thorough in Japan than in France.

The bureaucracy's partisanization, therefore, is important in accounting for the minister's reactive role in agency personnel matters. Other factors that have lessened the need for direct ministerial involvement are discussed below.

---

6 Interview with Karasawa Shunjirō, July 4, 1980. This position was shared by many other LDP dietmen who had had extensive dealings with the MOE.

7 For an excellent analysis of this development in France, see Ezra Suleiman, *Politics, Power, and Bureaucracy in France* (Princeton: Princeton University Press, 1974), pp. 352–371.

Admittedly, the AVM and other ranking officials have the major responsibility for making personnel recommendations, but they perform this role in a manner highly deferential to the minister, who has the formal authority over all agency personnel decisions.[8] For example, in formulating a list of recommended appointments for approval by the minister, the AVM who is in close touch with him carefully takes into account his superior's known views. If they are not available, he tries to anticipate the minister's reactions, for he does not like to be rejected by the minister. In all probability, the AVM will not go against the minister's strongly held views, for the minister who takes the trouble to make his wishes known to his AVM is an assertive minister who expects his AVM to respect his authority. Supervisors, even Japanese ministers, do not like to be ignored by subordinates.

Moreover, as former MOE AVM Saitō Sei put it, "The minister does not leave everything to his AVM; in fact, many a minister does speak out on personnel matters."[9] For illustration let us take Kaifu Toshiki, minister of education, 1976–77. He recalled: "I usually relied on my AVM and *kanbōchō* for most personnel matters. Of course, I made my general views known to them." At the same time, he intervened on behalf of several officials who in their formal education and civil service examinations passed were not up to the usual level found among the elite *kyaria* (career) officials, who typically graduated from the Tokyo University Law School and passed the Higher Civil Service Examination, Class A (*Kokka kōmuin shiken jōkyū kō*).[10] With the backing of the minister and key *Bunkyōzoku* members, these "underdog" candidates were promoted to posts normally reserved for those with the highest qualifications.[11]

---

[8] Interview with Kaifu Toshiki, April 27, 1979.

[9] Interview with Saitō Sei, April 19, 1979. Saitō was director of the National Museum of Tokyo at the time of interviewing.

[10] The *kyaria* designation is given to those who passed the top-level civil service examination. In general, these *kyaria* officials occupy the higher posts of division chief, deputy bureau director, bureau director, and AVM, although occasionally non-*kyaria* (non-career) officials rise to become division chiefs. Normally, the highest post a non-*kyaria* official can hold is deputy division chief (*kachō hosa*). Frequently placed in staff offices such as the Minister's Secretariat and general affairs divisions, however, veteran non-*kyaria* officials perform vital functions as sources of information on agency precedents and regulations and as teachers for new *kyaria* officials. I am grateful to former MOE AVM Iwama Eitarō and Yoshitake Hiroki, a veteran non-*kyaria* MOE official, for enlightening me on non-*kyaria* officials and their importance.

[11] Interview with Kaifu Toshiki, April 27, 1979.

Often the AMV's proposed list of appointments is not acceptable to the minister in toto, notwithstanding the precautions taken by the AVM in accordance with the rule of anticipated reactions. When this happens, the list has to be revised taking the minister's views into account, as has happened in all agencies. Moreover, as far as the AVM and key bureau director–level posts are concerned, it is the norm in all agencies for the outgoing vice-minister to make his selections in close consultation with the minister. Thus, more often than not the top-level appointments are based on the joint decisions of the minister and the AVM, subject to other factors, of course, as we shall see. In a conflict between the two, the minister usually wins. Faced with several equally qualified candidates, the outgoing AVM is often unable to reach a clear-cut recommendation. When this happens, the matter is referred to the minister for resolution.[12]

As mentioned previously, from the minister's standpoint, and the party's as well, the bureaucratic process of recruitment and socialization is not foolproof; nor is agency personnel decision making always based on the rule of anticipated reactions. Moreover, other considerations (e.g., factional and personal) prompt the minister to deviate from the reactive role and assume an interventionist posture. Some ministers go as far as to assume a direct decision-making role over personnel matters, especially high-level appointments, relegating their agency subordinates to a supportive, secondary role. The activist minister's personality is such that he must participate in all major aspects of agency affairs, including personnel decisions. He may be directed by his party to "streamline" or reshape the ministry to respond better to the party's new priorities. He may be similarly directed by the prime minister and by his faction.

Factional efforts to "colonize" the bureaucracy are particularly intense with the so-called distributive, extractive, and regulative agencies such as the Ministry of Agriculture, Forestry, and Fisheries (MAFF), MOF, Ministry of Construction (MOC), and MOT[13] because their jurisdictions encompass the sectors of society and industry pivotal to the electoral and financial bases of the party and its factions. To enrich their coffers and enhance their respectability in the eyes of powerful sectoral groups, all factions make vigorous colonizing efforts, although the power-

---

[12] Interview with Amagi Isao, April 20, 1979. Amagi, a former MOE AVM, is widely considered one of Japan's leading experts on higher education.

[13] These functional categories are borrowed from Richard L. Siegel and Leonard B. Weinberg, *Comparing Public Policies* (Homewood, Ill.: Dorsey Press, 1977), pp. 3–5.

ful "*jinmyaku*" (terrains of personal connections) historically found in the "lucrative" agencies are largely linked with powerful, "mainstream" factions. Factional ministers, of course, play a central role in these efforts, and the principal tool used is their personnel power.[14]

Personnel activism may also be assumed by an ambitious *jitsuryokusha* (man of power) minister. With his eyes on the party presidency (which also means the premiership under the present LDP-dominated system), he may seek to establish or strengthen his own bases of power within the key economic and foreign-policy agencies whose policy decisions directly affect the powerful sectors of industry and business. He is well aware that big business support is critical to his intraparty constituency building and his planned upward mobility.[15] Not only the prime ministerial hopefuls but also other *jitsuryokusha* dietmen make use of their appointment power during their ministerial tenures to establish footholds in the agencies in charge of disributive, extractive, and regulative functions for the groups critical to their constituency building. To be wooed, endorsed, and funded by these groups, ministers need to be widely recognized as powerful members and preferably *gosanke* of the appropriate *zoku*. To attain and maintain this coveted staus of privilege and power, they must have not only access to but also influence in the relevant agencies.

Whether reactive or activist in his approach to agency personnel decision making, the minister has the formidable removal power—not just a formal authority but one he actually exercises against his subordinates for a variety of reasons ranging from personality conflict to insubordination to his authority and policy. Whether a division chief on an elite mobility ladder or a senior bureau director "scheduled" to succeed the outgoing AVM, once a *kyaria* official incurs the ire of the minister, he is taken off the promotional track temporarily or even permanently. If the superior is determined that the insubordinate official must go, his exit is simply a matter of time. As the former MOE AVM Kobayashi Yukio put it. "If the minister is convinced that he cannot work effectively with his AVM, the career official must go."[16] The minister's

---

[14] For discussion of factional *jinmyaku* in the MOF and among its celebrated graduates, see Ōkura Mondō, "Ōkurashō no jinmyaku o kiru" [Networks of personal connections in the MOF exposed], *Hōseki* 8, no. 2 (February 1980): 334–348. Ōkura is the pseudonym of a newspaper reporter covering the MOF and fiscal affairs.

[15] Chitoshi Yanaga goes as far as to argue: "Candidacy for the premiership is unthinkable without its [big business'] tacit approval, and the Prime Minister's days are numbered if his policies or methods no longer meet with its approval." See his *Big Business in Japanese Politics* (New Haven: Yale University Press, 1968), p. 33.

[16] Interview with Kobayashi Yukio, February 18, 1980. For a dramatic demonstration

personnel authority used negatively is a foremost deterrent to bureaucratic defiance of him and his policy, as many interviewed officials privately admitted. This negative power may be the single most effective tool in the minister's arsenal.

In contrast to the American bureaucracy, which allows lateral entries from extrabureaucratic sectors, outsiders are rarely brought into the higher bureaucracy in Japan. Among the available candidates of the bureaucracy, however, the activist Japanese minister has a considerable choice because of the intensifying competition that bureaucrats must face as they move upward. Cooperative officials can be singled out for appropriate rewards; the uncooperative can also be properly dealt with. Subservience to the minister, a politician and an LDP dietman, is widely looked down upon and even condemned by the elite bureaucrats interviewed, but this position is in the realm of *tatemae*. What borders on *honne* (reality) is a great deal of "tail-wagging" by bureaucratic "climbers" keenly conscious of increasing competition ahead of them.[17]

Contrary to popular assumptions, key personnel decisions in all agencies are affected and even dominated by external inputs. They come from a variety of sources, including the agency's distinguished graduates, such as the former AMVs; powerful clientele groups; and the LDP. The most powerful of these sources, the party leaders and organs, include the prime minister, who concurrently is the leader of a mainstream faction; the director of the Cabinet Secretariat (*Naikaku kanbō chōkan*), who is the prime minister's chief aide in the government; the agency's former ministers; faction leaders and their factions having special relationships with the agency; high-level party functionaries, including the secretary-general and chairmen of the PARC and the Executive Board (*Sōmukai*); the chairman and deputy chairmen of the ministry's PARC counterpart; and leaders (*gosanke*) and other influential members of the appropriate party *zoku* who constitute the informal power structure behind the formal leadership of the PARC division.

Usually, of these party actors, the agency's PARC counterpart (*bukai*) and its leaders, especially *zoku gosanke,* are most involved in that agency's personnel decisions.[18] Although the level of *bukai* and *zoku*

---

by a health-welfare minister of this removal power, see Ashizaki, *Kōseishō,* pp. 138–141. In 1965, Kanda Hiroshi, then health-welfare minister, fired two top officials of the ministry (AVM and Health Insurance Bureau director) over a controversy widely attributed to the minister's judgmental blunder. He exercised this power shortly before his expected departure from the cabinet.

[17] *Imai Kazuo-shi danwa sokkiroku,* no. 15, p. 120. See also Takeuchi, *Konna kanryō,* p. 39.

[18] According to a former MOF Budget Bureau director, members of the specialized *zoku*

participation varies among agencies, all ministries consult in one way or another with their PARC counterpart groups and leaders who oversee them.[19] The principal personnel decisions in the MOE must be blessed with endorsement by the *Bunkyōzoku gosanke* headed by Sakata Michita, a former MOE minister. Once an MOE official is branded by the party Education Division and its *Bunkyōzoku* as persona non grata, his rise to the top is effectively doomed, notwithstanding his minister's support. If his defiance of the party is viewed as blatant, he must go.[20]

For the activist minister, therefore, party intervention is a powerful constraint on his personnel power when there is a disagreement between him and the party. If the two unite, of course, no official or group of officials in the agency can thwart them unless the officials are powerfully backed by a faction leader or the prime minister. The roles of the minister and *zoku gosanke* depend largely on the minister's power and standing within the party. A minor politician, inexperienced in agency affairs, will carefully consult with and even defer to the elders of the party *zoku gosanke* who have been closely involved with agency affairs and personnel. The more powerful the minister is, the more he will try to assert his authority over personnel decisions.[21] In most cases, however, even the powerful minister, except perhaps for such as Kōno Ichirō, who terrified the MAFF and MOC, will consult with the relevant *zoku* leaders before making final personnel decisions on key posts, including the AVM.

As far as the bureaucrats are concerned, the extensive party participation is not always bad; it sometimes works to their advantage because of the factional basis of all party organs, including the PARC divisions and *zoku.* In a move against an influential *kyaria* official, the minister may be backed by PARC division members who belong to his factions, but he may be opposed by other factions closely tied to the official. These antiminister factions may come to the official's aid and may succeed in blunting and even nullifying the minister's sharp blow—as the

---

*gosanke,* better informed and more experienced in some policy matters than the frequently rotated bureaucrats and the minister new to agency affairs, are involved in personnel matters of the ministry. See Hashigushi, *Shinzaisei jijō,* p. 196.

[19] Interviews with LDP dietmen, including Karasawa Shunjirō (July 4, 1980), Ishibashi Kazuya (July 8, 1980), and Arita Kazuhisa (April 16, 1979). See *Imai Kazuo-shi danwa sokkiroku,* no. 14, p. 93, and no. 15, pp. 165–166.

[20] Interview with Nishioka Takeo, February 19, 1980.

[21] This generalization applies to all agencies. In the MOE, Nadao Hirokichi (1956–57, 1958, 1963–64, and 1966–68), Araki Masuo (1960–63), Sakata Michita (1968–71), and Okuno Seisuke (1972–74) are considered to be among the activist MOE ministers who often made key personnel decisions with little consultation with the party's education dietmen.

Tanaka faction was often able to do for pro-Tanaka officials in the two agencies extensively "colonized" by Tanaka, the MOC and the MPT.

Contrary to Kakizawa's assertion mentioned earlier, all ministries, not only partisanized but also more independent agencies, have had activist ministers who see their personnel authority as a power to be exercised when necessary, not a formal prerogative that they cannot touch in reality. Reading a variety of published accounts and interviewing a wide range of individuals including ministry officials, former ministers, and reporters, one encounters too many interventionist and activist ministers to exclude personnel power from the minister's repertory of effective powers. Upon assuming the Education portfolio in 1953, Ōdachi Shigeo, considered one of the most powerful MOE ministers, made clear that he intended to abide by the prewar personnel norm he cherished: *"Daijin ga kawattara kachō ijō wa kubio aratte matte ita monoda"* (When a new minister is appointed, all the officials at the division chief level and higher would wait for his arrival, fully ready to be replaced).[22] More recently, the newly appointed MAFF minister Matsuno Raizō severely chided the director of the Minister's Secretariat when the latter paid a courtesy call on the new minister: "The new minister has come. Logic dictates that you should ask the minister about your future status, with a letter of resignation in your hand."[23]

Ōdachi's subsequent personnel decisions lived up to his convictions. In a major shake-up of the agency's senior staff, he removed several key "intellectual" officials, appropriately known as *kōdanha* (lectern faction), who had collaborated with SCAP in the postwar educational reforms. Replacing these reformists were prewar Ministry of Home Affairs officials who were committed, like Ōdachi, to correcting the excesses of SCAP's educational reforms. Tanaka Yoshio, a purged *Naimushō* official and onetime deputy chief of education in the Manchukuo government, was appointed the new AVM, and the directorship of the key Elementary-Secondary Education Bureau went to Ogata Shin'ichi, a member of the prewar *Naimushō* Special Political Police (*Tokkō*). As a result of Ōdachi's reorganization, the old adage *"Mombushō wa naimushō no kyōikukyoku"* (The MOE is the Education Bureau of the Ministry of Home Affairs) gained renewed currency.[24] Ad-

---

[22] Totsuka Ichirō and Kio Toshikazu, eds., *Mombushō* [The Ministry of Education] (Tokyo: Hōbunsha, 1956), p. 96. The contributors to this volume were then members of the MOE press corps.

[23] *Asahi*, May 24, 1979.

[24] Totsuka and Kio, *Mombushō*, pp. 22–44 and 96.

mittedly, this shuffle occurred in a key agency of "reverse programs," after the Americans left. Even after the turbulent decade of the 1950s, however, the agency's personnel decision making has frequently been subjected to the intervention of the minister and his party, though not on the scale of what was then known as the "Ōdachi tornado."

What about other partisanized agencies, such as the MOC, MAFF, MOT, MPT, and Self-Defense Agency (SDA)? They do not widely deviate from the pattern of political and ministerial intervention that has often befallen the MOE. Let us take the MOC, whose foremost function is distributive and regulative. Like other agencies, the MOC has its own bureaucratic traditions governing personnel decision making. They are adhered to for the most part, but not always. Those who depart from them with impunity are usually the so-called *jitsuryokusha* ministers, who have frequently headed the agency. By tradition, the highest career official, the AVM, is picked by a group of the past occupants of the post. The MOC AVM has a smaller role in the choice of bureau directors and lower officials than his counterpart in other agencies, for his immediate subordinates have a primary responsibility. In "administrative" (*jimukan*) *kyaria* posts, the appointments are made by the director of the Minister's Secretariat, the agency's second-highest career post, as with other postwar offspring of the prewar *Naimushō.* "Technical" (*gikan*) *kyaria* officials are appointed by the chief technical officer (*gikan*), the agency's highest technical official. A typical *jimukan* is a law school graduate; a *gikan* is trained in engineering and has passed the technical component of the higher civil service examination. The appointments for the so-called non-*kyaria* officials are handled by the chief of the Personnel Division in the Minister's Secretariat.

As noted above, the MOC's *kyaria* personnel is composed of *jimukan* and *gikan* classes. Neither group monopolizes all higher posts; rather, there is a careful division of these between the two classes. For example, the Road Bureau (*Dōrokyoku*) directorship is reserved for a *gikan,* as are the directorships of the regional construction bureaus (*chihō kensetsukyoku*), but other key posts such as the directorship of the Minister's Secretariat are held by members of the *jimukan* class. The top career post of AVM is held by the two classes on an alternating basis. In MOC personnel decisions, as with other ministries, a premium is placed on such factors as work performance, seniority, and education. No private-university graduate can hope to rise to the top career post, although he may have a small chance to become a bureau director.[25]

---

[25] Kanryō kikō kenkyūkai, ed., *Kensetsushō zankoku monogatari* [The Ministry of Construction inside out] (Tokyo: Ēru shuppansha, 1979), pp. 139–140.

This elaborate body of traditions notwithstanding, the agency has often been subjected to the minister's intervention; it too was hit by a personnel tornado of the Ōdachi type, administered in 1962–64 by Kōno Ichirō, one of the most powerful ministers to rule in the MOC. Upon assuming office, Kōno shocked the agency by announcing to a staff gathering: "I will not ask about your past. Those of you who will cooperate with me should stay. Those who will not cooperate, will oppose me, or are incompetent are requested to leave." He then instructed his AVM Yamamoto Saburō: "The MOC is lethargic and needs an infusion of new blood. We should transfer about ten officials out of the agency. We need to have the Police Agency send us about five of its men, and I will talk to them myself."[26] The three men brought in from the Police Agency assumed pivotal posts, including director of the Minister's Secretariat. Not only central bureau chiefs but also directors of the regional construction bureaus were affected by Kōno's shake-up, which violated the agency's traditional rules governing assignments for the agency's two categories of administrative and technical officials. A number of key regional bureau directorships went to administrative officials, much to the consternation of the technical class. Several discontented officials of technical background resigned from the agency in protest; they included a chief technical officer and a director of the Roads Bureau.[27]

Between 1964, when Kono's reign ended, and 1976, the MOC was headed by members of the prime minister's faction (the Satō faction for 1964–72 and the Tanaka faction for 1972–76; even after Tanaka's fall from the premiership, a member of his faction headed the MOC until 1976). With the backing of the prime minister, the mainstream faction ministers played the dominant role in key personnel decisions to establish and consolidate control over the agency. (By law, the minister's appointment of the AVM and bureau directors is subject to cabinet approval.)

The key personnel task of the early MOC ministers under Satō was to eliminate the remnants of Kōno's influence (Kōno was Satō's archrival), and by the end of the 1960s, the agency's pivotal posts were held by officials markedly sympathetic to the Satō faction. When Tanaka, one of Satō's key lieutenants, took over the premiership in 1972, his ministers proceeded to effect a "Tanakanization" of the agency. This was a fairly simple task because many of the pro-Satō faction officials were already close to Tanaka and his group within the Satō faction. As a result

---

[26] Kusayanagi, *Kanryō ōkokuron*, pp. 65–66.

[27] Kanryō kikō kenkyūkai, *Kensetsushō*, pp. 30–32.

of this personnel policy, "All key MOC posts," in the words of reporters covering the MOC, "were occupied by those backed by Tanaka."[28]

Hence, for much of the 1970s, well after Tanaka's departure from the premier's office, the MOC was widely known as "the stronghold of the Tanaka faction." Tanakanization of the agency had proceeded to such an extent that, even after Tanaka resigned from the office, a regional bureau director could boast at a Tanaka faction rally, "We [in the agency] consent to every petition from members of the Tanaka faction." This remark reached the ears of the then MOC minister, Chūma Tatsui, a member of the Fukuda faction. The irate minister "confided" to a group of reporters that he "would fire that impudent fellow." The director who had boasted, alarmed by his minister's threat, went to the Tanaka faction for assistance, which was promptly provided. The minister's attempt was effectively thwarted by the intervention of the Tanaka faction—an interesting testimony to the faction's influence over the MOC and its ability to frustrate even the agency head.[29]

The MAFF also has been frequented by assertive ministers who have played an active role, both positive and negative, in top personnel decisions. This activism is attributable in large part to the LDP's sensitivity to agricultural policy issues and the party's dependence upon the powerful National Agricultural Cooperative (*Nōkyō*) for financial and electoral support. According to former MAFF career official Takeuchi Naokazu (1942–65), this tradition of ministerial participation in agency personnel matters started during the tenure of Hirokawa Kōzen, thrice minister of agriculture in the Yoshida cabinet.[30] It was also during Hirokawa's incumbency that what Takeuchi calls "the politicization of agricultural policy-making" (*nōsei no seijika*) was set in motion.[31] Though not on a par with the Finance and MITI portfolios, the MAFF post is considered a major cabinet post and has often gone to powerful dietmen. One such minister, Akagi Munenori, who twice served in the MAFF post, said in his inaugural speech before ministry officials:

> It is said that art is long and life is short. You must think that "agriculture lasts long and the minister's life is short." You fellows don't last long either. My term is at most one year, but I can fire you through evaluations of your work performance. The truth is that "agriculture is long and the bureaucrat's life is short." Thus, I would

---

[28] Ibid., p. 92.
[29] Ibid., pp. 92–93.
[30] Takeuchi, *Konna kanryō*, p. 39.
[31] Ibid., p. 13.

like you to look at the farmer's face, not mine.[32]

Many a minister has lived up to the threat so bluntly put forward by A-kagi. Therefore, a group of reporters covering the MAFF concluded that although, on the whole, agency "personnel decisions appear to be fair, from time to time there are frustrated and extraordinarily successful careers, all made possible by the intervention of the minister. This is brought home so well in the adage, 'To be or not to be, it's all up to the minister' (*Shinumo ikirumo daijin no mune sanzun*)."[33]

Like the MOE and the MOC, the MAFF has had its share of "Ōdachi tornadoes," the most pernicious and most vividly remembered of which was inflicted by none other than Kōno Ichirō. When in 1954 he first assumed the cabinet post for the agency he had covered as an *Asahi* reporter for ten years, he astounded the agency officials by inviting them "to quit if unable to go along with my way of doing things."[34] The very first action he took was to get his old MAFF confidant Yasuda Zen'ichi out of an obscure post and promote him to the post of director of the Minister's Secretariat. Together with Yasuda, Kōno exercised a firm control over all major personnel decisions, promoting those who cooperated with him and demoting others.[35] This is precisely what he later did in the MOC, as mentioned earlier.

Kōno served in the MAFF twice, in 1954–56 and in 1961–62. In the intervening years he still kept tabs on the agency's personnel matters not only as a powerful faction leader but also as the undisputed doyen of the party's agricultural policy group (*Nōrinzoku*), which oversaw the MAFF. He intervened in support of his protégés and against those inimical to him and his faction. Understandably, some ministers, and especially those of anti-Kōno factions, resented his meddling, but many compromised and even went along with this potentate, thus ushering in the widely followed MAFF tradition that allows powerful former ministers a major voice in high-level personnel decisions.[36]

Through his activist personnel policy, Kōno established what was then widely known as the "Kōno *jinmyaku*," a powerful network of his supporters, which lasted as the dominant force in the agency well into the 1960s. It stands to reason that for much of the 1950s and 1960s the

[32] Kusayanagi, *Kanryō ōkokuron*, p. 113.

[33] Kanryō kikō kenkyūkai, ed., *Nōrinshō zankoku monogatari* [The Ministry of Agriculture, Forestry, and Fisheries inside out] (Tokyo: Ēru shuppansha, 1978), p. 33.

[34] Ibid.

[35] Ibid., pp. 35–36.

[36] "Jiki jūyō posto o yosōsuru" [Predicting forthcoming occupants of key posts], *Shūkan yomiuri* 39, no. 23 (June 1, 1980): 168.

MAFF was frequently referred to as "the bastion (*gajō*) of the Kōno faction." His death in 1965, however, saw the beginning of the Kōno *jinmyaku*'s demise, which started with Akagi Munenori's decision to "transfer" the chief Kōnoist "villain," Yasuda, to a post considered lower in the agency's pecking order than the bureau directorship he had to relinquish. The "demotion" decision was reached and announced while he was out of town on agency business. Akagi was a leading member of the Kawashima faction. By 1973–74, the last of the pro-Kōno officials retired, signaling the end of the Kōno *jinmyaku* in the agency.[37]

In the 1970s also, the MAFF had a variety of powerful ministers who assumed an activist posture in personnel decision making; even the less activist ministers moved with impunity against key agency officials because they were considered uncooperative or because of personality conflicts. They include Kuraishi Tadao, who in 1971 ousted a director of the MAFF's Fisheries Agency (*Suisanchō*), widely recognized as "a man destined to become the AVM"; and Adachi Tokurō, a senior member of the Tanaka faction who in 1972 fired a director of the Livestock Bureau (*Chikusankyoku*) for his actions allegedly detrimental to normalization of Sino-Japanese relations, the prime foreign-policy objective of the new Tanaka cabinet.[38]

The right-wing *Seirankai* of LDP Young Turks was a key cross-factional party group that during the 1970s sent the MAFF a string of its members to assume powerful decision-making roles as ministers and PVMs.[39] Particularly noteworthy are two *Seirankai* elders, Nakagawa Ichirō and Watanabe Michio, who, as MAFF ministers and members of the agricultural policy group *gosanke,* played the dominant decision-making role in all agency policy matters, including the very important rice-price setting.[40]

Nakagawa, though an assertive minister respected by his agency subordinates, delegated personnel policy-making to his lieutenants, only occasionally intervening in key personnel decisions. Watanabe, however,

---

[37] Kanryō kikō kenkyūkai, *Nōrinshō,* p. 39.

[38] These two cases are detailed in ibid., pp. 39–47.

[39] For discussion of the *Seirankai*'s ties with the MAFF, see Tahara Sōichirō, *Nihon no kanryō 1980* [Japan's bureaucrats, 1980] (Tokyo: Bungei shunjū, 1979), pp. 224–237. As in the MOE and other partisanized agencies, the PVMs of the MAFF also played a powerful role in agency affairs during the 1970s.

[40] "Nōsei o gyūjiru Nakagawa Ichirō to Watanabe Michio no jitsuryoku" [The power of Nakagawa Ichirō and Watanabe Michio, who control agricultural policy], *Shūkan yomiuri* 39, no. 23 (June 1, 1980): 165–167.

operated quite differently; he actively intervened in almost every major personnel decision. Twice the MAFF PVM (1970–71 and 1973–74), Watanabe fully lived up to his motto: "I don't feel good unless I do everything myself."[41] Sharply deviating from the traditional norms of agency personnel decision making, Watanabe effectively ignored those usually consulted within and outside the ministry, who included former ministers and AVMs and LDP agricultural policy dietmen (*Nōrinzoku*). The only exception was his AVM, Ōkawara Taiichirō, a close friend from prewar military days, who served as his foremost aide and confidant.[42] Already familiar with the backgrounds of many agency officials, Watanabe carefully went over the files of not only bureau and division chiefs but also lower officials before reaching his decisions. Thus, according to a *Mainichi* reporter covering the MAFF, the agency's July 10, 1979, list of new appointments "bore strong imprints of Watanabe's touch."[43] As informed *Yomiuri* and *Mainichi* sources put it, "Personnel decision making within the MAFF during Watanabe's tenure was effectively his."[44]

The preceding discussions have focused on three of the substantially partisan agencies—the MOE, the MOC, and the MAFF—noted for the major and even dominant roles of their ministers in agency personnel decisions. What about the reputedly assertive, less partisan economic agencies such as MITI and the MOF, where internal ranking orders of succession (*joretsu*) and "tracks of upward mobility" are supposedly more carefully adhered to, thus limiting the minister's input in personnel decision making?

Although these agencies have not been hit by personnel "tornadoes" of the Kōnoist or Ōdachian genre, they too have had their shares of assertive ministers who have played key roles in personnel decisions. Admittedly, these agencies have enjoyed the reputations of being more independent of and assertive toward the LDP and its ministers than the more partisan ministries, but because of their importance in the polity and their extractive, regulative, and distributive functions, they have attracted as their chief executives many *jitsuryokusha* dietmen, frequently leaders and veteran members of mainstream factions, who play interventionist roles in agency personnel decision making. As one interviewed

---

[41] *Mainichi*, July 21, 1979.

[42] "Nōsei o gyūjiru," p. 167.

[43] According to press reports, Watanabe's "favorite readings" included the staff directories for the MAFF and the MHW, which he had headed immediately prior to his MAFF assignment. See *Mainichi*, July 21, 1979.

[44] Ibid.; and "Nōsei o gyūjiru," p. 167.

MOF division chief put it: "There is much more political and ministeri-al involvement in MOF personnel decision making than meets the eye or is popularly assumed.  To be promoted beyond the division chief level, you really need the backing of a politician; the support of your minister would be most helpful."

Because of the variation found in their styles and levels of involve-ment in personnel policy, the economic ministers defy a simple generali-zation.  *Jitsuryokusha* ministers aspiring to the party presidency and recognizing the strategic importance of these agencies to their political careers attempt to develop close ties with key officials and even place their men in strategic posts.  Ikeda Hayato, Satō Eisaku, Fukuda Takeo, Tanaka Kakuei, Takeshita Noboru, Watanabe Michio, Miyazawa Kiichi, Abe Shintarō, Kōmoto Toshio, Nakasone Yasuhiro, and Tanaka Rokusuke, who all held one or both of the key economic portfolios (MITI and Finance), belong to this category.

Of course, *jitsuryokusha* ministers are by no means alike in their styles and extent of participation in agency personnel matters.  Those widely perceived to have realistic chances of attaining the top party-government post carry far more clout with their agency subordinates than do other presidential hopefuls, and thus their personnel preferences are rarely resisted by the career officials.  Some ministers, such as Ikeda, assume, often with success, the foremost decision-making role in all agency matters, including personnel; others, such as Nakasone, pursue a minimal policy of cultivating close personal and factional ties with promising elite bureaucrats.  Even these "minimal" ministers, however, often intervene in personnel matters critical to their protégés or allies.  Then, there are the likes of Ikeda and Fukuda, who have major advan-tages in personnel matters because of their long, respected tenures in the agencies they now head.  Both Ikeda and Fukuda, who had held ranking positions in the MOF (AVM in the case of Ikeda and Budget Bureau director in the case of Fukuda) before entering elective politics, literally took over the agency's personnel decision-making role as far as key deci-sions were concerned.  Chalmers Johnson, a chronicler of MITI, com-mented on Ikeda: "Ikeda...was always an activist minister in whatever ministry he headed; and he became famous for shaking up the Ministry of Finance in order to remove fiscal conservatives who were blocking his plans for rapid economic growth, and also in order to enlist the ministry in support of his own political ambitions."[45]

---

45 Johnson, *MITI*, p. 53.

Even *jitsuryokusha* dietmen without the advantage of career experience in the MOF, such as Satō and Tanaka, are by no means bystanders in agency personnel matters. Depending upon their personal inclinations, skills, and factional strengths, among other things, they can be and often are powerful personnel decision-makers, whose role can even be characterized as one of close involvement and active input. For illustration, let us take Tanaka, who, according to a source close to the MOF, "established a firm grip over the MOF bureaucrats during his three-year tenure in the Ikeda and Satō cabinets."[46] Though more concerned with cultivating close personal and symbiotic ties with the bureaucrats,[47] the youthful Tanaka (a good deal younger than most division chiefs) did not tolerate uncooperative officials. According to an informed source: "Kōno [Ichirō] had no monopoly over the policy of caring for those officials the minister likes and treating coolly those he dislikes. This policy was also used by the former prime minister Tanaka when he was consolidating his foothold in the MOF as minister, but he was not as gaudy as Kōno." A retiring MOF bureau director in Tanaka's disfavor had to find employment in the private sector, unable to do do so with a public corporation. Two other bureau directors in Tanaka's favor who retired at the same time were "allowed" to remain in the public sector.[48]

Even the powerful MOF and MITI are not always blessed with "first-class" (*ichiryū*) dietmen as their ministers who are independently powerful enough to successfully ward off outside (e.g., LDP and other ministries) attempts to dispute or undermine agency powers and decisions; "second-class" (*niryū*) politicians also frequent these prestigious agencies. Contrary to popular assumptions, however, it is simply wrong to lump them in the category of impotent ministers hopelessly manipulated by the elite economic bureaucrats, for there is wide variation among these ministers.

Because of the important functions performed by these agencies, the prime minister, the foremost decision-maker in cabinet formations, makes every effort to place his trusted lieutenants in the key ministerial posts, and espeically the all-important MOF post. Thus, many of the so-called *niryū* ministers come from the prime minister's faction and typically serve as his agents or as proxies through whom he deals with these

---

[46] Kanryō kikō kenkyūkai, ed., *Shin-ōkurashō zankoku monogatari* [The Ministry of Finance inside out: a revised version] (Tokyo: Ēru shuppansha, 1981), pp. 14–15.

[47] His generous gift giving (typically, salted Hokkaidō salmon, Niigata rice, and cash) is a well-known Tanaka trademark.

[48] Kanryō kikō kenkyūkai, *Nōrinshō*, p. 34.

pivotal economic agencies. This was true of several MOF ministers of the 1970s who served in the Tanaka, Fukuda, and Ōhira cabinets.[49] A prime example of the MOF ministers of this category is Ueki Kōshirō, a MOF Budget Bureau director–turned–dietman who served under Tanaka. Backed by the prime minister, these ministers more often than not assume an activist posture in agency personnel affairs to insure that the prime minister's policy priorities are respected and adhered to.

Moreover, there are *niryū* dietmen ministers, not even members of the prime minister's inner group or factions, who skillfully exercise their personnel authority—usually playing an interventionist or veto role—in the powerful economic agencies. Fukuda Hajime, a former minister of MITI and later of the MHA, provides an interesting illustration. Though a Tokyo University Law School graduate who passed the prewar civil service examination, he joined the Domei News Agency, for which he covered Southeast Asia. Upon returning to Japan, he briefly pursued a corporate career. He entered elective politics in 1949.

When he assumed his first cabinet assignment in MITI under Ikeda, his Enterprise Bureau director was none other than Sahashi Shigeru, a most outspoken and controversial official of the postwar bureaucracy, whose power within and without MITI was widely recognized. Fukuda arrived in MITI at a time when Sahashi and his "Sahashi battalion" were at full steam to secure Diet approval for their pet project, the Temporary Law for the Promotion of Specified Industries (*tokutei sangyō rinji sochihō*), a controversial measure to aid sectors of industry considered weak from the standpoint of national security. Without the needed backing from appropriate circles, the bill was having a rough sailing in the Diet, which prompted the blunt Sahashi to criticize his minister for not campaigning vigorously in its support.

Fukuda, irate but calm, decided to teach the impudent Sahashi a lesson at an appropriate time. That occasion came when the AVM Matsuo Kinzō offered to step down in 1963. Not only Sahashi's performance record but also the agency's tradition of succession dictated that he succeed the outgoing Matsuo. (Until recently it was customary for the Enterprise Bureau director to step up to the AVM post.) Sahashi, however, although widely recognized as Matsuo's logical successor, was passed over, against the recommendation of the outgoing AVM. Instead, Fukuda picked Imai Zen'ei, Sahashi's foremost rival and the other sur-

---

[49] Kanryō kikō kenkyūkai, *Shin-ōkurashō*, p. 16. For discussion of this theme, see Fukutomi Tōru, *Daijin eno chōsen* [Challenge to cabinet ministers] (Tokyo: Arō shuppansha, 1972), pp. 93–96.

viving member of Sahashi's class of 1937, on the grounds that, in Fukuda's own words, "MITI is a service agency, and in terms of [the candidate's] personal character Imai is the most appropriate person to become the next MITI AVM."[50] The retiring Matsuo and others tried, to no avail, to talk the *tōjinha* minister out of his scheme, arguing that it would "upset the established personnel rule" of the agency.

There was another aggravating factor for Sahashi, who in his autobiography portrayed himself as an *"ishoku kanryō"* (this can be translated as "an exceptional bureaucrat" or "an abnormal bureaucrat"). When he was chief of the Heavy Industry Bureau, Sahashi reportedly incurred the wrath of the Ōno faction, to which Fukuda belonged, by failing to thank the faction leaders properly for a favor. For an export promotion project, MITI then needed a special budgetary allocation from a fund administered by the agency. To tap this fund, MITI had to have MOF approval. Faced with the MOF's recalcitrance, Sahashi turned to the Ōno faction for intervention in support of his project. After the proposal was successfully cleared with the MOF, Sahashi "overlooked" paying proper gratitude to the chiefs of the Ōno faction, who subsequently branded him "an ungrateful fellow."

The coveted AVM post went to Imai, just as Fukuda had planned, and Sahashi was pushed over to the directorship of the Patent Agency—undoubtedly a humiliating blow. Rather than leaving the agency, as many would have done when a member of their class (*dōnenpai*) moved to the top career post, Sahashi stayed on, hoping to succeed his classmate Imai.[51] The cabinet reshuffle of December 1964 did not bring about the expected change in the MITI portfolio, and Fukuda was retained as Ikeda's MITI minister, again frustrating Sahashi's hoped-for move up. As a way out, the patient Sahashi had to turn again to the Ōno faction elders, through his MITI *senpai* who were close to the faction. The campaign paid off, and when in 1965 Sakurauchi Yoshio joined the new Satō cabinet as MITI minister, Sahashi was finally allowed to accede to the AVM post, with the acquiescence of the Ōno faction and the outgoing Fukuda. Significantly, to achieve his objective frustrated by a politician-minister, Sahashi had to work through politicians, thus "paving the way for political intervention, most dreaded by

[50] Hayashibara Kazuhiko, *Uchimaku tsūsanshō* [MITI inside out] (Tokyo: Ēru shuppansha, 1978), p. 97. Hayashibara was a *Sankei shimbun* reporter covering MITI.

[51] For discussion by Sahashi of the traditions of bureaucratic personnel policy-making, see his "Kanryō shokun ni chokugensuru" [Candid advice to you bureaucrats], *Bungei shunjū* 49, no. 9 (July 1971): 108–115.

bureaucrats, in top-level agency personnel decisions."[52]

Incidentally, when Fukuda assumed for the second time the MHA portfolio in 1974 (he first held the post in 1972), he again proved himself to be the formidable personnel decision-maker in the agency where by convention the retiring AVM and his predecessors play a major role in the selection of the new AVM.[53] Fukuda's touch on the MHA's personnel decisions was most conspicuous in the choice of the successor to the outgoing AVM Kamata Kaname. Kamata's personal preference was Shudō Takashi, then director of the Taxation Bureau, rather than Shudō's rival and Fiscal Bureau chief, Matsuura Isao. The two bureau directors had entered the MHA in 1947, but there was one crucial difference: Shudō graduated from Kyūshū University Law School; Matsuura was a product of the Tokyo University Law School. The law degree from Kyūshū, though highly respectable, is generally considered a liability in the agency where nearly every *kyaria* official is a Tokyo University law graduate. Yet, for reasons beyond the scope of this study, the retiring AVM, Kamata, backed Shudō and was supported by his *senpai* in this decision. Shudō's succession was widely anticipated within the agency as a matter of course.

When Kamata submitted his recommendation to his minister for approval, Fukuda vetoed it, saying that personnel decision making was his prerogative, not to be shared with his subordinates. Rejecting Kamata's choice, Fukuda picked Matsuura to succeed Kamata. Several factors were responsible for his decision, according to a source close to the MHA. Fukuda was a highly independent-minded politician who disliked to be instructed by his subordinates. Matsuura, considered an expert in fiscal administration and noticeably obliging to the LDP, was backed by several LDP dietmen, who had made their endorsement known to Fukuda. Moreover, Matsuura himself had carried on a vig-

---

[52] The above description is based largely on accounts by Hayashibara. See *Uchimaku tsūsanshō*, pp. 96–98. Significantly, the *ishoku* bureaucrat Sahashi was later "fired" by MITI minister Miki Takeo. See Asahi shimbunsha, ed., *Jimintō: hoshu kenryoku o kōzō* [The Liberal-Democratic party: the structure of conservative power] (Tokyo: Asahi shimbunsha, 1970), p. 135.

[53] For discussion of the role assumed by the agency's former AVMs, Kobayashi Yosoji, Okuno Seisuke, and Shibata Mamoru, see Kusayanagi, *Kanryō ōkokuron*, p. 45. Kusayanagi's highly acclaimed account of the MHA is based on his interviews with several assistant division chiefs of the agency. For discussion of MHA personnel decision making, see also Ijichi, "Jichi kanryō," pp. 78–83. I am grateful to several MHA officials who enlightened me on many aspects of Japanese bureaucracy in general and the MHA in particular. They include Katō Eiichi, Nakamura Keiichi, Asahi Nobuo, Tashiro Ken, Katō Tomiko, and Abe Takao.

orous, apparently successful campaign that included personal pleas with the minister.[54] The outgoing Kamata did not lose out completely, for he managed to squeeze from Fukuda a promise that the minister would not stand in the way of Shudō's succeeding Matsuura. As in MITI under Fukuda, two members of the same entering class successively held the topmost career post, departing from the traditional personnel practice of Japanese bureaucracy.[55]

Even minor ministries, far removed from distributive, regulative, and extractive functions, have not escaped the intervention of assertive ministers in agency personnel decision making. One such office is the Administrative Management Agency (AMA), which performs the staff functions of screening plans of organizational change from line agencies and proposing guidelines for administrative reform and streamlining. As with many other postwar agencies, the AMA's bureaucracy is composed of two groups of officials: (1) "native" recruits (*haenuki*) who have risen from the bottom of the agency hierarchy, and (2) those "on loan" from other agencies, "non-nativists," many of whom return sooner or later to their original agencies.

Because of the staff duties the AMA performs, it is natural for the line agencies to try to install their "lookouts" in key offices of the AMA. Often placed in the strategic and planning sections of the AMA's Minister's Secretariat, these non-nativists indeed serve as ears and eyes for their parental agencies. Kimura Takeo, an AMA chief appointed to supervise Satō's administrative reform effort in 1967–68, recalled: "Whenever I tried to do something involving, say, the MAFF or the Ministry of Health and Welfare [MHW], the guys from these agencies wasted no time in informing their old ministries [of the reform plans being proposed in the AMA]. Naturally I would hear from these ministries, which complained [about the plans] and wanted this or that [part of the plans] scrapped."[56]

This was the situation Kimura had to contend with in the AMA. As he tried to proceed with his reforms, the non-nativists "skillfully and ably resisted [his] ideas." Understandably, however, he found the *haenuki* officials more cooperative. To make the agency more responsive, Kimura decided to undertake a massive personnel shake-up in two major steps—one aimed at the disruptive non-nativists and the other at

---

54 Ijichi, *Jichishō*, pp. 80–82.

55 Ijichi, "Jichi kanryō," pp. 81–82.

56 Kimura Takeo, *Nihon o ayamaru kanryō* [Bureaucrats misleading Japan], *Getsuyōkai repōto*, no. 487 (Tokyo: Kokumin seiji kenkyūkai, 1970), p. 25.

the pliant *haenuki* officials. He later reminisced:

> I felt that it was imperative to separate the non-native officials from
> the key positions they were holding and move them far away from
> my own staff [in the Minister's Secretariat]. In the course of the
> reshuffle every non-native official was affected. I then watched them
> for six months. As far as [major] division chief posts were con-
> cerned, I picked my own men [to fill them]. They were my pawns,
> so to speak. Moreover, I named a Kawai to head a major bureau.
> There was a reason for this. He is Kawai Yoshinari's son. I thought
> I could fire him any time if I had to, for he had a place to go to
> [after leaving government service]. Thus, there wouldn't be anything
> for me to worry about [i.e., finding a place for him outside the agen-
> cy] if I had to let him go.[57]

It was by no means a simple task, however, for Kimura to place Kawai,
then a mere deputy division chief, in the key bureau directorship.
Kimura later recalled:

> The then AVM expressed his willingness to step down, but I told
> him that because I was not familiar with agency details he should
> stay on until after the Diet session was over. He consented and sub-
> sequently retired from the agency when the Diet session ended. One
> of the bureau directors moved up to assume the AVM post. He
> brought to me the name of the guy he had in mind to take the
> bureau directorship he had just vacated. I took a look at the file, but
> I couldn't approve the recommendation, so I sent him out. He came
> back to me [with the request] every day for three days. I turned him
> down every day. Then he asked me if I had somebody in mind [to
> take the director's post]; I mentioned Kawai [Miyoshi] who then was
> an assistant division chief (*shuji*) in the Statistics Bureau and is now
> a bureau director. He said that it couldn't be done and the agency
> had never had such a two-step promotion decision. He further ar-
> gued that such a decision would disrupt the AMA's seniority order
> and create a big problem. I then said, "I see," and told him to leave.
> The same thing happened several more times. Finally, I asked him
> if he would still oppose my man; he said yes. "Well, we have a
> problem here," I said. "We don't see eye to eye. One of us has to
> go. Because I cannot resign, you will have to go." He said he would.
> All pale, he walked out. Next day he came back [not with the prom-
> ised letter of resignation but] with the man I was pushing all along.
> The point of all this is that the minister can do anything if he is so
> determined.[58]

---

[57] Ibid. The senior Kawai, chairman of the Komatsu Industries and a *zaikai* elder, was
an LDP member of the Diet's upper house and a minister of health-welfare.

A fitting summation of the preceding discussions is offered by Kusayanagi Daizō, a veteran journalist who has long covered several ministries, including the MAFF:

> Whether or not the minister can control his agency depends on how freely he can exercise his personnel power. In the postwar political history [of Japan] Kōno Ichioro tore down the wall guarding bureaucratic personnel decision making, and the MAFF and the MOC felt the impact of his intervention. Since then the LDP dietmen-ministers have attached much importance to deepening their personal ties with agency bureaucrats [by using their appointment powers]. This has meant, among other things, that the bureaucrats must perform their duties, taking into account the minister's intentions. The bureaucrats can even be compared to contestants in the so-called spoon race at school athletic meets. They may run fast and, in fact, may even be the first to reach the goal line, but if they drop from their spoon the small ball called "the minister's trust," they are taken off the track of upward mobility.[59]

---

[58] Ibid., pp. 23–24.

[59] Kusayanagi, *Kanryō ōkokuron,* pp. 44–45.

# V

# Ministers: Bureaucracy's "Lame Ducks"?

One of the widely held axioms regarding bureaucracy has it that organizational "permanence" is a principal foundation of bureaucratic
power. Bureaucrats know that they outlast political executives and treat
them accordingly. Viewed in this context, much of the difficulty the
American department secretaries encounter in dealing wtih career
officials makes sense. They are often "strangers" brought in from outside and superimposed on the bureaucracy (and they are treaed as such
by their subordinates), although many are career officials promoted to
the top posts because of their professional and political credentials. Re-
gardless of their backgrounds, when the political executives depart from
their posts, the agency officials will in all probability never see them
again. Once out, they lose all influence over the offices they headed.
Hence, the American system lends itself to a great deal of bureaucratic
chicanery and recalcitrance against the secretary's aggressive meddling
with agency affairs or his policy innovation incompatible with agency interests as seen by the career officials. In the words of Adolf A. Berle:

> Incoming political officeholders can only work—at least in their early
> period of office holding—through the machinery the bureaucracies
> have set up and administer. Each cabinet secretary is almost, though
> not quite, helpless in the hands of his inherited bureaucrats if he an-
> tagonizes them. If they seriously disagree with policies he puts for-
> ward, they do not even need to enter into public controversy. They
> need merely drag their feet or silently oppose by delaying, requiring
> further study, seeking interpretations, raising practical objections,
> and leaking information to opposition senators, congressmen, and
> press commentators. . . .
>   In any case, most men dislike having their habits disturbed, and
> bureaucrats perhaps more than others. So they expedite the
> machinery if they are in favor, and retard it if they are not, awaiting
> the inevitable time when the top power holders either leave office or
> come around to their point of view.[1]

---

[1] Adolf A. Berle, *Power* (New York: Harcourt Brace Jovanovich, 1969), p. 317. For a
detailed study of these problems faced by political executives, see Hugh Heclo, *A Govern-*

Similar arguments have been advanced by many Japan scholars to lend credence to the concept of "ministerial impotence."[2] These arguments are seen as carrying greater validity in Japan, for the Japanese minister's typical tenure, shorter than that of his American counterpart, is approximately one year. A majority of Japanese ministers serve short terms. Frequent cabinet shufflings, often to consolidate interfactional harmony, make the high rate of ministerial turnover inevitable.

However, every agency has had a fairly large number of ministers whose tenure was considerably longer than the typical term. Many have served terms of three or four years, although the likes of Dean Rusk (nine consecutive years in the United States Department of State) are unheard of. In the MOE, Araki Masuo, Ikeda's education minister, who led vitriolic campaigns against the JTU, was in office for three consecutive years, 1960–63; so was Sakata Michita, who as Satō's minister played a leading role in the initiation of major reforms in the system of higher education and in developing an ambitious program of support for private education. Okuno Seisuke, widely considered one of the most activist education ministers of postwar Japan, held the post for two years, 1972–74. Then, there is Nadao Hirokichi, who has the unbroken record of four separate terms in the MOE; he was in office for a total of three years. These four ministers, widely viewed as powerful education ministers, together were in office for a total of eleven years, almost half of the agency's entire postindependence history. The MOE is by no means atypical. Significantly, more often than not these long-term ministers or repeaters were activist ministers who kept a tight rein on their agencies.

The attempts to apply to Japan the widely held assumptions about the U.S. pattern of secretary-bureaucracy relations overlook some basic systemic differences between the Japanese and the U.S. polities and their implications. In contrast to the American polyarchy, characterized by its Madisonian governmental structures and a two-party system that contribute to the power of the permanent bureaucracy, Japan is a parliamentary democracy whose principal feature is what Walter Bagehot referred to as "the close union, the nearly complete fusion, of the executive and legislative powers."[3] Moreover, it is one continually dominated by the

---

*ment of Strangers: Executive Politics in Washington* (Washington, D.C.: Brookings Institution, 1977).

[2] For example, see Ezra Vogel, *Japan as Number One* (New York: Harper and Row, 1979), pp. 57–61.

[3] Walter Bagehot, *The English Constitution* (New York: Doubleday, n.d.), p. 69.

same political party. Admittedly, the Japanese bureaucracy is permanent, but "the bureaucrat's life is short," as the former MAFF minister Akagi Munenori put it, and is subject to the minister's personnel power, as discussed in the preceding chapter. Unlike the United States and many other Western polyarchies, the LDP's durability or "permanence" as Japan's government party is well proven; it has continuously enjoyed the majority position for more than thirty-six years, and this status is not likely to change in the near future, notwithstanding the party's recent electoral setback.

These facts have ramifications for minister-agency relations, detailed below, and therefore the Japanese cabinet minister, unlike many of his U.S. counterparts, does not fade into obscurity when he leaves the agency. The termination of his ministerial tenure by no means spells the end of his influence and linkage with the agency. These considerations powerfully deter career officials from subjecting their incumbent minister to what often befalls American political executives, whom Hugh Heclo describes as "substantially on their own and vulnerable to bureaucratic power."[4]

Even after he leaves the agency, the Japanese minister will retain his seat in the Diet as a member of the majority party because his cabinet credentials vastly improve his standing with his constituents, thus virtually guaranteeing his reelection. His status within the party, and, especially, the PARC is also favorably affected by his ministerial experience, which in turn will strengthen his standing vis-à-vis the agency he headed.

If he was a member of the ministry's corresponding PARC division and its *zoku* before his ministerial appointment, not only will he return to that policy group but also his status within the *zoku* will vastly improve because of his ministerial experience. He will not hold any formal leadership post within the division, for its chair and vice-chairs are held by the junior members of the division. Rather, he will function as an elder statesman whose views carry much weight in division decision making on matters of the policy, budget, and personnel of the ministry he headed. If he was already a powerful member of the division and its *zoku* before his ministerial assignment, he will in all likelihood be elevated into the inner circle of *zoku* potentates, *zoku gosanke,* who collectively constitute the party's actal leadership group for the agency they over-

---

[4] Heclo, *Government of Strangers,* p. 112. This generalization is derived from interviews and informal discussions with MOE, MOF, MPT, MOC, and MHA officials at the assistant division chief (*kachō hosa*) and higher levels.

see. As a member of this powerful party group, the former minister will continue to participate in the party's legitimation and authorization of policy and personnel decisions involving the ministry.

If the outgoing minister was not a member of the relevant PARC division and its *zoku* when he was made minister of the agency under the division's supervision, he will, upon relinquishing the cabinet post, most likely affiliate himself with the division where his ministerial experience will be valued by other members of the division. Thus, he will continue to participate in agency affairs, playing an important role in agency policy and personnel decisions.[5]

The former minister assumes other PARC-related duties affecting the ministry. He may be given a PARC leadership position; he may be made a member of the PARC Deliberative Council (*Seichō shingikai*), which is responsible for screening policy proposals coming from the PARC divisions before they are sent to the Executive Board (*Sōmukai*) for approval. The more typical and important pattern he follows is to chair a key PARC investigative committee (*chōsaki*) charged with policy matters concerning the ministry.[6] This investigative committee, rather than the appropriate PARC division, functions as the primary party participant in long-range policy deliberations by his ministry. Also, this investigative unit of the PARC is charged with the task of initiating and developing a long-term party policy.

For example, the Education System Investigative Committee (*Bunkyō seido chōsakai*), one of the two PARC organs dealing with edu-

---

[5] For discussion of the role played by former ministers of agriculture in MAFF policy and personnel decisions, see *Shūkan yomiuri* 39, no. 23 (June 1, 1980): 168. For a similar situation in the MHA, see Ijichi, "Jichi kanryō," pp. 78–83. For the MHW, see Ashizaki, *Kōseishō*, pp. 159–160. For every ministry the corresponding party *zoku* elders include former ministers. For other useful sources of information on former ministers' roles in the MOC, the MHW, the MOE, and the MOF, see "Suzuki yosan o arau" [The Suzuki budget inside out], pt. 3, *Asahi,* January 3, 1981; and *Jimintō seichōkai,* pp. 43–135 and 183.

[6] Upon leaving the Education portfolio in 1972, Takami Saburō said, "Even after my resignation from the education minister's post, I am going to remain on the Investigative Committee on the Educational System and render my assistance to my successor" (*Sankei shimbun,* June 8, 1972). At the time of the 1982 controversy over revised Japanese texts toning down Japan's prewar aggression in Asia, the MOE worked closely with former MOE minister Tanigaki Sen'ichi, then deputy chairman of the LDP ICES, who had access to Prime Minister Suzuki as a senior member of the Suzuki faction and played a role in the government's decision making on the issue. See Yamasaki Hidenori, "Misutā kyōkasho Morozawa Masamichi no kōkokushikan" [Mr. Textbook Morozawa Masamichi's views on imperial history], *Ushio,* no. 282 (October 1982), p. 77. Interviews with former ministers (e.g., Okuno Seisuke, Kaifu Toshiki, and Hasegawa Takashi) shed light on postministerial activities LDP dietmen are engaged in for the ministries they served in.

cation policy and overseeing the MOE, is responsible for such long-range matters as "reform of the school system"; the Education Division, the other education-related PARC organ, is normally charged with short-term, operational aspects of the MOE and its policy. As of 1982, the Education System Investigative Committee was chaired by Kaifu Toshiki, education minister of 1976–77, and the senior vice-chairman was Tanigaki Sen'ichi, who headed the MOE in 1979–80. This pattern is typical for other policy areas.

For some dietmen, one-year cabinet assignments may well be the pinnacles of their public careers, but many—competent and ambitious ones—go beyond their initial ministerial portfolios. They are not only appointed to other cabinet posts, often more prestigious and lucrative than their previous portfolios, but also have opportunities to hold important party posts that allow them distinct advantages in dealing with the bureaucracy, including the ministries they headed.

Because of the constant intraparty, intragovernmental circulation of LDP dietmen, the bureaucrats never know what post is in store for their ministers. Placed in a strategic and powerful party or government post, the former minister can do a lot, either positively or negatively, for the agency and its oficials. As chairman of the powerful PARC he could make it difficult and even impossible for the ministry to get the needed party and MOF backing for its new costly program. Even as chairman of the party's Diet Measures Committee (*Kokkai taisaku iinkai*) he could affect the outcome of party and legislative debates on a ministry bill. As minister of finance, he can be a powerful supporter or a vitriolic critic of the line ministry's budget request. Obviously, he can damage or contribute to the budget in many ways. Holding a key staff post close to the prime minister, such as director of the Cabinet Secretariat, the former minister can help or hurt the career of the high agency official, for bureau director–level and higher appointments are subject to cabinet approval, and the director of the Cabinet Secretariat can have a major input in that process if he is so determined. He is normally the prime minister's right-hand man.

The widely held assumption of "transitory ministership" and "permanent bureaucracy" often overlooks the surprisingly large number of former ministers who return to the same agency for second or even multiple terms. To mention several, Hirokawa Kōzen was thrice the MAFF minister in the Yoshida cabinet in the 1950s. The same post was twice held by Kōno Ichirō, in 1954–56 and 1961–62. His successor of the 1960s, Akagi Munenori, also held the MAFF portfolio twice. Ikeda Hayato occupied the Finance portfolio twice and the MITI post three times in the 1950s. Mizuta Mikio was minister of finance in four different cabinets—two under Ikeda and two under Satō—in the 1960s. The SDA has had several repeaters, including Masuhara Keikichi (thrice), Nishimura Naomi (twice), and Esaki Masumi (twice). In the MOE, Nadao Hirokichi headed the ministry four times in the 1950s and 1960s. Sakata Michita, who held the MOE post in the turbulent years of 1968–71, was seriously considered for the same post in the Suzuki cabinet. The MHW twice had Hashimoto Ryōgo as its chief, in 1951–52 and 1958–59. Kanda Hiroshi served in the MHW under four prime ministers—Ishibashi, Kishi, Ikeda, and Satō. Fukuda Hajime twice held the MHW post in the 1970s, first under Tanaka and then under Miki.

Most of these ministers are considered to be among the influential agency chiefs of postindependence Japan. This list of returned ministers is by no means exhaustive; it can easily be expanded. The central point here is not the number of dietmen who head the same ministry more than once; rather, it is the implication that the frequency of returning ministers has for career officials' attitudes toward their ministers. As one interviewed official put it, "We have to take the minister seriously not only because of his expected involvement in agency affairs as a member of the PARC division and committees but also because we cannot rule out the possibility that the outgoing minister will return to our agency."

As the foregoing discussions show, the typical Japanese minister, in a functional sense, does not really sever his ties with the ministry. In some cases, such as those of *zoku* members and *gosanke,* ties with the agency are even strengthened after departure. Therefore, the widely practiced bureaucratic ranking of LDP dietmen that places former ministers in the topmost category, worthy of special agency consideration and treatment, makes sense.

All agencies rank the politicians and deal with them accordingly. This ranking order is one of the key indiacators of their behavior toward the elected legislators. Typically, the top category, Class A, is reserved for the party's top brass, consisting of the president (who concurrently serves as the prime minister), the secretary-general, and chairmen of the PARC and the Executive Board; former ministers; executives and other influential members (*zoku* and *gosanke*) of the agency's corresponding PARC division and investigative committees; and leaders and veteran members of the intraparty factions or groups that have intimate ties with the agency, such as the Kōno faction and *Seirankai* in the MAFF. Dietmen of lesser importance who have had dealings with the agency, usually former PVMs, are included in Class B. The rank and file members of the parliamentary LDP are assigned to Class C. In the agency's efforts to mobilize LDP support for its policy proposals, much of its energy is put into securing the backing of Class A members, and especially former ministers. Therefore, it is only natural that in agency policy-making and budgetary process they have a special status that is usually denied to those with lower rankings.

This ranking system has interesting symbiotic implications for the party and the agencies (especially those charged with "lucrative" distributive functions, such as the MOC and the MOT). For illustration, let us take the MAFF, one of the foremost distributive-regulative agencies. According to press sources close to the MAFF, party influentials on the agency's Class A list not only play a part in the formulation of the agency's budgetary requests to the MOF and the government budget bill pertaining to the agency but also are allowed major inputs in determining specific MAFF-sponsored construction projects for the forthcoming fiscal year. In current practice, the members of the top category must be informed of the contents of the proposed construction projects before the agency's budget bill is acted upon in the Diet. Those on the B list are briefed on the day before the upper house takes up the bill.[7]

Matsuno Raizō, the controversial former SDA minister later implicated in the so-called F4E-Fighter bribery scandal, provides an interesting illustration of the power a former minister can exercise in the affairs of his old agency.[8] A key member of the Satō faction and considered one of the rising stars of the party, Matsuno occupied the Self-Defense post in 1965–66 under Prime Minister Satō. While in office, he exercised his powers as agency chief to such an extent that he was widely viewed as one of the most assertive defense ministers, certainly on a par with Nakasone Yasuhiro, who headed the agency in the early 1970s. In mid-1966, after a tenure of one year, he left the SDA to assume the MAFF portfolio, reportedly to direct a systematic purge of MAFF officials friendly to the Kōno faction, the archrival of the Satō faction.

Even after he left the SDA, Matsuno continued to have a powerful influence over the agency and its key personnel decisions. A case in point is a massive purge of ranking officials including Kaihara Osamu

---

[7] Kanryō kikō kenkyūkai, *Nōrinshō*, pp. 128–129. See also "Kanryō doko o muku" [Future directions of bureaucracy], pt. 9, *Mainichi,* January 11, 1979. For a similar situation in the MOC, see Kanryō kikō kenkyūkai, *Kensetsushō*, pp. 102–104.

[8] The following account is based largely on published sources, including the transcripts of an interview with Kaihara Osamu, former director of the Self-Defense Agency Minister's Secretariat, printed in *Asahi,* January 19, 1979; *Asahi,* May 24, 1979; Kanryō kikō kenkyūkai, *Nōrinshō*, pp. 40–42; and Honda Yasuharu, *Nihon neo-kanryōron* [A study of the neo-bureaucracy in Japan], vol. II (Tokyo: Kōdansha, 1974), pp. 137–142.

(then director of the Minister's Secretariat, the second-highest post next to the SDA AVM) and his protégés that occurred in 1967. This reshuffle was widely attributed to the personal intervention of Matsuno, who then held no cabinet post and whose major formal party responsibility was chairmanship of a PARC investigative committee on elections. Unhappy with Kaihara's adamant opposition to the F4E-Fighters he was promoting for purchase as part of the givernment's Third Defense Buildup Program, Mastuno requested then SDA chief Masuda Kaneshichi, also a member of the Satō faction, to remove the anti-F4E elements, and especially Kaihara, from the agency. Reportedly, he was backed by his faction chief and then prime minister, Satō.

The assertive Kaihara, whose brilliance was widely recognized within and without the agency, was often known by his sobriquet, Emperor Kaihara, for the prestige and power he enjoyed. He was ousted shortly before his "scheduled" promotion to the highest career post of AVM and was transferred to the largely ceremonial post of staff director for the Cabinet Defense Council. When asked in 1979 to account for the enormous influence Matsuno had over the agency he had headed, Kaihara responded: "Everybody [in the agency] would rush to Matsuno with requests because he was chairman of the LDP PARC [the post he held in 1974–76]. Moreover, being a hierarchical organization, the SDA has the tendency to say yes to whatever its former chiefs demand."[9] In other words, Matsuno, a former SDA minister who later moved up to hold one of the key party executive posts, was a Class A politician as far as the SDA was concerned.

Admittedly, not every outgoing minister has in store for him the kind of postministerial career and influence that Matsuno enjoyed after he left the SDA until his fall forced by the bribery scandal, but many do. This likelihood of the minister's postministerial upward mobility and continued influence in agency affairs helps deter his agency subordinates from defying him and his policy preferences. The familiar bureaucratic techniques of recalcitrance and chicanery, based upon assmptions of bureaucratic longevity and the minister's transiency, are more avoided than used in Japan. In a case of bureaucratic sabotage of the minister's cherished project, the minister, even after his departure from the agency, can properly deal with the ringleader.

Even in Japan, there are some ministers who lack the requisites of the "durable minister" and are subjected to the plight that often haunts the American agency chief. These transients include a variety of

---

[9] *Asahi,* January 19, 1979.

ministers—for example, an "old-timer" who, before his expected retirement from politics, is given a minor cabinet post, his first and last, for his long but mediocre service to his party and faction; or a minister whose preministerial areas of interest and specialization do not have anything to do with jurisdictional matters of the agency and who, upon departure from the ministry, is not expected to assume any role of importance in the ministry's PARC counterpart. Ministers in this category, however, are few. Also, the career officials have no sure way of telling whether these ministers are going to be active in the PARC or not after leaving the agencies. This uncertainty helps deter the bureaucrats from committing any acts considered defiant of the minister.

The most transient of all is a "nonpolitical" minister brought into the government from outside the LDP Diet contingent. According to the constitution (Article 68), nondietmen "outsiders" may join the cabinet as long as they do not constitute a majority of its members. Notwithstanding this provision for infusion of "new outside blood," however, the typical cabinet is composed wholly of dietmen who, as dictated by the norms of party government, belong to the majority LDP. From time to time, however, outsiders who are not members of the parliamentary LDP have been appointed to cabinet posts for a variety of reasons. Fujiyama Aiichirō, appointed foreign minister in 1957 and elected a year later to the Diet, was a "big business" (*zaikai*) leader brought into the Kishi cabinet as a major link between that major sector of Japanese politics and the government, whose then top foreign-policy task was a restructuring of the Japanese-American alliance system. Ōkita Saburō, a retired EPA bureaucrat whose brilliance and expertise in economic affairs are widely respected by the key sectors of the Japanese "establishment," was appointed foreign minister by Prime Minister Ōhira Masayoshi at a time when several knotty questions of Japanese-American trade relations required serious answers. A few other ministries, including the MOF and the MOE, share the distinction of having "nonpolitical" ministers.

In the postwar period, the largest share of the "nonpoliticals" has gone to the MOE. During the entire SCAP era, the agency was headed by scholars-turned-ministers whose "liberal" views of education were highly valued by the SCAP authorities bent on their far-reaching reform of Japan's elitist and authoritarian prewar education. The MOE's latest, and only postindependence, encounter with the nonpolitical, scholar type came in 1974, when Nagai Michio, a former professor of educational sociology, headed the agency until 1976. A liberal educator widely respected by centrist and left-wing circles, including the JTU, Nagai assumed the Education portfolio with the encouragement of Prime Minister Miki

Takeo, who considered Nagai's popular image to be consonant with the low-profile consensual politics of the Miki government.[10]

The outside ministers, though without a base of power in the party because they hold no seats in the Diet, are given cabinet posts largely because of their expertise and standing in their areas of specialization, as noted above; but they face myriad problems as they attempt to perform their multifaceted roles as ministers. With the exception of the likes of Ōkita Saburō, a former bureaucrat, the nondietmen ministers are new to bureaucratic politics and find it difficult, if not impossible, to deal effectively with their agency subordinates, who consider their inexperienced minister to be ill prepared to fight for authorization and appropriation for new agency programs.

The bureaucrats' assumptions are not farfetched in view of the ministers' inexperience in party and Diet politics and lack of clout in the party and its PARC organs. With the growing power the PARC divisions and their *zoku* have over the bureaucracy, the outside ministers find it increasingly necessary to cooperate with the party. Their pliancy toward the party is significantly prompted by the usual hands-off posture of the prime minister who appointed them to the cabinet. Moreover, the career officials view them as transients who do not belong to the nation's governing elite and will in all probability not be seen again. For these reasons, the nonpolitical ministers are easily susceptible to bureaucratic slighting, defiance, and control.

These problems that confront outside minsters were vividly typified during Nagai's two-year term, which, as one informed source put it, "may well be the most turbulent interlude of his brilliant public service." Because of his pro-JTU record (as a critic of the MOE and its policy, he regularly lectured at JTU meetings prior to his cabinet appointment), the LDP's distrust of him was inevitable. He was often excluded from crucial party-MOE policy sessions. He was unable to command much deference from his agency subordinates, who often contradicted him, even in public. Viewing him as a lame duck—one about to leave the agency at any time—the conservative MOE career officials turned a deaf ear to his reform ideas. Sandwiched between the party *Bunkyōzoku* and the MOE bureaucracy over some of the most controversial policy and personnel

---

[10] He had been an editorial writer for the *Asahi shimbun*, whose editorial position is often incongruent with that of the *Nihon keizai shimbun*, reputedly a pro-MOE newspaper. He frequently served as a guest lecturer for JTU workshops and was widely considered persona non grata by the MOE and the LDP. His appointment to the MOE post, therefore, caused quite a stir in the MOE and among the conservative, anti-JTU LDP dietmen.

cases of recent years, Nagai was all alone, with Prime Minister Miki maintaining his characteristic low-profile policy of neutrality.[11] As noted by Okuno Seisuke, Nagai's predecessor in the MOE and a key *Bunkyōzoku* member he had to contend with, "A non-LDP minister without a Diet seat cannot be effective in dealing with agency officials; the actual organizational leadership is assumed by the AVM."[12]

---

[11] For discussion of the policy and personnel issues during Nagai's incumbency, see Yung Park, *Jimintō to kyōiku kanryō,* pp. 16–20.

[12] Interview with Okuno Seisuke, April 23, 1979. Upon leaving the MOE, Okuno became chairman of the PARC Investigative Committee on the Educational System, the key party post he held during Nagai's tenure in the MOE.

# VI

# Ministers and Mobilization of External Support

In the pluralistic political system of contemporary Japan, as with other competitive polities, administrative agencies must overcome a host of institutional and organized obstacles, both within and without the government, to have their policy programs authorized, funded, and accepted as legitimate governmental programs. Agency policy proposals must be coordinated with and approved by the appropriate LDP PARC divisions and their elders. If the proposals are seen as impinging on the jurisdiction of other ministries, the affected agencies also must be brought into the consultative process, and any conflict with them must be settled. The plethora of agency clientele groups and other interested organizations must be persuaded to support or, at least, acquiesce in its policy proposals. Because of the growing importance of interest group politics in Japan, outside clientele support is particularly important. Budgetary authorization must be sought from the MOF, the agency of budget making and appropriation, which inherently frowns upon budgetary requests for all new programs. The proposals must then be blessed with approval by the LDP PARC and other key party committees, including the Executive Board, and the prime minister and his cabinet, before they can go to the Diet for its legitimation. Controversial proposals are often vehemently resisted by the leftist opposition parties in the Diet, although a majority of government bills, dealing with routine policy matters, are unanimously adopted. Policy coordination with the opposition in the Diet, therefore, also occupies an important place in the agency's strategy and efforts to seek external support and has taken on an added importance in recent years because of the Diet's growing reactive powers of delaying, amending, and rejecting government bills.[1]

---

[1] For discussions of the major actors of Japanese politics whose support or acquiescence must be sought before agency programs can be instituted, see "Rippō no arikata" [The way lawmaking should be], *Jurisuto,* no. 331 (October 1, 1965), pp. 10–31. This is a transcript

All these actions to enlist outside support and adjudicate conflict with other sectors of the policy system require much of the agency's time and energy and constitute an integral part of the agency's policy-making process. No agency wants its policy efforts to result in futility. All agencies want to produce policy decisions that will be accepted or tolerated by other segments of the policy system, for they know that their policy efforts will be unsuccessful without this systemic support or acquiescence and without the respectability and legitimacy that come from such endorsement.

Notwithstanding the lack of careful empirical studies of bureaucratic interactions with the external environment, a notion of the bureaucracy's pattern of external mobilization and conflict adjudication has gained wide currency in and outside Japan. At the most general level, it can be expressed as "bureaucratic primacy." In this perspective, rooted in the traditional bureaucracy-dominant notion of prewar Japan, the bureaucracy's mobilization of the political (political parties and Diet) and private sectors is viewed as a simple, minor chore, with interagency coordination requiring most of the mobilizational and adjudicative efforts. Moreover, the middle-level officials of agencies (division head and their deputies) are assumed to be the key actors of external mobilization and coordination. According to Kawanaka Nikō, a leading Japanese scholar of this school, all private groups and even those

of a panel discussion by prominent Tokyo University scholars, including Katō Ichirō, Rōyama Masamichi, and Azuma Sakae. Also useful is Misawa Shigeo, "Seisaku kettei katei no gaikan" [An outline of the policy-making process] in *Gendai nihon no seitō to kanryō* [Political parties and bureaucracy in contemporary Japan], ed. Nihon seiji gakkai (Tokyo: Iwanami shoten, 1967), pp. 5–53. An English translation of this article is available in Hiroshi Itoh, ed., *Japanese Politics: An Inside View* (Ithaca: Cornell University Press, 1973), pp. 12–48. Misawa's "systemic" analysis closely follows the popular notion of "bureaucratic primacy." In examining the bureaucracy's relations with its environment, I have benefited much from my discussions and interviews with a large number of Japanese interest group representatives, scholars, government officials, dietmen, and Diet and LDP staff members including Ichikawa Shōgo, Maki Masami, Shimokawa Yoshio, Murakawa Ichirō, Arai Ikuo, Kimura Shūzō, Taki Yoshie, Nakajima Yoneo, Takagi Kōmei, Sasaki Sadanori, Uchida Susumu, Iwama Eitarō, Yasujima Hisashi, Kida Hiroshi, Kawanaka Ichigaku, Kumagai Kazunori, Genjida Shigeyoshi, Nishida Kikuo, Katō Eiichi, Umakoshi Tōru, Uchida Mitsuru, Muramatsu Michio, Kitamura Kazuyuki, Yamamoto Takayuki, Yamazaki Katsuhiko, Nagata Naohisa, Kobayashi Kazuyuki, Kimura Hitoshi, Hashimoto Akira, Sugihara Masayoshi, Itō Michio, Imamura Reiko, Okabayashi Takashi, Kusaba Muneharu, Satō Teiichi, Kuroha Ryōichi, Nakagawa Sumito, Mochizuki Shōsaku, Iwasawa Yoshitaka, Nakamura Ichirō, Morita Kōichirō, Hashimoto Seiichi, Sasaki Haruo, Omi Kōji, Okano Yutaka, Takada Akiyoshi, Sakamoto Harumi, Toyama Toshirō, Aoki Masahisa, Shirakawa Katsuhiko, and Yagi Jun.

representing the strategic industries are placed in a state of subjugation vis-à-vis the state bureaucracy—so much so that they can do little more than petition (*chinjō*) the government for minor or technical changes in its proposed policy, which to all intents and purposes is a legitimate, completed policy.

In this view, therefore, Japan is far from a pluralistic polity where public policy is typically hammered out of vigorous negotiations and bargaining between the government and private interest groups. In this statist notion, the critical part of the bureaucracy's external mobilization and conflict resolution is working out administrative-level (*jimuteki*) interministry understanding and agreement. Once this is done, the rest is simple. Again according to Kawanaka, interagency administrative agreements hold such a sacrosanct place in the policy process that the "fait accompli" can even be imposed on other sectors—both political and private—of the policy system if the more "civilized" process of *nemawashi* fails to "convince" them.[2]

The data collected from various LDP, bureaucratic, and interest group sources suggest that the assumption of bureaucratic centrality grossly simplifies contemporary Japanese policy-making. Not only are the bureaucrats not the primary actors in the critical stages of external support mobilization and conflict resolution but also interagency understandings without due regard for the views of other sectors of the policy system are simply inconceivable under existing circumstances. In other words, the process of support mobilization and conflict resolution is far more complex and expanded than asserted in the bureaucratic dominance thesis. It necessitates the participation of not only career bureaucrats but also their LDP patrons (especially their dietmen-ministers). In important controversial and costly programs, the minister's role is more ofen than not pivotal. Simply put, it is the minister's successful mobilizational campaign that often drums up the necessary authorization, funding, and support for such programs. As widely observed by interviewed former ministers, including Okuno Seisuke (education minister and justice minister), "The minister's status and powers in the agency are significantly affected by how well he performs his mobilizational role in support of agency programs."[3] In short, an effective mobilizer and

---

[2] Kawanaka Nikō, "Nihon ni okeru seisaku kettei no seiji katei" [Political process of policy-making in Japan], in *Gendai gyōsei to kanryōsei* [Contemporary administration and bureaucracy], vol. 2, ed. Taniuchi Ken et al. (Tokyo: Tokyo daigaku shuppankai, 1974), pp. 6–20.

[3] Interview with Okuno Seisuke, April 23, 1979.

persuader carries much weight with agency officials and plays a major role in agency policy-making. In the words of Misawa Shigeo, a leading student of Japanese policy-making, "A minister considered 'competent' by the bureaucrats performs such an important task in the promotion of the agency's 'private interests' that his 'decisions' come to play too big a role [in the determination of agency policy programs]."[4]

The minister's pivotal role in the agency's support mobilization and policy coordination and its effect on his intraagency position is the central theme to be developed and illustrated in this chapter.

The assumption of bureaucratic centrality views the administrative agency's external environment as intrinsically supportive and, at least, acquiescent and glosses over a large measure of competitiveness and even a propensity for conflict that Japan's postwar pluralization has introduced into the political and governmental systems. These developments have made the agency's support mobilization correspondingly complex and difficult.

A fitting commentary on the pluralizing Japanese polity and its effect on the bureaucracy's support mobilization is offered by Kakizawa Kōji, an MOF bureaucrat-turned-dietman, in his discussion of the diminishing of the MOF's power as a result of the pluralization of the budget-making system. He characterizes the occupation era as operating under a "unipolar system" (*ikkyoku kōzō*) in which the MOF held the dominant role in budget making by playing the SCAP and line ministries against each other. The end of the occupation in 1952 ushered in a decade of "bipolarity" (*nikyoku*), during which the MOF had to contend with the other "pole," consisting of line ministries and LDP politicians. The era of bipolarity ended around 1965, to be replaced by that of "tripolarity" (*sankyoku*), during which the LDP, the MOF, and line ministries made up the dominant triadic budget policy system. The pluralization continued, and in the middle of the 1970s the triadic structure gave way to a quadripartite (*yonkyoku*) system in which the four budgetary protagonists (the LDP, the MOF, line ministries, and the opposition parties) attempt to articulate their own institutional interests as well as those of their clientele groups.[5] Kakizawa's summation, though doing injustice to the LDP's preeminence in budgetary politics, nevertheless correctly points to the extent of pluralization that has taken place in the postwar Japanese political system.

---

[4] Misawa, "Seisaku kettei," p. 24.

[5] Kakizawa, "Kokkai to kanryō," app. 6.

Under the existing pluralistic system of Japan, to achieve their policy objectives all agencies must successfully deal with at least three key external sectors. The first segment of the agencies' environment is political and consists of the LDP, the opposition parties, and the Diet, which is the major forum for the political opposition. Second is the bureaucracy—other line ministries and the budget-making MOF, which must be persuaded to finance agency programs. Finally, there is an array of private interest groups—both clientele groups and "negative constituencies" hostile to agency actions. The following sections examine each of these sectors of the polity that any agency must cope with and the role performed by the minister in each stage.

### Political Sector

The foremost institution in the political sector that the bureaucracy must persuade and bargain with is of course the LDP, the party continuously in power since 1948, whose dominant status in the polity has not yet attracted the wide scholarly attention it deserves.[6] Several bases of growing LDP power and policy roles have been mentioned in the preceding chapters and hence require no elaboration here. Largely attributable to the simple fact of the LDP's electoral longevity, they include policy expertise, information, experience, power over agency personnel decisions, the strengthened PARC and its elaborate substructure, and legitimate authority derived from the constitutional norms of legislative supremacy and party government.

In view of the party's powerful role, what many interviewed officials referred to as "the politicization [which really refers to partisanization] of administration" (*gyōsei no seijika*) is not surprising at all. This is reported by both incumbent and former officials of not only heavily partisanized agencies but also such traditional bureaucratic giants as the MOF and MITI. The MAFF is characterized as an effective "support arm" for the LDP and its *Nōrinzoku* (farm dietmen), and contemporary agricultural policy-making is seen as "a highly politicized process decidedly controlled by the party's political considerations."[7] Several former MOE bureau directors and AVMs and an MOF budget official whose jurisdiction included MOE budgets spoke of the education bureaucracy as seriously eroded by the LDP's authority, expertise, and political needs. One official who headed all major MOE bureaus depict-

---

[6] The major exception is Muramatsu's pioneering study, *Sengo nihon no kanryōsei*.

[7] For a recent study in English along this line, see Aurelia George, "The Japanese Farm Lobby and Agricultural Policy-making," *Pacific Affairs* 54, no. 3 (Fall 1981): 409–430.

ed the LDP as "the senior partner" and the MOE as "the junior partner" of the official education policy-making system.[8] As for the MHW, also a highly partisan agency, an interviewed source described the agency as "suffocating" (*kurushii*) under LDP pressures. As he put it, "it is not only that the powerful Japan Medical Association [JMA] goes to the LDP" over the heads of agency officials; "the LDP is also cognizant of the growing electoral importance of health and welfare policy." Commenting on the MOT, a group of reporters who had long covered the agency wrote: "The relationship between the MOT and the [LDP] dietmen is not a 'dependency relationship' (*mochitsu motaresu*), for the legislators are much more powerful. The 'honorable dietmen' are so strong that they often impose unreasonably difficult tasks [upon the agency]."[9]

Policy-making in the Ministry of Foreign Affairs is also highly susceptible to the political considerations of the LDP and especially its leaders. Of course, the respective roles of politicians and bureaucrats vary depending upon issues involved, as with other ministries. "If the issue is routine and noncontroversial, involving essentially a continuation or marginal, incremental change of the status quo," according to Haruhiro Fukui, "the decisions (or nondecisions) may well be made 'bureaucratically'—mainly by the bureaucrats, with little intervention from politicians or interest groups." On important, politically sensitive and highly controversial foreign policy issues, however, LDP leaders assume the central role, "with the bureaucrats playing a subordinate or marginal role."[10]

What about the traditionally assertive economic bureaucracies such as the MOF and MITI? Hashiguchi Osamu, former MOF Budget Bureau director, in his perceptive discussions of "the political penetration of administration," attributes the LDP's growing policy role to its long tenure as the majority party and to the powers that come from this, such as policy specialization and personnel power over agency officials.[11] Imai Ka-

[8] For an exploration of this notion, see Park, "Kyōiku gyōsei ni okeru jimintō to mombushō." See also Park, "Party-Bureaucracy Relations in Japan: The Case of the Ministry of Education," _Waseda Journal of Asian Studies_ 1 (1979): 48–75; and "Education Policymaking in Contemporary Japan: A Study of the Liberal-Democratic Party and the Ministry of Education," a paper presented at the Japan Seminar, Center for Japanese Studies, University of California, Berkeley, May 19, 1978, 83 pp.

[9] Kankryō kikō kenkyūkai, _Un'yusho_, p. 90.

[10] Haruhiro Fukui, "Policy-making in the Japanese Foreign Ministry," in Robert A. Scalapino, ed., _The Foreign Policy of Modern Japan_ (Berkeley and Los Angeles: University of California Press, 1977), pp. 4–5.

[11] Hashiguchi, _Shinzaisei jijō_, pp. 196–197. For a perceptive analysis by a _Nihon keizai_

zuo, also a former bureau director in the MOF, has written extensively about what he calls "party intervention in administrative affairs," as well as the shift of effective decision-making power over agency personnel from the bureaucracy to the party sector. Imai diagnoses the resulting bureaucratic tendency of "tail-wagging" (*o o furu*) to the LDP as a contagious disease of the postwar Japanese bureaucracy.[12] In budgetary and fiscal powers too, former MOF official Sakakibara Eisuke sees the party as dominating the MOF bureaucracy. He views the PARC as performing a directive role over the MOF Budget Bureau, and the PARC Taxation Investigative Committee as having a similar power over the MOF Taxation Bureau.[13]

The EPA is not much better off. Not only in substantive policy-making but even in the presentation of the government's annual *Economic White Paper* (*Keizai hakusho*), the EPA is subjected to political intervention by the prime minister, agency chief, and LDP economic policy dietmen, who, as a senior EPA division chief put it, are "extremely specialized experts" and often have a better command of "micro-level policy knowledge."[14] One Environmental Agency (*Kankyōchō*) division chief, commenting on the hierarchical relationship between the LDP and the bureaucracy, went as far as to conclude, "Under the present system,

*shimbun* economic reporter of contemporary financial policy-making and of the party's role in it, see Ichioka Yoichirō, "Zaisei kin'yū seisaku kettei no katei to kōzo" [The process and structure of financial policy-making], in *Naikaku to kanryō,* pp. 88–94.

[12] *Imai Kazuo-shi danwa sokkiroku,* no. 15, p. 166. According to gossip circulating within the MOF, a righteous official (a tax policy specialist) on an elite mobility track was indignant over what he felt was an unfair income-reporting system for politicians. He committed the unfortunate sin of trying to do something about the matter. Though widely believed to be a bright, competent official, he was eventually taken off the upward mobility course; he never reached the top post within the Taxation Bureau, not to mention the topmost career post of AVM. The moral of the episode, well recognized by MOF officials, is that no MOF official in disfavor with a powerful LDP dietman can hope to be promoted to a coveted top post. See Moriyama, "Ōkurashō shuzeikyoku," pp. 289–291.

[13] Sakakibara Eisuke, *Nihon o enshutsusuru shinkanryōzō* [A portrait of new bureaucrats directing Japan] (Tokyo: Yamate shobbō, 1977), pp. 130–131. See also Sakakibara Eisuke and Noguchi Yukio, "Ōkurashō nichigin ōchō no bunseki" [The dynasty of the Ministry of Finance and the Bank of Japan: an analysis], *Chūō kōron* 92, no. 8 (August 1977): 96–150. For similar arguments by a former MITI division chief, see Uchida Genkō, "Taikenteki kanryōron" [An empirical view of bureaucrats], *Chūō kōron* 85, no. 5 (May 1970): 54–67. For discussion by an economic reporter of the LPD's domination of taxation policy-making, see Moriyama, "Ōkurashō shuzeikyoku," pp. 284–300.

[14] "Ima keizai kanryō wa nanio kangaeteiruka?" p. 44. See also Arai Tadao, "Kanchō ekonomisuto jidai no shūen" [The end of the era of government economists], *Ekonomisuto* 55, no. 19 (May 10, 1977): 27–28.

long conditioned by the LDP's long-lasting power, the central ministries cannot avoid being staff sections for the LDP PARC."[15]

Similar observations have been made regarding MITI. The daily newspaper reporters who covered the agency when it was "reigned" over by the so-called Sahashi battalion are now struck by the dramatic changes that have befallen the once assertive, powerful economic bureaucracy. Gone are the outspoken officials who passionately debated problems of capital liberalization and the need for Japanese advantages in international competition. As a *Mainichi* economic reporter put it, "MITI officials nowadays have their mouths closed like clams," and "when they open their mouths, they do so to complain" about their lowered status. The *Mainichi* MITI correspondent went on to note:

> The recent revision of the Anti-Monopoly Law is a good example [of the aforementioned change in MITI]. While the LDP Sepcial Investigative Committee on Revision of the Anti-Monopoly Law [chaired by Yamanaka Sadanori] was working on the LDP revision draft, MITI revealed its position only on a piecemeal basis. Even during the interministry coordination on the bill, MITI did not try to let its position be known....
>
> Because the revision was proceeding under the complete control of the LDP, it is most likely that MITI's strategy focused on efforts to coordinate with the LDP dietmen concerned rather than on public relations activities.[16]

Namiki Nobuyoshi, a former MITI economist and brain truster who "prematurely" left the agency in 1975, also provides us with an instructive glimpse of what has occurred in his agency. Though disgruntled with his partisan superiors who made impossible his *"hanamichi"* (glorious exit) from the agency, his lashing out at them is by no means personal. It is fully consistent with the widely held view of MITI as anything but *"gekokujō no honba"* (the home of the rule by lower officials) that it once was.[17] In Namiki's view, MITI no longer has room for either policy specialists or opinions incongruent with the agency mainstream dictated by "political considerations." In other words, MITI is seen as dominated by those subservient to political power—no longer a haven for "truth seeking economist-officials."

---

[15] "Kanryō doko o muku: kesareta hōan" [Future directions of bureaucracy: the bill that was struck out], *Mainichi,* July 16, 1979.

[16] Toda Eisuke, "Mokuhyō o miushinatta tsūsan kanryō" [MITI bureaucrats who have lost their aims], *Ekonomisuto* 55, no. 22 (May 31, 1977): 26.

[17] The following account draws extensively on an article by a *Mainichi* reporter, Arai Tadao. See his "Kanchō ekonomisuto," p. 30.

This development, shared by other economic agencies, as seen above, is also attributable to what an informed observer calls "political constriction" (*seijitekina shimetsuke*) of bureaucracy, which was given a major impetus by the LDP's electoral dip in the second half of the 1970s.[18] In contrast to the earlier eras when the party's stronger parliamentary status permitted it to be tolerant of assertive and even outspoken bureaucrats, the fierce LDP competition with the opposition parties (*hokaku hakuchū*) of the late 1970s forced the party to demand unquestioning loyalty and sacrificial devotion from the bureaucrats. As Namiki put it:

> Some people say that at a time of political confusion created by close conservative-progressive contest [as now], it is all the more imperative for the bureaucrats to demonstrate their ability to objectively mediate [between the two competing political forces], but these people are dead wrong. [The bureaucrats] all cower and are increasingly busy protecting their hides.[19]

Because of the powerful role the LDP plays in contemporary Japanese policy-making, it should not surprise anyone that policy coordination with the party—its influentials, factions, and policy-making organs—constitutes the singularly important segment of the bureaucracy's external mobilization and policy coordination. For any major governmental policy program, whether initiated by MITI or the MOE, the party is the first and the foremost of all obstacles that must be surmounted.[20] Contrary to the popular assumption, based on the notion

---

[18] Ibid. For discussions by veteran political reporters of how the growing LDP-opposition competition limits the bureaucracy's policy-making and legislative discretion, see Ashizaki, *Kōseishō,* pp. 125 and 146–156; Ijichi, *Jichishō,* pp. 128–129; and Shioguchi Kiichi, "Tenkanki no kanryō" pp. 142–145.

[19] Arai, "Kanchō ekonomisuto," p. 30.

[20] The following discussion draws heavily on interviews and discussions with LDP dietmen, Diet staff members, government officials (incumbent and retired), and reporters and commentators. Interviews with Murakawa Ichirō, Mori Yoshirō, Ishibashi Kazuya, Yasujima Hisashi, Hasegawa Takashi, Taki Yoshie, Itō Michirō, Suefuji Masahiro, Yagi Jun, Okano Yutaka, Shirakawa Katsuhiko, and Kuroha Ryōichi were most instructive. For a useful study of the LDP's growing role over MITI policy-making, see Yazawa Shūjiro, "Tsūsanshō ni okeru seisaku kettei katei" [Policy-making process in MITI], in Zenshōkō rōdō kumiai tsusan gyōsei kenkyūkai [The Commerce and Industry Labor Union's Research Institute on International Trade and Industry], ed., *Towareru tsūsanshō* [Questions about MITI] (Tokyo: Ōtsuki shoten, 1983), pp. 220–262. The Yazawa study and others included in this volume were commissioned by the union, whose membership includes about 20 percent of MITI's workforce. Even the short-lived Taishō Japan experienced factors contributing to the primacy of party government. For interesting parallels between that era and contemporary Japan in terms of party-bureaucracy relations, see Daikakai, *Naimushōshi,* vol. 1, pp. 768–771. Katō Eiichi, an MHA bureaucrat–turned–professor of politics at Tsukuba University, views "the Mejiro Palace" (Tanaka and his network) as

of "bureaucratic dominance," that views coordination with the party as a perfunctory part of the bureaucracy's external mobilization, all agencies take the utmost care in dealing with the party. All interviewed sources viewed bureaucratic-party policy coordination more as careful consultation, negotiation, and bargaining than as the party's reactive "stamp of approval" readily given for an agency policy formulated.

The ministry's policy coordination with the party starts in the earliest stages of agency policy-making. It needs to be stressed anew here that the bureaucrats are very much governed by "the rule of anticipated reaction" (*jishu kisei*) in all stages of agency policy-making and party-bureaucracy policy coordination, starting with the initial and foremost decision of whether the matter on hand should be taken up or not. If their prudence and their assessment of the party's (and the Diet's) probable reaction suggest that the party is not ready for the sort of action the agency has in mind, nothing will happen. If not sure of the party's probable reaction, an informal and even formal scouting of the party must be made, before any decision-making action can be undertaken within the agency. Only after a preliminary "go sign" is attained from the party does the agency proceed with its intraorganizational decision making and coordination. Of course, before any major directional change can be made during this intraagency process, the relevant PARC organs must be consulted and their understanding sought.

A multitude of party offices must be persuaded and mobilized in support of an agency program. First, there are the PARC and the appropriate organs under it, including the Policy Deliberation Commission

---

"*honne no seifu*" (real government) of Japan. Naturally, the Mejiro Palace is the foremost party-government element that agencies must persuade and bargain with before their major policy programs can be undertaken. For his fascinating analysis of the contemporary Japanese power structure, see Katō Eiichi, "Toshi no fukushū" [Cities' revenge], *Chūō kōron* 98, no. 6 (June 1983): 72–89. Katō's argument was somewhat underscored by Tanaka himself when he boasted that he was "a legal consultant" for governmental ministries. In his own words: "Every morning many officials come to my place. They are not particularly concerned with my health. They come to ask about laws. They bring their proposals and ask, 'Will the proposed revision of this law pass the Diet?' They bring many other problems. In short, I am a consultant on laws, budgets, and systems." See Tahara Sōichirō, "Tanaka Kakuei motosōri dokusen intabyū" [Solo interview with former Prime Minister Tanaka Kekuei], *Bungei shunjū* 59, no 2 (February 1981): 118–145. For recent studies of the LDP's growing policy role, see Michio Muramatsu and Ellis S. Krauss, "Bureaucrats and Politicians in Policy-making: The Case of Japan," *American Political Science Review* 78, no. 1 (March 1984): 126–146. The article is based on extensive interviews conducted by Muramatsu and his team. See also Uchida Kenzō, "Mōhitotsu no seifu: jimintō" [One more government: the LDP], in *Nihon no sietō*, a special expanded issue (no. 35) of *Jurisuto*, pp. 18–23.

(*Seimuchōsakai shingikai*), the division, and the investigative committee. This stage, dealing with the PARC organs, is the most crucial part of the agency's coordination with the party. Especially important are both the formal officers (chairman and vice-chairmen) and the senior members (*zoku* and *zoku gosanke*) of the PARC division and investigative committee, who constitute the specialist core of the party's Diet contingent in a given policy area. Also important are former ministers of the agency, who for the most part are now well established as *zoku* members and even *gosanke* members. As Edwin Reischauer has noted, the PARC divisions "serve as the chief area for the initial melding of the differing views held by the party's Diet members and for the coordination of their views with the expert opinion of the ministerial bureaucracy." Of course, behind the formal PARC committee meetings, "there will often be extensive consultations among Diet members especially interested in the specific legislation and between them and the concerned ministry and bureaucrats."[21]

Because of the careful and elaborate consultations between ministry and PARC division officials that go into the agency's policy-making and bill drafting, the policy measure or bill produced by the ministry faces little opposition from the PARC organs when it is formally presented to them for approval. This prompt PARC ratification has induced many observers to conclude that the PARC is a perfunctory legitimating mechanism for whatever the government bureaucracy proposes to do. In reality, as many interviewed dietmen and bureaucrats noted, the government proposals that come before the PARC organs for formal, final ap-

---

[21] Edwin O. Reischauer, *The Japanese* (Cambridge: Harvard University Press, 1977), p. 287. As early as 1965 some prominent Tokyo University scholars recognized the growing role and involvement of the LDP PARC in governmental policy-making. In the words of Katō Ichirō, "I hear that in recent years their [government-PARC] power relationship has significantly changed. PARC divisions have come to exercise considerable power, performing a role similar to that of SCAP GHQ during the [American] occupation. Some government draft bills might have to be introduced in the Diet following revisions by the PARC; some government proposals, which have already gone through deliberative councils [*shingikai*] and other organs, might be rejected by the PARC." Ogawa Ichirō concurs, saying that if agencies bring to the PARC proposals not acceptable to the party, agency officials are "sometimes subjected to a kangaroo court" (*tsurushiage*). Commenting on policy matters involving judicial reform (*shihō seido kaikaku*), Miyazawa Toshiyoshi notes that proposals likely to be rejected by the PARC are not even pushed to begin with. See "Rippō no arikata," pp. 18–19. For a recent study of the LDP PARC and *zoku* dietmen, see Kanazashi Masao, "Jimintō seichōkai to 'zoku' giin" [The LDP Policy Affairs Research Council and *zoku* dietmen], in *Nihon no seitō* [Japanese political parties], a special expanded issue (no. 35) of *Jurisuto*, pp. 173–178.

proval are government-party measures that naturally will encounter no opposition from the PARC members who participated in their formulation.[22]

Once the influential *zoku* dietmen are persuaded and their inputs registered in bill drafting, and the *zoku*-dominated PARC divisions have given their blessings, the rest is simple, provided that the policy matter is not too controversial and does not require a huge budgetary outlay. This is so because the recommendation by the relevant PARC division carries much weight with other policy-making organs of the party because of the party's internal "rules" based on specialization and reciprocity. The recommendation goes to the PARC Policy Deliberation Commission, which, like other PARC and party organs, represents a factional balance. When cleared there, it is forwarded to the Executive Board (*Sōmukai*), whose membership, composed of veteran dietmen with extensive ministerial experiences, also represents both a factional and regional balance. Approval by the Executive Board completes the party stage of the policy process, and the bill goes back to the government where it is endorsed by the cabinet before it is introduced in the Diet.

For politicized policy issues or complex issues that defy easy consensus decisions by PARC organs, the process of bureaucracy-party coordination is often very complicated and prolonged, involving the top echelons of the party and the government. The policy issue may be referred to the Executive Board or to a conference of top party officials that includes the secretary-general and even the president (prime minister) or to a meeting of factional leaders. A meeting of the prime minister and other major factional leaders is often the final policy arbiter. All these mechanisms represent a factional balance and therefore serve as the means for achieving an intraparty, interfactional consensus that will be binding on all party members in parliamentary voting. There are times, however, when even these high-level mechanisms fail to produce an intraparty consensus. The prime minister then assumes the final responsibility for decision making and its political consequences, as Kishi did in 1960 over the controversial revision of the American-Japanese security treaty.

For the reasons outlined above, it is imperative that, insofar as controversial programs are concerned, the initiating agency include in its coordinative and mobilizational efforts not only the relevant PARC policy *zoku* and its *gosanke* but also top party leaders—factional leaders and

---

[22] Interviews with Okuno Seisuke, Yasujima Hisashi, Okano Yutaka, Shirakawa Katsuhiko, Kudō Iwao, and Mori Yoshirō.

the prime minister. Of the party leaders, of course, the key individual to be mobilized is the party president, who also is the prime minister. The prime minister's role depends upon the policy issues and his personality; he can be a powerful and often the decisive factor determining the fate of a bureaucracy policy proposal.

This perspective obviously does not square with the notion of *gekokujō*, or *zokkan seiji*, that belittles the prime minister's role in policy-making and views him as standing at the apex of the legitimating hierarchy. "More and more," as Donald Hellmann has suggested, "the Prime Minister has come to exercise in fact the comprehensive powers that reside formally in that position."[23] This has been particularly true with foreign-policy issues, and the notion of "two presidencies" in the United States, to distinguish the powerful, activist "foreign-policy presidency" from the restrained "domestic-policy presidency," may also be a useful concept in understanding the policy behavior of the contemporary Japanese prime minister. As the spokesman for the nation and the government in international affairs, "the Prime Minister's authority and visibility provide unique opportunities to draw public support for his views." With various tools available to him, including the appointment power over top party and government personnel,[24] "he can do much to check opposition and to build intraparty unity on foreign-policy goals,"[25] as Tanaka did in 1972 over the normalization of Sino-Japanese relations.[26]

It has increasingly become the norm for the prime minister to assume personal responsibility for, or at least to identify with, one key policy achievement—more often a foreign-policy than a domestic-policy decision—during his administration. No conceptualization of contemporary Japanese foreign policy-making that failed to take into account the powerful role assumed by the prime minister would be valid.[27] All key foreign-policy decisions of postwar Japan are associated with the prime ministers: the formation of the U.S.-Japan alliance, 1951–52

---

[23] Donald Hellmann, *Japan and East Asia* (New York: Praeger, 1972), p. 56.

[24] Yomiuri shimbun seijibu, ed., *Sōridaijin* [Prime Minister] (Tokyo: Yomiuri shimbunsha, 1972).

[25] Hellmann, *Japan and East Asia.*

[26] For discussion of Tanaka's intraparty consensus-building on the China issue, see Yung Park, "The Politics of Japan's China Decision," *Orbis* 19, no. 2 (Summer 1975): 562–590.

[27] For discussion of the Satō case, see Fukutomi, *Daijin,* pp. 17–23. For an account by his chief aide, see Kusuda Minoru, *Shuseki hishokan* [Chief aide] (Tokyo: Bungei shunjū, 1975), pp. 105–194.

(Yoshida); the normalization of Japan-USSR relations, 1956 (Hatoyama); the revision of the U.S.-Japan security treaty, 1960 (Kishi); the Okinawa reversion, 1972 (Satō); the normalization of Sino-Japanese diplomatic relations, 1972 (Tanaka); and the signing of the Sino-Japanese peace treaty, with its so-called anti-hegemony clause, 1978 (Fukuda).[28]

Even in domestic policy, the prime minister is by no means a bystander if the issues are very controversial or require large budgetary support from the government. His intervention, though not readily forthcoming because of his reluctance to get involved in the more pluralistic and competitive domestic-policy area,[29] usually makes a decided difference. For illustration, let us take the so-called *Jinzaikakuhōho* (the Law to Obtain Talented Manpower) of 1974, initiated at the prodding of the LDP *Bunkyōzoku* and intended to drastically raise teachers' salaries. Faced with serious opposition from other ministries, and especially the tight-fisted MOF, MOE minister Okuno Seisuke, aided by the *Bunkyōzoku,* intensely lobbied Prime Minister Tanaka, who agreed to intervene.[30] In the words of Iwama Eitarō, then MOE bureau director in charge, who also played a major role in the efforts to mobilize party and governmental support, "Without Tanaka's intervention, the *Jinkakuhō* [i.e., *Jinzaikakuhoho*] would not have come about."[31] The ministries must enlist the prime minister's support not only against other competing ministries and the MOF but also against powerful interest groups

---

[28] For discussion of Fukuda's central role in the signing of the 1978 treaty, see Tahara, *Nihon no kanryō,* pp. 21–34. For Miki's efforts to deal with the issue of anti-hegemony, see Yung Park, "The 'Anti-Hegemony' Controversy in Sino-Japanese Relations," *Pacific Affairs* 49, no. 3 (Fall 1976): 476–490. For Hatoyama's role in the 1956 Japanese-Soviet negotiations, see Donald Hellmann, *Japanese Foreign Policy and Domestic Politics* (Berkeley and Los Angeles: University of California Press, 1969). For Kishi's role in the 1960 U.S.-Japan security treaty negotiation, see George R. Packard, *Protest in Tokyo: The Security Treaty Crisis of 1960* (Princeton: Princeton University Press, 1966), and Robert Scalapino and Masumi Junnosuke, *Parties and Politics in Contemporary Japan* (Berkeley and Los Angeles: University of California Press, 1962), pp. 125–153. For Satō's role in the Okinawa reversion case, see Kusuda, *Shuseki hishokan,* pp. 135–164; Watanabe Akio, *The Okinawa Problem: A Chapter in Japan-U.S. Relations* (Melbourne: Melbourne University Press, 1970); and Nihon kokusai seiji gakkai, ed., *Okinawa henkan kōshō no seiji katei* [The political process of Okinawa reversion negotiations] (Tokyo: Yūhikaku, 1975).

[29] One major domestic-policy area the prime minister traditionally stays away from is the fixing of rice prices, an extremely controversial and politicized matter. See "Kokkai no tōshitachi [Warriors of the Diet]: Mitsuzuka Hiroshi," *Kankai* 7, no. 10 (October 1981): 101.

[30] Yamada Hiroshi, *Jinzaikakuhoho to shunin seido* [The law to obtain talented manpower and the system of department chairmen] (Tokyo: Kyōikusha, 1979), p. 61.

[31] Interview with Iwama Eitarō, February 29, 1980.

that are in the habit of going directly to the prime minister for support. The available literature abounds with examples of direct group-lobbying of the prime minister by, almost exclusively, powerful business groups with "unrestricted" access to him.[32] The so-called Third Capital Liberalization Program (*Daisanji shihon jiyūka*), instituted in September 1970, is a case in point.

Obviously, by the early 1970s, the leadership of "big business" felt secure enough to go ahead with a program of further capital liberalization in response to demands from abroad. This was evident from an action taken by Kobayashi Ataru, a *zaikai* elder who then chaired the MOF's Foreign Capital Council (*Gaishi shingikai*). Even before the MOF could work out specific plans, he announced that he would like to see a program of extensive liberalization adopted. This was followed by the revelation by Okumura Tsunao, then chairman of the *Keidanren* Committee on Foreign Capital, of his "private proposal" that the new "liberalization should involve at least three hundred categories of business."

Shocked at the sudden development, the MOF hastily reacted. In its responses, however, it was governed by its traditional fear that the importation of foreign capital would drive many fragile domestic firms out of business and that the responsibility for that would naturally fall on the government, which has the legitimate authority to select areas for capital liberalization. Thus, the MOF countered with a liberalization plan that included only two hundred categories. Not sharing the MOF's apprehension and more sure of successful international competition, however, *zaikai* leaders pressed on with their initial demand and turned to Prime Minister Satō for support. He obliged, and the completed government plan of liberalization contained three hundred categories of enterprises, as had been urged by *Keidanren*.[33]

Let us look at another example of direct business lobbying of the prime minister—of Prime Minister Ōhira Masayoshi, who like Satō was considered a consensus-seeking, low-profile prime minister. In 1979, Mitsui, a leading corporate giant, involved in an Iranian petrochemical project that had been interrupted by Iran's political turmoil of 1979–79, had to raise a huge additional fund to cover the cost inflation. Unable to raise this sum on its own, Mitsui had to seek government investments in

---

[32] According to *Yomiuri shimbun* political reporters' accounts, the chairman and vice-chairmen of *Keidanren* "have the habit of rushing to" (*tondeiku*) the prime minister when they have problems. See Yomiuri shimbun seijibu, *Sōridaijin*, p. 148.

[33] Ibid.

the venture. To qualify for government participation, however, the Mitsui project needed to be elevated to a "national project," which required the participation of not only Mitsui but also others representing the iron-steel and electric industries. Decisions regarding such elevation and investment required coordination among the industries, among the four economic agencies (MITI, the MOF, the MFA, and the EPA), and between the private sector and the government. Even before interministry agreements could be worked out, however, Prime Minister Ōhira and Mitsui had reached an understanding that committed government support to the "expanded" project, and the economic bureaucracy was relegated to the role of elaborating and implementing the Ōhira-Mitsui compact.[34]

The primary responsibility for the bureaucracy's coordinative and mobilizational effort targeting the party falls on high-level officials, and especially the bureau directors.[35] The ministry's consultation and coordination with its PARC counterpart (division) is generally handled by the bureau director. It is he who undertakes an assessment of the party's mood and the likelihood of its receptivity to his bureau's policy. He consults with the chairman of the PARC division and *zoku* elders; he, accompanied by his own division chiefs, attends all major PARC division meetings, defends the proposed measure, and answers questions from the division members (especially the so-called nonregulars who show up when controversial issues giving them higher voter visibility are before the PARC division), just as he does in the Diet meetings. Whether or not the PARC division decides to endorse the ministry proposal depends largely on the skills and efforts of the bureau director. This picture of his primary role is a contrast to the 1950s, as portrayed by many former officials, in which division chiefs played the central role in coordinating with the party.[36]

It is not too difficult for the ministry to have its policy proposals or bills "anointed" with the PARC division's approval, as long as party inputs are properly taken into account. Policy conflicts develop from time to time between the two, however, although the contemporary norm is for the ministry to make concessions to appease the PARC division. In persuading and bargaining with the division and its elders, the bureau

---

[34] This account draws on discussions by a group of informed observers including an LDP staff member. See Kyōikusha, *Kanryō,* pp. 112–124.

[35] Muramatsu, *Sengo nihon,* p. 217.

[36] Interview with Naitō Takasaburō, May 8, 1980; and interview with Yasujima Hisashi, February 29, 1980.

director does not work alone, for he is aided and supported by his AVM, PVM, and minister. When the going gets tough, however, the minister assumes the major responsibility for coordination and becomes the key spokesman for the agency. (This theme is further discussed later in this chapter.)

Once division leaders (not only formal leaders, who include the division chairman, but also informal leaders such as *zoku* members and *gosanke*) are won over, the ministry can count on their support in dealing with the nonregulars of the PARC division who may still have reservations about the proposed measure. Similar reinforcement can be expected from the divisional leaders in coping with party opposition in the stages and organs beyond the PARC division. Typically, the chairman of the PARC division assumes responsibility for managing the ministry measure through the PARC Policy Deliberation Commission and the Executive Board, both filled with veteran dietmen with cabinet experience.

Though aided by his *zoku* elders and a contingent of ministry officials that includes the bureau chief and the director of the Minister's Secretariat, however, the division chairman is still hampered in his mobilizational efforts by his junior standing (*jingasa*) and his limited intraparty clout. It is at this stage that the minister becomes highly active and useful and takes over the responsibility for defending the agency proposal. He appeals to and lobbies top party functionaries, and especially the chairman of the PARC and the Executive Board, who together have a decisive voice in settling issues of intraparty and party-bureaucracy conflict. He attends top party meetings such as the conference of three executives (*tōsanyaku kaigi*) and argues for the ministry bill. For highly politicized issues, his lobbying must eventually include factional leaders and the prime minister; once the prime minister's endorsement is secured, he and his key aides (e.g., director of the Cabinet Secretariat) lend helping hands to the minister as he tries to persuade factional leaders. Although on occasion the prime minister summons the ministry's career staff (AVM and even bureau directors) for consultation, major ministry efforts to persuade the prime minister are usually carried on by the minister. If he is a member of the prime minister's faction or close to him (as was the case with Okuno Seisuke under Prime Minister Tanaka), the minister will naturally use this special relationship in his attempts to persuade the prime minister to intervene on the agency's behalf.

Several LDP dietmen interviewed by Nathaniel Thayer commented on the power that decisions by top party leaders carry. In the words of Kosaka Zentarō, "Pushing a plan through the party organs takes a long time. A short cut is to take your ideas to the top party leaders, to get their understanding, and let them do the pushing for you." According to Koyanagi Makie, "Real decisions come from above, formal decisions come from below." Fukunaga Kenji spoke of an advantage in getting the support of faction leaders and the Executive Board. According to him, "many times a minister if it is a bill, a party committee chairman if it is a party matter, or an individual politician if it is a personal plan," plays the central role in soliciting high-level intraparty blessings.[37]

The so-called university campus disturbance of 1968–69 provides an illustration of the central role played by ministers in agency dealings with the party sector over controversial policy issues. At the peak of the disturbance, ignited by an incident involving the Tokyo University medical school, most of the nation's institutions of higher learning and even some high schools were affected, and nearly seventy institutions were under siege by radical students. Riot police were called in, and violent confrontations with the students followed. The early 1969 entrance examinations were canceled at several schools, including Tokyo University, which annually provides an overwhelming majority of the new recruits for governmental ministries.

Though divided in its view of how to respond to the highly volatile situation, the MOE bureaucracy—dominated by moderates—was hesitant to take "hasty" actions that would further escalate the riotous situation and insisted on working within the framework of existing laws and in accordance with the principle of "university autonomy." This "go slow" approach was deeply resented by the "hawkish" segment of the LDP *Bunkyōzoku*, who advocated not only legislative measures against radical students and disrupted institutions but also a fundamental reform of higher education that would preclude similar occurrences in the future. Responding to this demand, which, because of the deteriorating situation, had a wider backing in the party, the MOE decided to initiate an "interim" measure that would empower the education minister to take specific actions against institutions unable to deal firmly with campus disorders. This, however, did not go far enough to meet the demands of the hawkish party dietmen, who included the MOE's own graduate Natiō Takasaburō and PARC chairman Nemoto Ryūtarō.

The final government-party bill introduced and passed in the Diet in August 1969 was largely along the MOE's moderate lines, which were backed by the "dovish" members of the party and its *Bunkyōzoku*. The moderates' victory was attributable to a variety of factors. Undoubtedly,

---

[37] Thayer, *How the Conservatives Rule Japan*, pp. 294–295.

one major factor was the effort by Education Minister Sakata Michita. Though "hawkish" on the JTU, Sakata, often dubbed "the intellectual member of the *Bunkyōzoku gosanke,*" was markedly dovish on the critical issues of 1968–69 and did not share the "radicalism" of his hawkish *Bunkyōzoku* colleagues. Backed by Prime Minister Satō, who wanted to see the crisis "minimized" for his own political reasons, the education minister played the key role not only in dealing with the MOE's own "hard-liners" (e.g., Miyaji Shigeru, then director of the Higher Education Bureau) but also in quieting the party's hawks, who wanted stronger language in the proposed legislation. Sakata vigorously lobbied party leaders, including factional chiefs and the chairmen of the PARC and Executive Board; he held numerous meetings with the PARC Education Division, the Investigative Committee on the Educational System, and *Bunkyōzoku* elders, who often chided and humiliated him for siding with the moderates. In short, without the minister's successful mobilizational efforts, the final legislation might well have taken a different shape.[38]

The contemporary Diet is also an important part of the bureaucracy's external environment whose blessings must be obtained for its policy programs. After all, under the present Japanese constitution, the Diet is endowed with the ultimate legitimating authority for all policy measures that require legislative sanction. The legislature, however, is a less powerful institution than the United States Congress, and its policy-initiating role is rather limited, although, surprisingly, bills originated by opposition dietmen are given legislative approval from time to time.[39] If one takes into account bills and laws incorporating ideas ini-

---

[38] The preceding account is based on information collected from various sources: interviews with MOE officials, LDP dietmen, and journalists, and published accounts including Yagi Jun, *Mombu daijin retsuden* [Profiles of education ministers] (Tokyo: Gakuyō shobō, 1978), pp. 203–214; Sugawa, "Daigaku mondai," pp. 100–104; "Hoshutō seiji to daigaku kaikaku," *Seikai,* no. 281 (April 1969), pp. 181–185; and *Asahi* and *Nihon keizai shimbun* accounts.

[39] This observation is particularly true with education policy. Interviews with Taki Yoshie and Sasaki Sadanori, April 25, 1980. Both were upper-house Education Committee staff members at the time of interviewing. Nakajima Yoneo and Takagi Kōmei, both members of the Diet lower-house staff, also enlightened me on the opposition parties' role in the Diet. For an excellent discussion of the opposition's policy role, see Kojima Kazuo, *Hōritsu ga dekirumade* [The process of lawmaking] (Tokyo: Gyōsei, 1979), pp. 139–188. Most interviewed individuals agreed that the contemporary Diet is a far more powerful institution than it was in the 1950s. Kimura Shūzō, formerly a foreign-policy expert on the Diet staff, felt that although the Diet's role in domestic-policy matters has certainly grown, the same thing cannot be said for foreign policy-making, in which its role has been rather minimal.

tiated by LDP members of the Diet, however, the Diet's role in policy initiation is greater. The norm, however, is for the LDP to coordinate its measures internally and then give them to the appropriate governmental ministers for elaboration and then submission in the Diet, although on occasion bills of importance and urgency defying successful interministry coordination are introduced as private members' bills (*giin rippō*).[40] The importance of the contemporary Diet is most visible, therefore, in its reactive roles of amending, delaying, and rejecting government-LDP bills.

A large majority of bills are easily disposed of in the Diet—mostly routine, minor bills, supported by all parties. For important and controversial policy measures, the rule of "anticipated reaction" plays a major role in the LDP government's strategy in handling the opposition in the Diet. The LDP, of course, uses its majority strength on occasion, but it does so with much reluctance, as the final resort. The party wants to avoid, if possible at all, what the vociferous media condemn as "the tyranny of the majority" because "undemocratic" tactics can precipitate not only intra-Diet resistance by the opposition parties but also larger, organized demonstrations and even anomic activities on the streets, which may have negative repercussions on the party's electoral performance.

Therefore, the LDP government must not only limit the number of controversial bills introduced in the Diet but also tailor the bills and make them as palatable to the opposition as possible, taking into account strongly held views and probable reactions. Even after bills are introduced in the Diet, it is not unusual for the LDP to make concessions to the opposition. This conciliatory pattern is now pronounced, even in budgetary matters, to the consternation of MOF budget officials long used to seeing products of their laborious work sailing through the legislative labyrinth unscathed.[41]

According to a recent *Yomiuri* account, the Diet's role in fiscal matters must now be viewed in more than reactive terms, for the legislature has become increasingly active, even in policy initiation. As the *Yomiuri* put it: "The lower-house Finance Committee's Subcommittee on Tax Reduction is now looking into issues of tax cutting. They are not only debating merits and demerits of a tax cut but also studying such policy specifics as tax rates. MOF bureaucrats now refer to the subcommittee as 'the real Bureau of Taxation.' "[42]

---

40 Interview with Nishioka Takeo, February 19, 1980.

41 Yamamura, *Ōkura kanryō,* pp. 56–66.

42 "Kanryōtachi no zasetsu" [Bureaucrats' frustrations], *Yomiuri,* July 6, 1982.

The common characterization of the Diet as a rubber stamp for governmental policy decisions is thus far too simplistic and fails to take proper note of the place the Diet and the opposition parties occupy in the contemporary Japanese policy-making process. The Diet's growing importance is poignantly underscored by Kida Hiroshi, former MOE AVM and now director of the MOE's National Institute for Education Research:

> In the early postwar years, the newly established Diet, not used to its new constitutional role, simply served as a rubber stamp for governmental bills, bestowing legitimacy on them. In the 1950s, however, the Diet gradually woke up and began to try to live up to its constitutional expectations. In the 1960s and 1970s the Diet became "overriding." There are many legislators, in all parties, who have long tenure in the Diet now. They are no longer policy amateurs. Based on their experience and expertise in their areas of specialization, they ask probing, tough questions [during Diet interpellations of government], some of which cannot be answered without a great deal of prior preparation. Nowadays all governmental ministries are much occupied with matters having to do with the Diet. I would say that Japan has come to approximate the American system, in which Congress is very assertive. I would even say that the Diet has become a big nuisance. Through their contacts with the Diet, government officials know very well where the politicians stand on policy matters. As far as controversial items are concerned [e.g., those on which the dietmen have reservations and a variety of strongly held views] the bureaucrats don't want to do anything new; they don't wish to propose any new bill. In this way, the Diet does limit our policy behavior.[43]

In a similar vein, Imamura Taketoshi, also a former ranking MOE official, compares the prewar and postwar Japanese bureaucracies:

> [When the Second World War ended], I was like a rat crawling around in the bottom of a sinking ship, for the supreme position we bureaucrats had enjoyed before the war was now given to the Diet in accordance with the new Japanese constitution. The situation surrounding the bureaucracy began to change shortly after the new constitution was adopted, and the constitutional designation [of the Diet as the supreme organ of the state] has become a reality now. I

---

[43] Interview with Kida Hiroshi, April 15, 1980. Even during the Taishō era, according to former *Naimushō* officials' recollections, the Diet was the formidable political actor. The known views and anticipated reactions of the Diet parties, and especially the majority parties, were dominant factors regulating *Naimushō* policy-making. See Daikakai, *Naimushōshi*, pp. 768–769.

managed to climb from the ship's bottom to the top of the mast. As I look around, however, I see that my position relative to the level of the ocean has not changed at all in the past thirty years. Be that as it may, in my view, this postwar constitutional change will certainly affect the pride of young bureaucrats.[44]

"All this," as Edwin O. Reischauer put it, "means that negotiations must be held with opposition parties."[45] As Kida and many other interviewed officials noted, for all ministries, Diet-related matters and strategy occupy a principal place in their mobilizational efforts. Recognizing that successful dealings with the Diet parties require accurate information about them and their policy views, all agencies accord high priority to their information-gathering activities in the Diet. Officials of legislative liaison are designated for this purpose. The General Affairs Division (*Sōmuka*), a key staff office in the Minister's Secretariat in all agencies, and its Diet porthole and listening post known as the Office of Government Witnesses (*Seifu iinshitsu*) are key intermediaries between the ministry and the Diet.[46]

Ministries also use other devices of information collection. Let us take the MFA. A contingent of five or six elite freshman officials are sent daily to the Diet to observe and report on its activities. "These notes [taken by them] are put into shape intelligible to others, and then duplicated and distributed" throughout the agency. This time-consuming practice is an important part of intraagency socialization and training for MFA officials, who are often chided for their ignorance of domestic politics. It also is a major method of gathering information about the Diet.[47]

In addition, higher officials of the line division gather information, as do their superiors, and especially bureau directors, who regularly interact with the dietmen of all parties. In mobilizational and coordinative efforts, the bureau director plays the primary role, and lower officials, even division chiefs, are generaly excluded from these political activities. The bureau director frequently visits not only the leading LDP members but also opposition members of Diet committees, to see where they

[44] Imamura, "Kyōiku gyōsei zakkan," p. 6.

[45] Reischauer, *The Japanese,* pp. 293–294.

[46] I am deeply indebted to Murakawa Ichirō of the LDP PARC for educating me on *seifu iinshitsu* and other devices of bureaucracy-Diet coordination, during my stay in Japan, 1976.

[47] "Hachijūnendai no nihon o ninau kasumigaseki no ekisupātotachi" [Kasumigaseki experts in charge of the Japan of the 1980s], an interview with Kunihiro Michihiko, deputy chief of the Foreign Ministry Minister's Secretariat, *Kankai* 7, no. 10 (October 1981): 227.

stand on policy issues, explain agency bills, and seek their support. Informal and even "covert" consultations are held, and "deals" are made, with key dietmen whose support would pave the way for smooth passage of agency bills. This is what one MOF division chief calls the "*urakata*" (behind-the-scenes) task of the agency's support mobilization.[48]

The importance the agencies attach to their legislative coordination is well attested to by the time and energy bureau directors expend on the Diet and its committees.[49] The principal complaint made by all interviewed bureau directors (incumbent and recently retired) was the inordinate amount of time and energy spent in Nagatachō, which houses the Diet and the LDP headquarters.

For controversial issues, whose handling requires close LDP supervision, the minister will often intervene on behalf of the agency and negotiate and bargain with key Diet members on both sides of the aisle. For a highly politicized bill whose passage in the Diet is in jeopardy, the initiating agency must deal with an expanding circle of dietmen, both LDP and opposition; the minister's intervention, if he is a man of influence and persuasion, is often pivotal to the passage of the bill. He must meet with key members of not only the Diet Management Committees (*Giin un'ei iinkai*) but also of the Diet Strategy Committee (*Kokkai taisaku iinkai*) of each of the parties. As party officials, including the secretaries-general and even presidents, invariably participate in the handling of highly controversial issues, it often becomes imperative for the minister to direct his lobbying to the top level of each of the parties.[50]

For important policy measures that are already designated as vital to the government and the party, the sponsoring ministry will have no difficulty in mobilizing the kind of government and party support necessary to successfully deal with the resistance of the opposition parties; but in the absence of such support, the ministry bill may not see its way out of the Diet without the minister's vigorous and successful mobilization and persuasive efforts. The minister, aided of course by his *zoku* colleagues, plays a critical role in elevating his agency bill to a measure considered vital to the LDP and thus worthy of an all-out party effort to secure its passage.

---

[48] "Ima keizai kanryō wa nanio kangaeteiruka," p. 45.

[49] Ibid. See also Ashizaki, *Kōseishō,* p. 103.

[50] For discussion of LDP and Diet machineries of interparty conflict resolution, see Murakawa Ichirō, *Seisaku kettei katei* [The policy-making process] (Tokyo: Kyōikusha, 1979), pp. 157–177.

The party's growing interest in the controversial ministry bill may also mean the agency's weakening grip over the bill—not only over how it should be handled but also over its contents. In other words, the party often assumes the final say over whether or not the bill should be amended, and if so, how, in response to the opposition's demands. At this stage of high-level political negotiations, the bureaucrats often take a back seat to their minister, who assumes the central role in the efforts to keep the bill from further watering down.[51]

**Bureaucratic Sector**

One prominent feature attributed to the Japanese bureaucracy is "vertical administration" (*tatewari gyōsei*).[52] This is the entrenched sectionalism of individual offices—"vertical structures" (*tatewari soshiki*) and their habit of "roping off" (*nawabari*) their own prerogatives and spheres of jurisdiction from outside interference. Interoffice competition and jealousies are found at all levels of bureaucracy, not only among individual ministries but even among divisions and bureaus within the same ministry.[53] In a recollection of his experience as a freshman official in the prewar days, former MOF bureau director Imai Kazuo provides telling testimony of intraagency sectionalism:

> Soon after I was appointed to my post in the government, I was sent to the next division to borrow some documents. As I recall it, they involved statistics compiled from all the prefectures of the country. I thought that the documents were no longer much needed by the division, for its study based on them had already been completed. The division officials, however, put up a fight and refused to oblige me. I can still recall the parting words of the division official I was talking to because they were so outrageous: "If these data are so essential, why don't you write to the prefectures and get it yourself?"[54]

Among ministries, *nawabari ishiki* (sectional consciousness) is far more serious, and competition and jealousies more frequent, prompting Chalmers Johnson to conclude, "Jurisdictional disputes among agencies over policy, appropriations, and priorities are the very lifeblood of the

---

[51] The above discussion draws on interviews with former cabinet ministers and parliamentary vice-ministers. Particularly useful was the interview with Okuno Seisuke.

[52] "Ima keizai kanryō wa nanio kangaeteiruka," pp. 49–50.

[53] Albert M. Craig, "Functional and Dysfunctional Aspects of Government Bureaucracy," in *Modern Japanese Organization and Decision-Making*, Vogel, pp. 15–17.

[54] Imai, *Kanryō*, p. 142.

Japanese bureaucracy."[55]

In Japan, therefore, coordination (*chōsei*) of government activities, if not the chief administrative problem, runs a close second. The Japanese have developed a variety of mechanisms of interministry coordination, some of which are quite familiar to other polities. Initial attempts at policy coordination are undertaken at the policy-drafting stage—usually by deputy division chiefs and division chiefs. If the issues are complex and controversial, interministry coordination, still conducted within the realm of *jimuteki* (staff) efforts, is moved up to the level of bureau directors and even AVMs. The so-called conference of AVMs (*jimujikan kaigi*), a weekly meeting of the top career officials of all agencies, however, is not an important coordination mechanism, notwithstanding the popular characterization of the conference as a forum "where common problems are confronted."[56] A highly ritualized forty-minute luncheon gathering, the conference is hardly an efficient device for coordinating top-level policy matters. It is largely a legitimator for policy decisions previously worked out and coordinated.[57]

The MOF's Budget Bureau is another mechanism of interministry coordination. Through its budget-making power and in attempts to avoid waste and duplication by line ministries, the Budget Bureau plays an important role in prodding and cajoling competing agencies to reconcile differences—a role particularly strong when the office enjoyed an undisputed status in budget making.[58] With its declining share of the budget-making power, however, the importance of the agency's coordinative role has also decreased.

In addition to these devices, bureaucratic proxies are also used to effect interministry coordination. Examples of this are deliberative councils (*shingikai*) and investigative committees (*chōsaki*), which, though often dominated by the graduates and allies of the sponsoring agency and thus supportive of its policy position, play an appreciable

---

[55] Johnson, *MITI*, p. 320.

[56] Vogel, *Japan as Number One*, p. 59.

[57] Thus, according to Watanabe Masao, former chief of the Cabinet Research Office (*Naikaku chōsashitsu*), "The conference of AVMs has been reduced to a mere skeleton." Quoted in Tahara, *Nihon no kanryō*, p. 13. Some important items, such as draft budgets, top bureaucratic appointments, and controversial items defying *jimuteki* compromise, normally bypass the conference of AVMs and go directly to the cabinet. See Okabe, *Gyōsei kanri*, pp. 100-101. Moreover, policy matters come before the conference after they have gone through the party organs; this is a serious check on the freedom of the AVMs' conference. Interview with Murakawa Ichirō, August 23, 1976.

[58] Uchida, "Taikenteki kanryōron," pp. 62-64. Uchida is a former MITI division chief.

role in interministry understanding.[59] Interministry consultative councils (*kyōgikai*), with memberships representative of all the ministries, are also created for the sole purpose of interministry coordination. These are all *jimuteki* mechanisms of interministry coordination among the career officials of the ministries concerned; however, they are not the only devices available to the ministries, for "political" mechanisms are also used, with increasing frequency, to achieve high-level coordination on important matters, as we shall see later.

As widely reported by interviewed bureaucrats and LDP dietmen, *jimuteki* efforts of interministry coordination have become increasingly difficult because of the LDP's growing policy role. A prominent feature of the contemporary Japanese political system, as previously noted in this chapter, is the system of tight linkages (*yuchaku*) that has developed between all ministries, on the one hand, and their corresponding PARC divisions and *zoku* members, on the other. Therefore, as an initiating agency coordinates its policy with other ministries and tries to enlist their support, it must also consult and coordinate with its PARC counterpart. This is a rule of high priority for all agencies. Even after initial blessings are secured from the PARC division, the ministry must keep it informed of major developments and seek its understanding at every important stage of coordination and support mobilization with other ministries (including the MOF), the Diet (and the opposition parties), and interest groups. Agency-party *nemawashi* and consensus building can be more complex and assume greater importance than those aimed at interagency coordination.

Other agencies consulted by the initiating agency because of their legitimate interest in the policy proposed also have to consult with and coordinate their policy postures with their own PARC division "patrons" if the matters on hand are sufficiently important and warrant such coordination. Because of the party's participation in interministry coordination from the very beginning, therefore, an agreement coming out of such coordination is most unlikely to be rejected by the relevant PARC divisions. In these bureaucratic efforts of coordination and consultation with the PARC divisions and other party organs, not only the higher officials of the ministries (normally, bureau directors and even the AVM,

---

59 For a comprehensive study of *shingikai* and its roles in Japanese policy-making, see Yung Park, "The Governmental Advisory Commission System in Japan," *Journal of Comparative Administration* 3, no. 4 (February 1972): 435–467; in Japanese, "Shingikai-ron" [A study of deliberative councils], *Jichi kenkyū* 48, nos. 5–6 (May and June 1972): 20–38 and 81–96.

but not division chiefs), but also the ministers play a major role. When the agency bureaucrats fail, ministers must be mobilized. If they happen to be powerful dietmen with much clout on the relevant party organs, the bureaucratic dependence on them will be far more pronounced.

A theme persistently brought up in conversations with bureaucrats and LDP dietmen is increasing bureaucratic dependence on the politicians in the process of interministry coordination and support mobilization. This is well corroborated by the published accounts of former bureaucrats. Interviewed MOF officials attribute this dependence to the line agency officials who, unable to get their requested budgetary funding through bureaucratic channels, rush to their dietmen-*sensei* for help. Line officials, on the other hand, put the blame on "spineless MOF Budget Bureau examiners who cannot say no to men of power." The truth most likely lies with both the "spineless" MOF and the "dependent" line agencies. In any case, it is a reflection of the growing power of the "perennial" majority party and its dietmen. As a senior MOF division chief recently noted, "an interministry conflict invariably goes up to the top level" for resolution.[60] Widely echoed by interviewed officials, this is a remarkable admission of the relative futility of lower-level coordination efforts; it also points to the large role assumed by the dietmen-ministers and what interviewed officials often call "our cheerleading dietmen-*sensei*."[61]

A variety of "political" mechanisms exist for interagency coordination. Ministers get together to iron out interagency differences; the cabinet and cabinet committees, and even the prime minister, are also entrusted with the coordinative task. A 1961 opinion survey, conducted by Watanabe Yasuo, of higher officials of three agencies (Finance, Home Affairs, and Agriculture-Forestry-Fisheries) shows that, when the bureaucratic (*jimuteki*) channels fail, 48 percent of the respondents favor a consultative procedure among the heads of agencies. Thirty percent mention the cabinet, and 15 percent would delegate the matter to the prime minister.[62] These findings point to the bureaucrats' preponderant reliance

---

[60] "Ima keizai kanryō wa nanio kangaeteiruka," p. 50.

[61] Chalmers Johnson, in his MITI study, writes: "[A] useful practice [of interagency coordination] is the recruitment of ministers and other senior political leaders from among former senior bureaucrats, thereby giving powers of coordination to leaders with expert knowledge of the bureaucracy, 'old boy' connections, and hierarchical relations with serving bureaucrats." Johnson, *MITI,* p. 321.

[62] Watanabe Yasuo, "Kōkyū kōmuin no ishiki" [Consciousness of higher public officials], in *Gendai gyōsei to kanryōsei* [Contemporary administration and the bureaucratic system], vol. 2, ed. Taniuchi Ken et al. (Tokyo: Tokyo daigaku shuppankai, 1974), pp. 457–458. In the early postwar years, ministry bureaucrats (usually division chiefs con-

on the intragovernmental devices involving the ministers. In the view of no less than 78 percent of the officials polled, the mechanisms dependent upon their ministers are the preferred methods of conflict resolution. Even in adjudication by the prime minister, his decisions reflect and follow careful consultations with the relevant ministers and thus their inputs.

The Watanabe survey, taken six years after the LDP was formed, makes no reference to party mechanisms of interagency coordination. The picture of interagency coordination drawn from the interviews with government officials and LDP sources conducted in the late 1970s, however, is one of growing party participation. The elders of the relevant PARC organs and *zoku* often assume the coordinating role for the agencies under their supervision. The PARC chairman, always a senior LDP dietman and often a faction leader, also has served as a mediator.[63] Other party mechanisms are ad hoc party committees of PARC investigative committees composed of LDP dietmen including former ministers of the agencies.[64]

Recent examples of these party devices include the LDP Special Investigative Committee on Measures Regarding International Economic Relations (*Jimintō kokusai keizai taisaku tokubetsu chōsakai*), chaired by Esaki Masumi, a veteran "trade policy" dietman who has held many key party and government posts (e.g., PARC chairman, Executive Board chairman, and MITI minister). Composed of *zoku* dietmen and former ministers with expertise in trade policy who represent the party's major factions and interests, the party committee has played the central role in

---

cerned) were admitted into cabinet meetings to assist their ministers. They were even allowed to address the cabinet on the issues on hand. Now, however, all agency bureaucrats are barred from cabinet meetings, making dietmen-ministers the only spokesmen for their agency interests. See Hashiguchi, *Shinzaisei jijō*, p. 187.

63 Fukutomi, *Daijin eno chōsen*, pp. 182–184. For discussion by a veteran political reporter of the coordinative role assumed by party actors (party *zoku*, functionaries, and faction leaders) in the MHA and the MOF, see Ijichi, *Jichishō*, pp. 134–202. For a case study by Tōhoku University students (under Professor Ōtake Hideo) of how LDP leaders (top party officials and cabinet members) assume a coordinative and decision-making role when politicized issues on hand defy administrative efforts of coordination, see Tōhoku daigaku hōgakubu ōtake zemi, "Kankyō gyōsei ni miru gendai nihon seiji no kenkyū" [A study of contemporary Japanese politics as reflected in environmental administration], *Chūō kōron* 97, no. 9 (September 1982): 82–112. Katō Eiichi, a former Home Affairs Ministry official, notes that "the bureaucracy's coordinative ability has vastly deteriorated in recent years," prompting the so-called Mejiro Palace of Tanaka and his followers to assume a larger role in interagency coordination. See Katō, "Toshi no fukushū," pp. 79–80.

64 Murakawa, *Seisaku kettei katei*, pp. 31–33. See also, Nihon keizai shimbunsha, ed., *Jimintō seichō*, pp. 40–46.

coordinating complex policy issues of market access for foreign goods that had been hotly debated by the economic agencies concerned, including MITI, the MOF, the MFA, the EPA, and the MAFF. The committee has also been a key medium for party and big business inputs into the formulation of market-access policy decisions.[65]

Another example of party committees in interministry coordination is the Special Investigative Committee on Revision of the Anti-Monopoly Law (*Dokkinhō kaisei ni kansuru tokubetsu chōsakai*) created within the PARC. Always chaired by the party's economic policy experts, such as Yamanaka Sadanori and Saitō Eisaburō, the committee has clearly assumed the dominant role in not only party-government but also interministry coordination, with a view to revising the controversial law.[66] This kind of party device, in not only economic policy but also other policy areas, has gained in importance in policy coordination, although it is frowned upon by the bureaucrats because it tends to constrict their policy discretion.[67]

Once interagency coordination is shifted to the political stage (LDP organs and dietmen), the minister becomes the key actor representing his agency. He assumes the central role in articulating its interests and mobilizing intraparty support for its policy. In these efforts, of course, he is aided by his agency staff, but they perform what many interviewed officials and cabinet members call "a supportive role" for the minister. Whether party adjudication of interagency conflict is handled by the relevant PARC divisions or by an ad hoc PARC investigative committee, it is the minister who visits and lobbies with influential members of these committees in an attempt to lead a party compromise closer to the policy position of his agency. The minister attends all major meetings of party coordinating committees and speaks for his agency. He approaches powerful party elders (e.g., the secretary-general, the chairman of the Executive Board, and the leader of the minister's faction) who are in a position to intervene with the party committees on the minister's behalf. He also assumes a major share of agency lobbying of his ministerial predecessors in the party and the elders of the relevant party *zoku,* whose backing is also crucial to the success of an agency program.

---

[65] "Kanryōtachi no zasetsu," p. 9. See also Minakimi Tatsuzō, "Tsūshō kanren hōrei no kaisei to un'yō kaizen o motomete" [In search of revision and improved management of international trade-related laws], *Keidanren geppō* 31, no. 5 (May 1983): 55.

[66] "Kongo no dokkin seisaku ni nozomu" [Our views on future anti-monopoly policy], *Keidanren geppō* 31, no. 4 (April 1983): 19.

[67] *Kanryōtachi no zasetsu,* p. 9.

In view of the foregoing discussions, it is not surprising that the notion "the centrality of bureaucratic channels in interministry conflict resolution" applies more to routine, minor, or noncontroversial policy issues over which the officials of the agencies can work out compromises without political intervention. In any agency, well over 90 percent of its affairs are routine and minor matters having to do with implementation and elaboration of the existing laws and regulations.[68] Most of these matters are strictly intraministry in scope and do not concern other agencies. Other matters do require coordination with other ministries, and many are indeed administratively handled. If the notion of bureaucratic centrality refers to the popularity or frequency of bureaucratic channels used, then it is undoubtedly an accurate concept. As far as important and controversial issues are concerned, however, they often defy administrative interagency coordination, even at the bureau directors' level, thus necessitating action by nonbureaucrats, including the ministers and even party functionaries and organs.

In any area of policy-making, needless to say, policy authorization is wasted effort unless accompanied by the necessary funding. Appropriation may well be the most important part of the policy process. Hence, the MOF, the finding agency of Japanese officialdom, has occupied a central position in the Japanese policy-making system; thus, to secure blessings from the MOF is a key part of the line agencies' efforts to mobilize external support.

Much of the literature (both in Japanese and English) on the Japanese budget-making system dwells on the powerful role played by the MOF, often to the exclusion of other actors of budget making. This emphasis is not too surprising in view of the important, often undisputed, role that the agency played in the prewar years, which was allowed to reemerge during the postwar occupation era. The notion of MOF dominance, as applied to contemporary Japan, however, overlooks some of the major changes that the Japanese budget-making system has experienced since the merger in 1955 of the two conservative parties into the LDP. Therefore, many of the earlier generalizations about the budget-policy system are no longer valid. Most interviewed Japanese sources take issue with the popular assumption that budget making is monopolized by MOF budget officials who make "marginal allowances for requests" of the LDP (its cabinet and dietmen).[69]

---

[68] Interview with Kida Hiroshi, April 15, 1980; and interview with Yoshitake Hiroki, July 8, 1980. Yoshitake was a veteran MOE official who served in the Minister's Secretariat and the Bureau of Elementary-Secondary Education.

[69] Vogel, *Japan as Number One,* p. 67.

Several broad generalizations based on the data from interviewed sources and published accounts by former officials can be attempted that distinguish the present budget-making system from its predecessors. First of all, as Kakizawa Kōji has already informed us, the budget system had become markedly pluralistic; it now consists of multiple actors. Second, as far as the powers of the LDP and the MOF are concerned, the balance has undoubtedly tipped in favor of the former, so much so that Sakakibara Eisuke, an MOF bureaucrat-turned-scholar, characterizes contemporary budget making as based on "the pattern of party domination" (*tōshudō-gata*).[70] In an elaboration of his party primacy thesis, Sakakibara offers the following outline of the budget-making process:

> Every ministry must first submit its estimates of budgetary requests to the PARC division in charge. Adjusted and approved there, they are then sent to the [MOF] Budget Bureau. In the process of revival negotiations (*fukkatsu setchū*) [between the MOF and the line ministry involved], the items that the PARC has designated as "Most Important" cannot be touched.
>
> The LDP PARC, therefore, has in reality come to stand above the Budget Bureau. This is well symbolized by the position that "negotiations among the three top party executives" (*tōsanyaku setchū*) publicly hold in the final stage of the revival negotiations. In principle, the process involved in the formulation of the government's budget bill requires intragovernmental coordination, and thus the final stage of that process should be negotiations by the ministers concerned (*daijin setchū*). The fact that issues of conflict, not settled by the ministers, are deferred to the party for resolution, vividly testifies to the contemporary budget-formation process characterized by "LDP dominance."
>
> The problem is not confined to budget making. Even in taxation policy, the LDP Taxation System Investigative Committee has become extremely powerful in the past ten years, and no reform of the taxation system can be undertaken without clearance with the party committee.[71]

---

[70] Sakakibara, *Nihon o enshutsusuru*, pp. 130–131. For discussion by a former Bank of Japan official of the MOF's declining power and of factors contributing to it, see Saitō Seiichirō, *Keizai kanryō no fukken* [Return to power of economic bureaucrats] (Tokyo: PHP, 1980), pp. 27–41.

[71] Sakakibara, *Nihon o enshutsusuru*, pp. 130–131. Commenting on the party's growing role in budget making, Imamura Yuzuru (former chief of the MHW's Agency for Social Insurance), noted, "Legislation and administration are no longer separate." Ashizaki, *Kōseishō*, pp. 141–142. Katō Eiichi of Tsukuba University has demonstrated that the party-dominated budgetary system has worked very much in favor of the rural prefectures

Sakakibara's description, though fully congruent with the views widely expressed by the interviewed officials and LDP legislators, is too brief a sketch of contemporary budget making, leaving out some important details that also point to the LDP's intimate involvement in the budgetary process. For example, all agencies carefully consult with their PARC counterparts in the course of preparing their initial budgetary estimates; any new major programs must be coordinated and cleared with the PARC divisions before they can be incorporated into their estimates. Moreover, the party's anticipated reactions must be taken into account by the ministry budget officials and, especially, bureau directors who have coordinating authorities over bureau budgets and are in close communication with the relevant PARC divisions. Therefore, the ministry's official budgetary estimates, when submitted to the PARC divisions for formal approval, already reflect the party's key concerns and inputs and hence do not encounter opposition from the PARC organs.

Attendant upon the growing party power in budget making and over the MOF is a change in the bureaucracy's tactics to secure funding for its programs. This is most conspicuous in the pattern of interactions between the MOF and line agencies, which has changed from one of bureaucratic centrality to one of bureaucratic dependence upon the LDP and its dietmen. In the early years of the postindependence era, the line agencies' budgetary efforts focused primarily on the MOF. As the party's budgetary role grew and intergency budgetary competition increased, however, all ministries found traditional bureaucratic methods and channels increasingly ineffective. For costly new programs, they now directed their primary energy to efforts to secure party support, and the MOF became the target of secondary importance. This was—and is—so because, as a former MOE AVM put it, "MOF budget officials are highly

---

that have consistently returned a large majority of LDP dietmen. The share of the national tax assumed by 38 rural prefectures (58 million people altogether) for 1980–82 was 29.6 percent; the remainder, 70.4 percent, was paid by 58 million residents of 9 urban prefectures. The national government's subsidies (*kōfukin*) to, and administrative investments (*gyōsei tōshi*) in, the urban prefectures amounted to only 40 percent of the total, the remaining 60 percent going to the rural prefectures. The Tanaka faction, the most powerful LDP faction, had 78 percent of ite Diet contingent coming from the rural prefectures. See Katō, "Toshi no fukushū," pp. 77–78. For commentaries by Niigata Prefecture's LDP dietmen on this unfair distributive system, see "Niigata senshutsu daigishi ōini kataru" [Dietmen from Niigata prefecture speak out], *Chūō kōron* 98, no. 12 (November 1983): 208–213. This distributive practice, as seen by former MHA official Katō and the LDP dietmen, is a significant deviation from the notion of "fair share" described in John Campbell, "Japanese Budget *Baransu*," in *Modern Japanese Organization and Decision-Making*, Vogel, pp. 71–100.

susceptible to LDP pressures." He went on to say:

> MOF budget examiners really started the practice of dealing directly with the party dietmen; they listen to them; they cannot say no to them. Although they are accommodating to the dietmen's demands, the budget officials have developed the tendency of ignoring pleas from [line] ministry officials [that are not backed by the party]. They are very responsive to those with power. As a result, the dietmen have become quite assertive and even haughty [vis-à-vis the bureaucrats].

Initial efforts to obtain necessary appropriations are of course made at adminisrative levels, even under what Sakakibara calls "the party-dominated system." When these fail, the agencies have to turn to their ministers and party patrons for support. The support of the ministries' PARC counterparts is readily forthcoming. This is so not because the PARC divisions are bureaucratic appendages in the party, as many writers have suggested, but because all major agency programs are worked out in a setting of intimate division-ministry consultation, as previously mentioned. Many of these programs may have been instituted at the prodding of the PARC divisions. Therefore, most of the agency's budgetary lobbying is directed to other sectors of the party, and especially top party executives who play the pivotal role in the final stages of budget formulation; to the prime minister, who though powerful, often frowns on getting involved in interagency budgetary wranglings; and to the MOF, which is also backed by its own LDP patrons, who usually include the prime minister.[72]

In the efforts to persuade and bargain with these key party and governmental sectors, the minister has come to play an increasingly important role. If a powerful, experienced dietman (e.g., a *zoku* member or *zoku gosanke*), he will assume the central role in mobilizing not only the party's budgetary influentials but also the MOF. Some of the minister's mobilizational activities are now quite institutionalized. One

---

[72] *Yomiuri,* July 10, 1982. According to Kojima Akira, a leading Japanese scholar of budgetary process, Tanaka Kakuei's budgetary activism, typified by frequent prime ministerial "directives" (*shiji*) and "decisions" (*saidan*), was more the exception than the norm. See Kojima Akira, "Yosan hensei katei no seiji kōzō" [The political structure of budget formulation], in *Naikaku to kanryō,* p. 69. The notion of bureaucratic dependence on the LDP for budgetary support is well corroborated by the data collected by Muramatsu Michio and his team from interviews with bureaucrats. The survey data show that LDP support is needed even in the preparation of intrabureau budgetary decisions; in new projects and revival negotiations with the MOF, LDP support is deemed absolutely mandatory. See Muramatsu, *Sengo nihon,* p. 154.

of these is minister-level negotiation (*kakuryō setchū*) between the ministers of the MOF and the line agency. *Kakuryō setchū*, however, lasting not more than thirty minutes for each ministry, is rather a routinized device consummating informal understandings previously worked out by the ministers and officials of the MOF and the line agencies.[73]

In the negotiations preceding this perfunctory *kakuryō setchū*, however, a powerful dietman-minister, backed by party influentials and leaders of the agency's PARC counterpart, can make a major difference. This is so because, as an interviewed MOF official noted, the budget officials (especially higher officials) and the finance minister tend to be quite concessionary toward the agency headed by a powerful dietman, although what Tsuji Keiichi, a former ranking MOF official, referred to as "the interministry moral code" (*yakusho kan'no jingi*) dictates that slicing of the pie be done in accordance with the notion of fair share.[74]

Another device of interministry budgetary coordination, which follows *kakuryō setchū*, is the so-called political negotiation (*seiji setchū*) among the three top party executives (secretary-general, and chairmen of the Executive Board and the PARC) and the ministers. Here, at the highest level for resolving budgetary conflicts, the controversial, costly agency programs denied funding through administrative and ministerial channels are taken up. In this stage of budget making, as an LDP insider observed, "the government makes large-scale concessions to the party and its considerations." This obliging posture is assumed largely because the MOF's budget bill will "not be approved by the party's Executive Board [the highest policy-making organ whose approval is required for all government bills, including the budget bill] unless party demands are accommodated."[75] Therefore, it is natural that the line ministers, and of course the finance minister too, carry on intense lobbying of the top party officials so that *seiji setchū* may result in actions favorable to their own agencies.

### Private Interest Groups

Interest group politics was not unknown to the "monistic" Japan of prewar years, where activities promoting sectoral interests were highly frowned upon by the state (the government) as contrary to the national

---

[73] Murakawa, *Seisaku kettei katei,* pp. 105–108.

[74] For transcript of the interview with Tsuji, see *Asahi,* November 19, 1978. Tsuji long served in the MOF before moving to the Administrative Management Agency, where he became AVM.

[75] Murakawa, *Seisaku kettei katei,* p. 110.

interest. It was not until the postwar period, however, that, in the words of Robert E. Ward, "Japanese society reached that point of saturation by interest group activities that characterizes the United States or the Western European nations."[76] Frank Langdon concurs, noting that interest articulation by groups is "the aspect of Japanese politics where modernization has made some of the most spectacular gains in recent years, especially since the end of the Allied Occupation in 1952.[77] Taguchi Fukuji also sees interest groups as "increasingly active in politics following the end of the occupation and especially after the formation of the Kishi government (in 1957)." As he puts it, " 'pressure politics' (*atsuryoku seiji*) can be said to be the basic feature" of the contemporary Japanese political system.[78] Not only have interest groups multiplied and become active but also they have become assertive and powerful vis-à-vis the official policymakers—both the LDP and the governmental bureaucracy—in the increasingly pluralistic Japanese polity.

For illustration, let us look at economic policy in two key bureaucracies, the MOF and MITI. In the 1950s the role of big business groups (e.g., *Keidanren* and *Nikkeiren*) in economic policy-making was undoubtedly minimal. In the words of a veteran *Mainichi* reporter covering the economic agencies, "important policy decisions involving budgetary and fiscal matters [in the 1950s] were nearly controlled by the bureaucrats" of the MOF.[79] This is very much in keeping with the notion of what the former MOF bureaucrat Kakizawa calls "the unipolar age," as previously discussed. By the middle of the 1960s, however, this picture changed considerably, the business sector having a larger input in budgetary and fiscal policy-making through its direct contacts with the bureaucrats and, especially, the increasingly powerful LDP and its leaders.[80]

The same development has occurred in MITI, which some pundits have referred to as "the headquarters of Japan, Inc."[81] By the middle of

---

[76] Robert E. Ward, *Japan's Political System,* 2d ed. (Englewood Cliffs: Prentice-Hall, 1978), p. 75.

[77] Frank Langdon, "The Making of Political Demands in Japan," *Pacific Affairs* 39, nos. 1–2 (Spring-Summer 1966): 37.

[78] Taguchi Fukuji, *Shakai shūdan no seiji kinō* [Political functions of social groups] (Tokyo: Miraisha, 1969), p. 158. For his discussion of Japanese interest groups in English, see his "Pressure Groups in Japanese Politics," *The Developing Economies* 6, no. 4 (December 1968): 468–486.

[79] Koizuka Fumihiro, "Jikoshuchōsuru wakate kanryō no yukue" [Future directions of assertive, youthful bureaucrats], *Ekonomisuto* 55, no. 30 (July 19, 1977): 37.

[80] Nishida Makoto, "Yosan kettei no uchimaku" [Budgetary decisions: an exposé], *Chūō kōron* 81, no. 3 (March 1966): 140–151. For discussion of this development by a former ranking MOF Budget Bureau official, see Hashiguchi, *Shinzaisei jijō,* pp. 195–196.

[81] A recent study has concluded that "MITI is not nearly as all-powerful as U.S. officials

the 1960s, heavy chemical industries had become deeply embedded in the foundations of Japan's industrial structure, and such key industries as steel, shipbuilding, and auto-making had become increasingly visible in international competition. As a result, their assertiveness vis-à-vis MITI also grew, and in the words of an informed economic observer, Japan's "industrial policy-making gradually shifted from the pattern of MITI dominance to that of private dominance (*minkan shudō*), and MITI's influence upon the economic sector grew weak."[82]

Take MITI's stance on the auto industry and anti-monopoly. As is well known, MITI has generally viewed the Fair Trade Commission's (*Kōsei torihiki iinkai*) advocacy of anti-monopoly as a nuisance.[83] MITI's basic philosophy has been that industry functions best if it is dominated by a few efficient firms that can reap the benefits of large-scale production. Some industries, however, have frequently ignored MITI's advice. In the 1960s, for example, MITI tried to persuade the then ten Japanese automakers to merge into two auto giants under the umbrellas of Toyota and Nissan. Only one company complied, joining Nissan. In the late 1960s MITI attempted to keep Honda, the motorcycle maker, out of auto-making. Honda defied MITI and grew into Japan's third largest automaker. MITI's success with its "policy of mitigated competition" has largely been in declining industries such as shipbuilding.

Not only in economic policy-making but also in other areas such as transportation, health-welfare, agriculture, and education, interest groups have become increasingly multitudinous and assertive, performing, with a growing vigor, functions of initiating, amending, and rejecting, thus limiting the traditional discretion of bureaucratic policymakers. Therefore, the mobilizing of support of, and coordinating of policy with and among, private interest groups have taken on added importance and become increasingly difficult tasks for the agencies. Gone are the days when governmental policy decisions could be imposed on interest groups as faits accomplis even when they did not take into account group positions.

---

often believe" and that its "leverage over Japanese firms has decreased since the early postwar period." See I. M. Destler and Hideo Satō, eds., *Coping with U.S.-Japanese Economic Conflicts* (Lexington, Mass.: Lexington Books, 1982), p. 286.

[82] Koizuka, "Jikoshuchōsuru," p. 37. See also Saitō, *Keizai kanryō*, pp. 163–192.

[83] Yanaga, *Big Business in Japanese Politics,* pp. 152–176. For valuable information on MITI's relations with industries I am indebted to Isawa Yoshitaka of the Japan Automobile Manufacturers Association and to Tsukahara Reizō and Tochigi Katsushirō, both of the Japan Chemical Industry Association.

Another complication for the contemporary bureaucracy is the marked tendency of interest groups to approach directly the locus of decision making (LDP and cabinet influentials) to articulate their interests and to counter undesirable bureaucratic proposals. This is particularly noticeable with groups that because of their electoral and financial muscles carry much clout with the party. They include not only powerful *zaikai* and industrial associations, the Agricultural Cooperative Associations (*Nōkyō*), and the Japan Medical Association (*Nihon ishikai*), but also a large variety of such less known groups as the National Association of Public School Superintendents of Instruction (*Zenkoku kōritsu gakkō kyōtōkai*) and the Japanese Federation of Auto Maintenance Associations (*Nihon jidōsha seibi shinkōkai rengōkai*), which have gained access to key points of LDP decision making, and especially the relevant PARC divisions and *zoku* elders.

As is widely known, big business groups enjoy a special access to the LDP that not many other organized interests do. At the top party and governmental level there is frequent and even regularized interaction with *zaikai* elders. For example, *zaikai* leaders—chairmen of *Keidanren, Nikkeiren, Nisshō* and *Keizai dōyūkai*—have monthly meetings with the top party executives. Around every faction leader, businessmen have formed clubs or supporters' associations that serve as a major conduit between the party and business. The following *Keidanren* account of the organization's efforts to influence Japan's internationalization of her market is very typical of big business's mode of operations:

> We have already explained our "proposals" and supportive "cases" to government and party leaders including the prime minister and relevant cabinet ministers, and the LDP Special Investigative Committee on Measures Regarding International Economic Relations (*kokusai keizai taisaku tokubetsu chōsakai*); we have solicited their cooperation in the efforts to improve [the governmental system of processing import and export items]. At the same time, we are holding numerous sessions of coordination with the proper offices and bureaus of the ministries concerned—the MOF, MITI, the MFA, the MAFF, the MHW, the MOT, the EPA, and the AMA.[84]

Even less known economic groups, such as small and medium-sized enterprises (SME), have also increasingly turned for support to the LDP,

---

[84] Minakami Tatsuzō, "Tsūshō kanren kyoninka kensa tono kaizen ni tsuite" [Concerning improvement of international commerce-related licensing, inspection, and other things], *Keidanren geppō* 31, no. 2 (February 1983): 26–27. For discussion of similar tactics used by one particular business interest, securities (*shōken*), see Nihon keizai shimbunsha, *Jimintō seichōkai*, pp. 55–59.

which recognizes the electoral and fiscal importance of these interests.[85] The creation (1948) within MITI of a Small and Medium-sized Enterprise Agency (*Chūshō kigyō-chō;* SMEA) was largely a response to SME demands for governmental protection and promotion. The party and its SME dietmen have increasingly assumed the role of articulating SME interest, prodding the SMEA into upping its fiscal support for the enterprises under its wing. In view of the party's vigorous backing for the SMEA and its clientele groups, it is not surprising that a *Sankei Shimbun* economic reporter went as far as to conclude, "The budgetary requests relating to SME matters are the only items always blessed with near-full funding [by the MOF] nowadays."[86]

A major perennial problem for MITI has been management of conflicts between big business and SME, and the LDP SME dietmen's intervention has increasingly complicated MITI's adjudicative process. Largely under LDP and SME prompting, MITI, in 1973, revised the Department Store Law (*Hyakkatenhō*) to discourage not only department stores but also *"sūpā"* (supermarkets or "general stores" that are in reality small department stores) from pursuing "expansionist" activities that drive small retail stores out of business.

The revised law, however, did not go far enough in meeting SME needs, for it regulated only large sūpā stores, leaving smaller sūpās free to carry their developmental activities into the traditional strongholds of small retail stores. The LDP intervened on behalf of the SME and urged MITI to expand the new law's jurisdiction to cover even small sūpās. MITI opposed the move, arguing that there already was a special measure that would alleviate the SME plight. In the SME and party view, however, the measure was not strong enough. Tired of MITI's dithering attitude, the LDP, with the backing of the opposition parties, speedily pushed through the Diet a private member's bill (*giin rippō*) that granted the MITI minister directive and punitive power over small sūpā stores that are "overly aggressive."[87]

---

[85] A foremost Japanese observer of interest group politics notes that in recent years interest groups have increasingly turned to PARC organs rather than to factions. See Hirose Michisada, "Seitō to atsuryoku dantai" [Political parties and pressure groups], in *Nihon no seitō,* a special expanded issue (no. 35) of *Jurisuto,* pp. 52–56. For discussion of the earlier activities of the major group representing small and medium-sized enterprises, the Japanese Political League of Small and Medium-sized Enterprises (*Nihon chūshō kigyō seiji renmei*), see Naoki Kobayashi, "The Small and Medium-sized Enterprises Organization Law," in Itoh, *Japanese Politics,* pp. 49–67. See also "Interest Groups in the Legislative Process" by the same author in the same volume, pp. 68–87.

[86] Hayashibara, *Uchimaku tsūsanshō,* p. 136.

[87] Ibid., pp. 136–137.

*Nōkyō* also has close ties with the party, which, in the words of one informed observer, "plays the dominant role in formulating and ensuring government policies protective and supportive of rural interests."[88] LDP *Nōrinzoku* members (farm politicians), key *Nōkyō* spokesmen within the party, occupy leading positions on PARC committees and subcommittees responsible for various aspects of agricultural policy. Supplementary channels of influence are available to farm interests through a variety of groups or leagues of LDP dietmen that function as intraparty and intra-Diet lobbies for specific farm interests such as rice, citrus, beef, and so forth.[89]

Like the business and agricultural groups, the Japan Medical Association (JMA), a key actor in health and medical policy, also has extensively worked through the party, which, though powerful over the bureaucracy, is markedly amenable to the association's demands. In the words of an MHW official, "The biggest reason why the MHW is weak in dealing with the JMA is that the politicians are completely controlled by the JMA and we bureaucrats are weak in dealing with the honorable dietmen."[90]

Another important factor governs the JMA's pattern of political activists. As Taguchi Fukuji noted, "The MHW bureaucracy is the greatest adversary the JMA must contend with."[91] This antagonistic relationship has grown out of the bitter struggle the JMA has waged in opposition to the government-imposed medical care system, which the association holds responsible for the decline in the social prestige of medical practitioners.[92] Moreover, MHW officials administer the specifics of what the JMA considers to be the degrading health care system, spotting and dealing with cases of "irregularity" by medical doctors.[93] In view of this

---

[88] Yamaji Susumu, "Atsuryoku dantai toshite no nōkyō" [Nōkyō as pressure group], in *Nōkyō ninjūgonen* [Nōkyō: a twenty-five year history], ed. Kondō Yasuo (Tokyo: Ochanomizu shobō, 1973), pp. 242–243.

[89] Tahara, *Nihon no kanryō,* pp. 224–252; Taguchi, *Shakai shūdan no seiji kinō,* pp. 237–278; and Kanryō kikō kenkyūkai, *Nōrinshō,* pp. 106–149.

[90] Cited in Tahara, *Nihon no kanryō,* p. 408.

[91] Taguchi, *Shakai shūdan no seiji kinō,* p. 190.

[92] JMA-MHW relations were not always bad. When the Health Bureau of the prewar Home Ministry was elevated to become a new MHW in 1938, it was "the JMA that played a major role in its independence." See "Bimyōna kankei: kōseishō to ishikai" [Delicate relationship: the MHW and the JMA], *Asahi,* September 4, 1959, p. 2.

[93] Taguchi, *Shakai shūdan no seiji kinō,* pp. 178–187. For an account by former JMA president Takemi Tarō of the association's long record of conflict with the MHW, see his "Ishikaichō nijūgonen" [Twenty-five years as JMA President], serialized in *Asahi,* March 30–May 2, 1982.

relationship with the MHW and the LDP's hold over the bureaucracy, it is only natural for the JMA to work mainly through the sympathetic party. As far as major controversial issues of health and medical policy are concerned, therefore, policy decisions usually evolve out of interactions among PARC health committees (both division and investigative committees), top party leaders, the MHW minister, the JMA leaders, with the MHW bureaucracy performing supportive, elaborative, and at best, mitigative roles.[94]

Not only such organized giants as the JMA and *Nōkyō* but also other highly specialized, narrow interest groups often limit bureaucratic policy discretion and make it impossible for the ministries to make policy decisions without careful consultation and coordination with them.[95] For illustration, let us take the MOE and educational interest groups. Organized interests the MOE must deal with can be grouped into two broad categories. Most of them fall into the category of "friendly clientele groups." They include various organizations representing elementary, secondary, and high schools and their administrators; private institutions at all levels; and national (state-run) and municipal universities and colleges. Then there are anti-MOE, anti-LDP groups, spearheaded by the JTU.

The agency appears to have a basically hierarchical orientation toward the friendly groups; that is, it sees itself as standing at the apex of a hierarchy of educational groups. From conversations with MOE officials, one gets the impression that they view these groups as supportive devices that can be readily manipulated.[96] This corporatist appearance (*tatemae*) belies the actual situation, which is often different and quite complex. In minor, routine issues, this hierarchical attitude is undoubtedly in agreement with the reality. On key policy issues vital to the groups, however, they have minds of their own and do not hesitate to contradict the MOE. If not happy with bureaucratic rulings, they too turn to what they correctly see as the real locus of education policymaking—the LDP and its influentials (especially, *Bunkyōzoku* members),

---

[94] Ashizaki, *Kōseishō*, pp. 56–68.

[95] For the auto-maintenance organization and other groups, see Utsumi, "Riken ni muragaru," pp. 141–159.

[96] For example, Tōyama Kōhei, then an assistant division chief in the MOE Bureau of Physical Education, referred to many educational interest groups as "*suishin dantai*" (promotional groups). Both Tōyama and his bureau director, Yanagawa Kakuji, said: "These organizations are not pressure groups. Of course, we get ideas and proposals from them and teachers. They petition (*chinjō*) us." Interviews with Yanagawa and Tōyama, May 16, 1979.

and the education minister. This has undoubtedly complicated the bureaucracy's dealings with these groups.

On matters concerning the antigovernment JTU, the bureaucracy's freedom is extremely restricted because of the LDP's long-standing political struggle with the militant union. Because of their mutual antagonism, of course, the MOE and the JTU do not carry on regularized interactions; but this does not mean that in formulating their policy MOE bureaucrats do not take into account the union's known positions and probable reactions. Whether proposed policies arise from the MOE's initiative or the party's directive, the agency officials are required carefully to coordinate their policy-making with the party. When MOE and JTU representatives meet, as they have from time to time in recent years, it is always the ministry's political component (the minister or, at least, the PVM) that represents and speaks for the agency.[97]

A variety of channels are used by administrative agencies to coordinate their policies with outside groups and enlist their support. Widely used in the preliminary stage of policy-making are, of course, deliberative councils (*shingikai*) or consultative councils (*kyōgikai*), which include in their membership representatives of key interest groups whose backing or acquiescence is needed. A major role performed by the council staff, all agency officials, is to lead council deliberation to conclusions desired by the ministry. In this the ministry is aided by proministry council members including "outstanding" former ministry officials.

In addition to these advisory councils, numerous coordinative and *nemawashi* sessions are held between agency officials and their interest group counterparts. Major responsibility for such coordination is shared by the chief of the division.[98] He is, however, largely confined to low-level coordination and negotiation, sensitive and controversial issues being handled by higher officials. Indeed, depending upon the complexity of the issues to be coordinated with external groups, the key agency actors responsible for such policy coordination vary. When the issues on hand are such that they defy the usual bureaucratic channels, or when the groups are formidable and powerfully backed by the party in power, interest articulation and support mobilization for the agency invariably fall on the dietman-minister. This is so not only with such partisan agencies as the MAFF and the MHW, traditionally susceptible to interest group and party pressures, but also with the elite economic bureaucracies of MITI and the MOF, traditionally assertive toward the political and

---

[97] For discussion of MOE ministers' dealings with the JTU, see Yagi, *Mombu daijin.*

[98] Muramatsu, *Sengo nihon,* p. 219.

interest group sectors. Many groups have become so powerful and "uppity" (*namaiki*), as one interviewed official put it, that their "responsible persons" (*sekininsha*) often tend to refuse to deal with agency officials other than their agency counterparts—ministers.

In a perceptive discussion of what he calls "the decline of the bureaucracy's status" (*kankai no chii no teika*), former MOF Budget Bureau director Hashiguchi Osamu identifies two primary factors responsible for this development. One of them, of course, is the semipermanent status of the LDP as the majority party. The other is the growing power of what he calls "*zaikai*" or "*keizaikai*" (economic community). The elevated status of big business and large corporations vis-à-vis other sectors of society is such that "the popular characterization of *zaikai* as the greatest 'power elite' of the postwar era is not farfetched at all." In the popular perception, company presidents (*shachō*) and managers (*keieisha*) not only enjoy an enhanced social status but also "possess the weight and stability often denied to cabinet ministers, whose typical term in office is one year, and to high-ranking bureaucrats, rotated every two years." Hashiguchi goes on to say, "Judging from mass media reactions, the view of *zaikai* as the aggregate of all business corporations, and the view of economic organizations [e.g., *Keidanren*] as the representatives of *zaikai*, carry tremendous weight." This situation, in Hashiguchi's view, "has brought about the deterioration of the bureaucracy's status" to such an extent that "the commanding position (*tōsei*) the prewar bureaucracy enjoyed...is now in the realm of legends."[99] Turning to his personal experience, the former Finance Ministry official gives the following account:

> In the decade of 1945–54, during which I was a deputy chief of the Banking Bureau's Banking Division (*Ginkōka*), my counterpart in a city bank was department chief (*buchō*) or deputy chief (*jichō*); my division chief's counterpart was a managing director (*jōmu*) of the bank. When I became Bank Division chief ten years later (1962), my deputy chief had to deal with the bank's division chief (*kachō*) [a step lower than the department chief), and my bank counterpart was still a *buchō*- or *jichō*-class official. The bank's managing director usually dealt with the deputy director (*shingikan*) of the Banking Bureau, and the senior managing director and vice-president of the bank dealt with our bureau director.[100]

---

99 Hashiguchi, *Shinzaisei jijō*, p. 195.
100 Ibid., p. 196.

In view of this, it should not come as a surprise that the agency's high-level and important dealings with leaders of industrial enterprises, not to mention elders of business associations, have now become a major responsibility of top-level officials, and especially the minister. If these negotiations involve not only interest groups but also the LDP and its influentials mobilized by these groups (the tendency of powerful groups to approach the party leadership has increased in recent years), only the minister can effectively perform the mobilizational and coordinative function.

For illustration, take the JMA and its "archrival," the MHW. The JMA's illustrious chairman for 1957–82, Takemi Tarō, was adamantly opposed to dealing with MHW officials other than the minister. Even the minister was treated in a highly condescending manner, even rudely.[101] Much of the routine negotiation and policy coordination is of course conducted between MHW officials and the corresponding staff of the JMA, but when these processes break down or key policy issues are concerned, the minister assumes the responsibility; he must deal with not only the JMA leadership but also party influentials who tend to be quite sympathetic to JMA positions. Taguchi Fukuji, in his lucid analysis of the JMA, provides an interesting illustration of the difficulties facing even the minister as he tries to perform his mobilizational and coordinative duty:

> On April 11, 1958, MHW Minister Horiki announced at a press conference, "I intend to see the [MHW-initiated] revision of the fee system for medical doctors implemented during my tenure." When that matter was brought up at a JMA Executive Committee meeting later, however, Takemi said, "But I hear that the party executives will not let that [the revised fee system] happen." He appeared very sure of party support on the matter. Later, on April 20, Takemi got an assurance from LDP vice-president Ōno, "You may feel at ease because we will not let the MHW do that" [revise the fee system]. On May 2, LDP Secretary-General Kawashima also assured JMA executive director Okabe, saying that "the new fee system cannot be proclaimed without approval by the three party executives and the cabinet." On June 3 of the same year [however], the Conference of Six Party Executives decided that "if the revision bill cannot be amended in a manner acceptable to the organizations concerned, we will [eventually] go ahead with the original MHW proposal." The *Journal of the JMA* later reported on the meeting: "The Six

---

[101] For a personal account of such experience by MHW minister Watanabe Michio, see Tahara, *Nihon no kanryō*, pp. 423–424.

Executives invited MHW Minister Horiki to the meeting and urged
him to postpone the implementation [of the original MHW proposal]
until after the formation of a new cabinet, but the MHW minister
adamantly refused, insisting on his own position [immediate imple-
mentation]. When told by LDP Executive Committee chairman Satō
to 'leave the matter to the Six Executives Conference,' the minister
reportedly got extremely upset and used abusive language not becoming of a minister." Horiki was never able to achieve his objective
and had to leave the cabinet post.[102]

## Summary

In contrast to its prewar predecessor, deeply permeated by the traditions of monism and statism, the contemporary Japanese polity is pluralistic and competitive. This is well mirrored in the changing relationship between the government bureaucracy and the rest of the political
system. The environment of today's bureaucracy is inhabited by multitudinous actors who are neither docile nor impotent. Some outside
groups, as noted above, are even vehemently hostile.

This situation is a significant contrast to the prewar years, when the
outside constituency was rather homogeneous and responsive. For much
of the post–Meiji Restoration era, and especially in the years preceding
the military ascendancy, agency policy-making was little restrained by
extrabureaucratic actors; the primary constraints on agency policy-
making were largely intragovernmental—to be specific, the MOF with its
appropriation powers, the line agencies in cases of conflicting jurisdiction, and the cabinet of government leaders. Extragovernmental policy
coordination and support mobilization, which involved weaker political
parties and interest groups, were not overpowering impediments for the
initiating agency.

This era of "bureaucratic primacy" is gone, having faded into what
former MOF Budget Bureau director Hashiguchi calls "the realm of
legends." Along with "bureaucratic power," such concepts as "party
dominance," "interest group pluralism," and "big business (*zaikai*)
power," have also come to dominate the lexicon of contemporary
Japanese politics. All these suggest formidable limitations imposed on
the bureaucracy by its environment. Successful extrabureaucratic policy

---

[102] Taguchi, *Shakai shūdan no seiji kinō,* pp. 195–196. For similar efforts by Environmental Agency (*Kankyōchō*) ministers to promote agency interests, see Tōhoku daigaku
hōgakubu ōtake zemi, "Kankyō gyōsei ni miru gendai nihon seiji no kenkyū," pp. 82–112.

coordination and support mobilization have now emerged as the foremost sine quibus non that the agency must meet to have its policy authorized, funded, and implemented. These functions are no longer monopolized by the agency bureaucrats. They are shared with the agency's political suzerains, and especially the minister. In important and controversial policy issues, the mobilizational and coordinative function is progressively pushed upward to the minister, who must now deal with not only the MOF, the line agencies, and the cabinet but also the LDP and its PARC committees, the Diet, and outside interest groups.

In mobilizing external support for his agency programs and in representing his agency at the political level, the minister is in a much more advantageous position than agency bureaucrats. Of course, the advantages are far more pronounced if he is a powerful dietman (*jitsuryokusha*). A veteran dietman, most likely from a safe district, the minister belongs to one of the major LDP factions and can count on the helping hands of his factional colleagues and leader. Moreover, he can deal with party functionaries and other ministers on an equal footing. This is by no means insignificant in this age of the growing sense of superiority on the part of dietmen-*sensei* vis-à-vis ministry officials (*yakunin*).[103] Being in the same party and having gone through similar processes of intraparty and intra-Diet socialization, these coequals know each other very well and are intimately familiar with skills and techniques of intraparty negotiations.

In dealing with the opposition parties in the Diet, the minister is also aided by his long legislative experience and by interactive skills acquired from his extensive association with the opposition members of his Diet committees. Moreover, in the course of his upward mobility the minister has developed personal and factional ties with party influentials (e.g., leaders of the key party policy-making organs such as the PARC and the Executive Board) that afford him special advantages in mobilizing external support or acquiescence for his agency programs. This point was brought home well by Kaifu Toshiki, minister of education in the Fukuda cabinet and known as "a rising star" of the LDP:

> Before I was appointed education minister, I had wide-ranging experience in the party and the Diet, including the chairmanship of the party [LDP] Diet Strategy Committee (*Kokkai taisaku iinkai*). This had given me a good knowledge of how the Diet and the party

---

[103] This theme was persistently brought up by both the bureaucrats and the LDP dietmen interviewed in 1978–80 and 1981. For comments to this effect by a key MITI division chief, see "Ima keizai kanryō wa nanio kangaeteiruka?" p. 46.

worked. It also allowed me opportunities to establish special relations with the key figures of the party. Thus, when I assumed the
Education portfolio, I was able to make good use of these assets in
my efforts to persuade party leaders and dietmen ino supporting the
MOE policies I believed in. On budgetary matters I managed to get
strong support from the Education Division and the [Education Sys-
tem] Investigative Committee [of the LDP PARC].[104]

In view of the clout and skills possessed by the minister, it is not
surprising that, as the former MOE AVM Kobayashi Yukio noted, "one
of the key roles performed by the minister is to persuade LDP
influentials to go along with his agency programs."[105] This is why all
agencies tend to bring up their cherished and usually costly projects for
authorization and implementation when they are blessed with powerful
ministers, although they have to pay a "price" for having them, as we
shall see below.

For illustration, let us take the MOE and one of its activist ministers, Okuno Seisuke, 1972–74. Commenting on Okuno's role in a major
MOE reorganization that resulted in the splitting of the Bureau of
Higher Education and Science into two bureaus—the Bureau of Higher
Education and the Bureau of Science and International Affairs—a
former AVM recalled, "Okuno was directly responsible for the creation
of the new Bureau of Science and International Affairs (*Gakujutsu
kokusaikyoku*); without him it would not have come about."[106] Several
other MOE programs are widely credited to Okuno's efforts.[107] Okuno is
close to the then prime minister Tanaka Kakuei, who played a dominant
role in budget making during his administration.[108] A noted fiscal expert
and a former AVM in the Ministry of Home Affairs who had had extensive dealings with the MOF, he commanded a great deal of respect from
budgetary policymakers, including the officials of the MOF Budget
Bureau.[109] It is not coincidental that his MOE subordinates deferred to
him and his leadership in agency policy-making and widely perceive him
to be one of the most active and assertive ministers of education.[110]

---

[104] Interview with Kaifu Toshiki, April 27, 1979. Kaifu's political career is detailed in
his interview with Itō Masaya. See "Bū-chan no seiji dōjō," pp. 178–186.

[105] Interview with Kobayashi Yukio, February 18, 1980.

[106] Interview with Kida Hiroshi, April 15, 1980.

[107] For discussion of Okuno's role in the passage of *Jinzaikakuhohō,* see Yamada, *Jinzaikakuhohō,* pp. 59–61.

[108] For discussions of Tanaka's activist role in budget making, see Tahara, *Nihon no
kanryō,* pp. 140–152; and Koizuka, "Jikoshuchōsuru," pp. 36–41.

[109] Interviews with MOF Budget Bureau and MOE officials.

[110] Interviews with Iwama Eitarō, February 29, 1980, and Shinozawa Kōhei, May 7,
1980.

Let us take another case illustrative of the minister's mobilizational and coordinative role—the MPT and its law providing for the so-called People's Loan system (*shomin kin'yū seido*), instituted in 1973 after much heated debate.[111] The law was designed to make small, low-interest, and short-term loans available to those who could use their postal savings as collateral. Understandably, the proposed program, popular among the vast majority of middle- and low-income consumers, was vehemently opposed by two very powerful sectors of the economy—the private banking institutions and *Nōkyō* (Agricultural Cooperative)—which saw the proposed move as cutting into their territory.

Their governmental spokesmen—the MOF for the banking interests and the MAFF for *Nōkyō*'s loan services—responded by launching what a *Yomiuri* political reporter called "a fierce attack" on the proposed program.[112] Even the LDP was split along the usual *zoku* (tribal) lines—the *Kin'yūzoku* (financial dietmen) and *Nōrinzoku* (farm dietmen) pitted against the *Yūseizoku* (postal and communications dietmen). Administrative-level efforts of interministry coordination got nowhere, and the MPT officials naturally turned to their minister, Hirose Masao, a former local postmaster and a bona fide member of the party's *Yūseizoku* who, before assuming the MPT portfolio, had held all key party, Diet, and government posts relating to postal and communication matters.

As he set out to mobilize intraparty and government support and coordinate with the disgruntled sectors, Hirose saw many problems. For one thing, being a member of the Ishii faction, he was not linked with a powerful faction. He was also dealing with the mighty coalition of *Nōkyō* and the banks, two electoral and financial backbones of the LDP that were powerfully supported by two formidable agencies of government, the MOF and the MAFF. These opponents countered the MPT plan with a proposal that interest rates for postal savings should be lowered in return for their acquiescence in the MPT People's Loan.

This scheme, because of its adverse implications for the MPT, was of course not acceptable to the ministry. Hirose, faced with the intransigence of the MOF and the MAFF, turned to and energetically pleaded with Kosaka Zentarō, PARC chairman and a senior member of the powerful Ōhira faction. Assuming the role increasingly familiar to PARC chairmen, Kosaka agreed to mediate among the three warring agencies and their constituencies. His role required more than

---

[111] Fukutomi, *Daijin,* pp. 183–184.
[112] Ibid.

mediation and coordination; it also required his siding with a particular position. Supportive in principle of the MPT plan, Kosaka succeeded in arriving at a compromise that was based on the premise that the MPT plan should not seriously jeopardize the business of banking and *Nōkyō* institutions and that required the three agencies to work out the specifics among themselves. Without Hirose's vigorous mobilizational efforts and Kosaka's sympathy, the People's Loan program of 1973 would not have come about.[113]

Okuno and Hirose are just two of the many contemporary ministers who have powerfully contributed to the implementation of major agency programs by effectively articulating agency interests and by successfully mobilizing party and government support. As an interviewed MOF budget official noted, "Surprisingly, behind every key agency program of recent years is an assertive and energetic minister who had much clout with the prime minister and other influentials in the LDP PARC." Hence he was "effective with not only other line agencies involved but also he Budget Bureau of our ministry."

In dealing with interest groups, also, the minister is aided by his ministerial status, his experience (parliamentary, governmental, and electoral) as a veteran dietman, his political skills, and his party, factional, and interest group affiliations. If he is a member of the ministry's corresponding party *zoku,* he has the major advantage of knowing, even intimately, leaders of the key groups under agency jurisdiction, as did Naitō Takasaburō, Takemi Saburō, Nadao Hirokichi, and Sakata Michita, who had extensive dealings with educational groups prior to their appointments to the Education portfolio.

Needless to say, the minister's connections with these groups helps him as he tries to articulate his agency positions. He is the highest "man of authority" (*ken'isha*) of the agency and as such can deal with his interest group counterparts as equals. With powerful groups and, especially, "negative constituencies" (e.g., the JTU for the MOE, and the JMA for the MHW), the minister is the only one who can authoritatively represent the agency in the crucial and controversial stages of policy coordination and adjudication because other officials, even the administrative vice-minister, are shunned by the groups as lacking full authority to speak for the agency.

Because coordination and conflict adjudication with interest groups inevitably entail dealings with their powerful LDP and Diet patrons, the minister's party, factional, governmental, and legislative ties are decisive

---

[113] Ibid.

assets not available to career bureaucrats. For these reasons, the bureaucrats increasingly have to turn to their political chieftain, notwithstanding their nagging doubts that, given his political and electoral bases and predispositions, he may be susceptible to party and interest group position and pressures as well. This characteristic of the contemporary minister will be explored in the following chapter.

One popular characterization of the minister's intraagency and extraagency roles has found its way into the literature on Japanese politics. In what might be termed "the notion of the mechanical minister," he is depicted as performing his extraagency roles strictly according to the ministry's scenario prepared by the career bureaucrats with hardly any input from him; he is allowed no unilateral deviation from the script. In short, this notion, clearly the dominant characterization of the contemporary minister, entails small intraagency roles and large extraagency roles for him. Akira Kubota, a scholar of Japanese bureaucracy, characterizes the typical Japanese cabinet minister as a "figurehead" who rarely assumes "an active leadership role in administering" the ministry "with respect to such matters as personnel and policy formulation." In the contemporary bureaucratic norm, he goes on to say, the "role expected of the minister is to defend the interests of his ministry in the context of the cabinet; a successful minister is the one who gets a big budget for his ministry and who persuades the cabinet to adopt his ministry's pet projects."[114]

Indeed, many agencies can claim to have ministers of this genre, although it is impossible to determine how many without undertaking careful studies of all the ministries involved. The impression gained from interviews with bureaucrats, however, is that the number is not very large, although the mechanical minister effective in his extraagency roles is the ideal type preferred by them. Moreover, according to interviewed officials, most "minimalist ministers" in their intraagency roles tend to be rather weak and ineffective chiefs who lack much clout over the sectors of the polity that the agency needs to persuade and bargain with. In other words, the puppet minister is likely to be an ineffective mobilizer and articulator for the agency.

As many interviewed party and government sources testified, the minister who has clout over the agency's environment is typically a powerful, assertive minister, even with regard to the agency's career officials. Furthermore, his ability to articulate agency interests and mobilize external support readily translates into intraagency power.

---

[114] Interview with Naitō Takasaburō, May 8, 1980.

Before he can defend and promote an agency program to the inquisitive LDP, MOF, Diet, and interest group actors, it must first be acceptable to him. It must be defensible and supportable. He must be convinced of its validity and purpose; he "must believe in" it, as Kaifu Toshiki put it.[115]

Cases abound in which ministry proposals failed to see their way out of the government, party, and Diet labyrinth because, either wholly or partly, of the passivity of ministers who were not convinced of their utility and legislatibility. Fukuda Hajime, MITI minister at the peak of the so-called Sahashi Battalion era (1963), was markedly cool to the Sahashi-initiated *Tokushinhō* (Temporary Law for the Promotion of Specially Designated Industries) bill, which was opposed by major sectors of the economic polity including a key segment of the LDP, the MOF, and big business.[116] The ill-fated bill, quickly dubbed "the sponsorless bill," was even without the backing of the minister of the agency that had prepared it.[117]

The minister, if a member of the relevant party *zoku,* is equipped with much of the expertise and information necessary to influence agency decision making. Moreover, as discussed in the preceding chapters, he is endowed with many other attributes that enable him to play an important role in decision making. He is also in possession of "political information" not readily available to the administrators. As a veteran party man and minister, he is well informed of the prevailing moods and opinions within the party and its major factions, the Diet, and the cabinet. Hence, he most likely has a well-developed sense of timing and strategy for successful securing of the needed intraparty, intragovernmental, and interest group consensus.[118] Thus, careful consultations with the minister and anticipation of his reactions become critical considerations governing the policy behavior and calculations of the career officials responsible for bill drafting. A miscalculation or slighting

---

[115] The preceding discussion is based on interviews with several former ministers. Arita Kazuhisa, though without any cabinet experience, was most knowledgeable about the contemporary minister's role. Former chairman of the *Nikkeiren* (Japanese Federation of Employers' Associations) Education Committee and a member of the upper-house LDP, he left the party to join the New Liberal Club. He later retired from elective politics. I am deeply indebted to him for taking time to educate me on the politics of education policy-making in Japan during my 1978–80 stay in Japan.

[116] *Asahi,* January 31 and March 13, 1963. See also *Nihon keizai shimbun,* February 27, evening; and March 13, 1963.

[117] Hayashibara, *Uchimaku tsūsanshō,* p. 97.

[118] Interviews with Kaifu Toshiki (April 27, 1979), Hasegawa Takashi (September 17, 1981), and Okuno Seisuke (April 23, 1979).

of the minister's intentions and views in the course of bill drafting and budgetary formulation may well mean unhappy consequences for a policy proposal.[119] All this suggests a major role—not only reactive and legitimating but also activist and input making—for the minister in agency decision making. In the words of an informed *Mainichi shimbun* observer:

> An agency blessed with a powerful dietman as its minister is able to strengthen its position vis-à-vis other sectors of government. On the other hand, this creates problems for the agency officials, for they must read his mind and act accordingly. They end up doing as they are told by the minister.[120]

Like other agencies, the Ministry of Transportation is aided in its support mobilization by a group of "rooters" whom some members of the agency's press corps (*kishadan*) have described as "*arigatakumoari katsu meiwakuna ōendan*" (valuable and troublesome cheerleaders).[121] They are, as the first half of the characterization suggests, effective articulators and promoters of agency interests. They also have minds of their own, making demands upon and expecting compliance from the agency bureaucrats.

No member of the present MOT *ōendan*, "valuable and troublesome," can ever top Satō Eisaku, the most illustrious of all MOT graduates and the most powerful of all the rooters the agency has had in its postwar history. Included among the powerful but troublesome agency friends is Sasagawa Ryoichi, who heads the well-endowed Japanese Association for the Promotion of Ships (*Nihon senpaku shinkōkai*). Widely known as "Don of Japan," Sasagawa effectively controls huge sums of grants and loans that the promotional association makes available to maritime and shipbuilding industries. Other members of the MOT's effective but bothersome *ōendan* include the agency's political appointees—not only the minister but also the PVM.

Some PVMs have established a more illustrious record than some ministers. Satō Takayuki, a personal aide to Kōno Ichiro and later MOT PVM in the third Satō cabinet, must head the list of activist MOT PVMs. In 1972 he drafted almost single-handedly the "Minister's

---

[119] Interview with Naitō Takasaburō, May 8, 1980.

[120] Arai, "Kanchō ekonomisuto," p. 27. For examples of the activist minister strong in both intraagency and extraagency roles, see: *Jimintō: hoshu kenryoku no kōzō*, pp. 35–37; and Kōno Hisashi, "Rōjinhokenhō no seiritsu katei" [The process involved in the formation of the law on health insurance for the elderly], *Jurisuto*, no. 805 (January 1–15, 1984), pp. 92–94.

[121] Kanryō kikō kenkyūkai, *Un'yushō*, pp. 28–50.

Memorandum on Aviation," which limits excessive competition by Japan's three airlines and specifies areas of business activities for each. This document, often known as the "Charter of Aviation" (*Kōkū kenpō*), continues to this date as the aviation policy of the Japanese government.

MOT ministers and even PVMs play an important role in mobilizing external support for agency programs; they also have a large voice in agency policy-making, as the case of Satō Takayuki suggests. As noted by members of the MOT *kishadan:* The MOT, perhaps because it has many kind-hearted bureaucrats, never commits vicious acts threatening to the minister and the PVM. Thus, it is only natural that the agency is easily dragged into following the pace set by the minister and the PVM."[122]

This pliant attitude toward the *arigatakumoari katsu meiwakuna ōendan* (party ministers and PVMs) may largely account for ups and downs often experienced by the MOT in its "administrative currents" (*gyōsei no nagare*).[123] In the 1960s Arafune Seijūrō, an LDP dietman from Saitama and then a member of the powerful Kishi faction, was appointed transportation minister. The new railway schedule released after his appointment showed that four express trains were to stop daily in Fukaya, a small city in his district that until then had been passed by. It was clear that the new minister was directly responsible for what many felt was "an outrageous decision" by the Japanese National Railways, whose administrative overseer is the MOT. In defense of the new train schedule, Arafune pronounced that "one or two stations" should not make much difference.[124]

---

122 Ibid.
123 Ibid.
124 Ibid., p. 90.

# VII

# Ministers and Articulation of Extraagency Interests

The minister not only is the chief executive officer of his agency but also must perform other roles while in office. He is a popularly elected legislator, and a longtime member of the majority party and an intraparty faction. Moreover, he is affiliated with one or more of the informal specialist groups (*zoku*) within the party. Thus, he has a multitude of constituencies outside his agency that he must cultivate—his election district and its dominant interests, his party, his faction, and a host of interest groups that his partisan, factional, and *zoku* affiliations require him to "nurse."

Interposed between the agency he heads and the external interests he is expected to serve, he must perform the difficult task of dual representation. As minister he represents and promotes agency interests to the outside constituencies, as discussed in the preceding chapter. At the same time, as an elected party-politician he must articulate and promote the interests of his political constituencies to the agency he heads. To effectively perform this political role of representing extraagency interests, he needs to do more than simply wear "the minister's hat." He must be an activist-minister—not only a watchdog within the ministry for his political constituencies but also an initiator, input maker, and prodder in agency policy-making. This the the central theme to be developed in this chapter.

All ministers are sensitive and responsive to party views, and especially those of their factions and the appropriate PARC divisions and *zoku*. This is inevitable because of Japan's system of party government, ministers' membership in the party, their factional ties, and their affiliations with the special policy groups in the PARC. Under the present system of party government, as former education minister Okuno Seisuke put it, "not only is the cabinet minister the head of his agency; he also is the chief representative of his party in the agency."[1] In the

---

[1] Interview with Okuno Seisuke, April 23, 1979.

words of Arita Kazuhisa, former LDP member of the upper house, "At present the majority party is the LDP and the (current) cabinet is formed by the LDP. Thus, it is natural for the education minister, a member of the cabinet, to feel "responsible to" and "listen to" the party in power and its policy positions.[2]

This perspective is widely echoed by LDP dietmen, whether they are incumbent cabinet ministers or not. The minister is expected to speak for and articulate his party's interests in agency policy-making. He is a key conduit for party-bureaucracy communication;[3] through him the party, its influentials, and its committees direct their policy preferences to the agency, although other channels are widely used (for instance, PARC division chiefs may deal directly with ministry bureau directors, as is often the case with the MOE and many other agencies).[4]

When party policy priorities are conveyed to the minister, he is expected to see that they are incorporated into agency policy. He cannot allow agency considerations to overshadow those of the party on important policy issues. In such partisanized agencies as the MOE, the MAFF, and the MHW, which perform functions vital to the party and its key political clientele groups, the minister's articulative and implementational role takes on added importance. The MOE, the agency responsible for socialization of youngsters through school education, has long been engaged in what many refer to as the party's "proxy-war" with the JTU and its leftist allies. The MAFF is the foremost office charged with looking after the interests of the nation's farm community, the backbone of the LDP's electoral support. As the MAFF must deal with the poweful nationwide agricultural cooperative *Nōkyō,* so the MHW (the agency of welfare and medical policy) is fated to contend with the powerful JMA, which the LDP simply cannot afford to alienate.[5] Similar constraints affect LDP ministers in the economic agencies (e.g., the MOF and MITI) because of close LDP-business ties.

In view of dietmen-ministers' deference and susceptibility to their party's needs, it is quite logical that Education Minister Kiyose Ichirō, 1955–56, boldly stressed in his inaugural address his intention to "place priority on party views" in MOE policy-making and portrayed himself,

---

[2] Arita Kazuhisa, *Nihon no kyōiku o kangaeru* [Thinking about Japan's education] (Tokyo: Daiichi hōki, 1976), pp. 200–205.

[3] Interview with Okuno Seiksuke, April 23, 1979.

[4] Interview with Yasujima Hisashi, February 29, 1980.

[5] This point is brought home well in the remarks by interviewed JMA officials and in the memoirs of former JMA president Takemi Tarō, serialized in *Asahi,* March 30–May 2, 1982.

even publicly, as "an obedient watchdog for my party," a shibboleth he faithfully adhered to in structuring the foundation of the postindependence "educational reverse course."[6] Nor is it unreasonable that Adachi Tokurō, a minister of agriculture in the Tanaka government (1972–74), had the habit of reminding his agency subordinates that he was "an MAFF minister dispatched by the LDP."[7] Nor is it surprising that the minister of finance often succumbs to party pressures, failing to live up to the role his Budget Bureau officials expect him to perform: not only to preach "budgetary responsibility" to the line agencies and their PARC and *zoku* mentors but also to successfully ward off their claims on the shrinking national treasury.

A recent case in point is Watanabe Michio, who held the Finance portfolio under Prime Minister Suzuki Zenkō. Although he tried to attain a balance between the conflicting party and MOF requirements, Watanabe did not vigorously resist the party demands in areas vital to the party and its traditional allies. MOF officialdom, in an attempt to curb the spiraling deficit, had doggedly insisted on lower price supports for rice growers. In this position the MOF was powerfully backed by the Second Ad Hoc Commission on Administrative Reform (chaired by Dokō Toshio), which recommended cutting governmental subsidies. Faced with vehement opposition from the party's "rice dietmen," however, the MOF backed down and proposed that, if the rice price support could not be reduced, the current level should at least be maintained. However, Watanabe, considered a key member of the party *Nōrinzoku,* overruled his agency recommendation and authorized an increase of 0.5 percent in rice support for 1982. Watanabe's justification for his action was, "We have to do this to get party support for the budget bill."[8]

Powerful dietmen-ministers, on their own or backed by the prime minister, may ignore with impunity party demands or rumblings about agency policy, but most ministers take party views very seriously, especially if these positions are widely supported within the party. Failure to accommodate a major party policy or even deviation from the established rules of party-government coordination (insofar as important policy matters are concerned) prompts warnings and even "disciplinary ac-

---

6 Totsuka and Kio, *Mombushō,* pp. 108–109.

7 Fukutomi, *Daijin,* p. 158.

8 *Yomiuri,* July 10, 1982. For discussions of *Daini rinchō's* attempts to reduce governmental spending, see Yomiuri shimbun seijibu, ed., *Dokyumento gyōsei kaikaku* [Administrative reform: a documentary account] (Tokyo: Chōbunsha, 1981), pp. 45–177; and James Elliott, "The 1981 Administrative Reform in Japan," *Asian Survey* 23, no. 6 (June 1983): 765–779.

tions" by not only the appropriate PARC divisions but also party elders and the Executive Board, whose functions include watching over cabinet ministers.[9]

For illustration let us take education policy, one of the policy areas in which the party has long held a powerful and even controlling voice. Matsunaga Tō, then a 70-year-old veteran LDP dietman who had served as the Speaker of the House of Representatives, assumed the Education portfolio in 1957, at the beginning of the so-called teacher's efficiency evaluation (*kinmu hyōtei*) controversy. During his tenure he was nicknamed *dōtoku kyōiku daijin* (minister of morals education) because of his commitment to the teaching of morals (a controversial posture widely opposed by "intellectual" and media communities, including the JTU); but on the issue of *kinmu hyōtei,* vehemently condemned by the JTU as an anti-JTU move, he was quite sympathetic to the teachers' union and even pledged that he would make final decisions regarding the controversial issue "in close consultation" with the JTU. At the same time, he was under the growing pressure of his party's Executive Board to "enforce *kinmu hyōtei* by all means." Notwithstanding his promise to the JTU, and prodded by the party, Matsunaga eventually did precisely what the party "directive" dictated—authorized the agency's implementational decisions for *kinmu hyōtei.*[10]

In 1959–60 (Kishi's second cabinet), the Education portfolio was held by Matsuda Takechiyo, an American-educated "nonconformist" dietman who defied his party's then policy of eschewing contacts with the JTU. Deviating from the party policy of shunning any act that might dignify and legitimate the anti-LDP union, the new minister not only met with JTU leaders to discuss matters of mutual concern including *kinmu hyōtei,* but even attended a JTU "study convention" (*kyōken taikai*) in defiance of specific warnings from the LDP Education Division. His actions were based on his conviction—one diametrically opposed to the LDP's dominant thinking—that outstanding policy issues of education could not be settled without a dialogue with the JTU, the nation's largest teachers' group. Although he made no substantive concessions to the JTU's demands, Matsuda's violation of the LDP's anti-JTU rule deeply disturbed the party and especially its hawkish dietmen. Shortly after a JTU *kyōken* that he attended, Matsuda was summoned to the LDP Executive Board, where he was chided for his antiparty behavior. He, however, refused to oblige his party and had additional

[9] Interview with Murakawa Ichirō, August 23, 1976.

[10] Yagi, *Mombu daijin,* pp. 147–148.

sessions with JTU leaders, insisting that his rapport with the JTU was beneficial to the nation's education.

In July 1960 the Kishi cabinet resigned after the riotous turmoil over the revision of the United States-Japan security treaty, and Matsuda was replaced by Araki Masuo, who led a three-year crusade against the JTU under Prime Minister Ikeda. In November Matsuda sought reelection in his crowded Ōsaka district (a district then entitled to three lower-house seats where a large majority of voters traditionally support non-LDP legislators). Interestingly, his party nominated no less than three LDP candidates to run in the districts—a departure from the norm—and Matsuda lost. Kobayashi Takeshi, then JTU chairman, who dealt with and "admired" Matsuda, claims that the former minister's defeat was his party's doing, a view shared by many informed observers of education.[11]

That the LDP dietman-minister cannot deviate from his party's policy or even the "institutionalized" code of party-government coordination was powerfully brought home even to Okuno Seisuke, that activist education minister (1972–74) held in confidence by the then prime minister Tanaka, over a plan to shift the existing six-day weekly school schedule to a five-day week. Okuno supported the plan and announced, obviously without careful consultation with the party's education dietmen (*Bunkyōzoku*), his desire to go ahead with it. In taking this action, he perhaps felt that because of the growing popularity of the idea in all major sectors of the education polity including the JTU, and his close ties with the powerful Tanaka, he could ride out potential party objections. Perhaps he misjudged his colleagues in the party *Bunkyōzoku.*

In any case, the disturbed *Bunkyōzoku* members, meeting in a hastily held joint session of the ED and ICES, told the assertive minister that not only was he out of step with the established procedure of party-government consultation but also his proposal was premature, lacking in careful studies and planning. Prime Minister Tanaka intervened on behalf of the party organs, not his education minister, by directing him to "exercise prudence in dealing with the controversial issue."[12]

"Party vigilance" over LDP ministers is not confined to the MOE. It is so with all agencies. When, in 1979, Moriyama Kinji, Ōhira

---

[11] The above account is based on ibid, p. 179; and Kuroha Ryōichi, *Sugaono sengo kyōiku* [Postwar education unmasked] (Tokyo: Gakuji shuppan, 1974), pp. 134–138. I am very much indebted to Yagi Jun and Kuroha Ryōichi, both distinguished journalists, who taught me so much about party-bureaucracy relations and education politics during my two-year stay in Tokyo, 1978–80.

[12] *Yomiuri,* May 8, evening, 1973; and *Mainichi,* May 9, 1973.

Masayoshi's transportation minister, went along with his agency officials by favoring a moratorium on actions against the Japan National Railway (JNR) workers then carrying out illegal work stoppages (he was obviously concerned with the adverse repercussions these punitive measures might have on the JNR, already deep in the red), he was quickly reminded by irate Executive Board members that "to mete out severe punishments to those involved in work stoppages is our party's basic policy."[13] Even such "apolitical" offices as the Ministry of Justice (MOJ) and the AMA are often subjected to the watchful eyes and intervention of the party—for example, the MOJ during the entire decade of the Lockheed-Tanaka controversy and the AMA at times of "administrative reform fever."

A contemporary minister, because of his double role as administrator and party dietman, is bound to find himself caught between conflicting party and agency priorities from time to time. How he behaves in such a predicament varies with a multitude of factors, including his standing in the party and his relations with the prime minister, the factional alignments; and the issues and agencies involved. Thus, his behavior defies easy generalizations. One powerful influence on his judgment, however, can be singled out—as several interviewed former ministers noted, for him the party and his factions are permanent and the ministerial portfolio is transitory. This is indeed a formidable restraint and militates against any serious departure from a policy position deemed essential to his party or faction. Although he formally relinquishes all party responsibilities when appointed to the cabinet, he still meets and interacts with his factional colleagues and members of the ministry's counterpart in the party PARC and does not want to be castigated for his "antiparty," "antifactional" behavior. Moreover, he knows that upon leaving the cabinet post he will return to (if a *zoku* member), or most likely join (if a non-*zoku* dietman), the appropriate *zoku* in the PARC.

Whether or not he is a member of the ministry's corresponding party *zoku*, he will try to accommodate the party's needs and wishes. If an inexperienced non-*zoku* dietman, the minister (unless he is a *jitsuryoku-sha* dietman who can successfully deal with, or ride out, party grumbles) will be particularly deferential to the judgments of the veteran *zoku* policy experts who to all intents and purposes are "party overseers" ("*omet-sukeyaku*" in the words of the former labor minister Hasegawa Takashi)[14] for his ministry. Commenting on the education minister's ar-

---
[13] *Asahi,* June 6, 1979.
[14] Interview with Hasegawa Takashi, September 17, 1981.

ticulative role for his party, a former newspaper reporter assigned to the MOE recalled:

> Many years ago I was in the office of the then education minister, interviewing him on a controversial item involving the MOE's curricular policy. His phone rang, and at the end of the line was a powerful dietman, obviously a *gosanke* member of the party *Bunkyōzoku,* who wanted to make sure that his position, widely endorsed by other conservative LDP dietmen, was included in the proposed MOE curricular guidelines. The minister, much younger than the caller and new to education policy, was most obliging. The final MOE guidelines adopted contained the change requested by that senior dietman.

If the minister is not cooperative with the party inasmuch as he must protect the agency's interests, the party *zoku* may simply bypass him and turn directly to the source of ministerial opposition—the bureau directors and division chiefs—who under party prodding may well turn out to be amenable to party positions. The officials' cooperative postures are governed by a variety of factors, one being career considerations. With eyes on the coveted top posts, as former bureaucrats have testified, they try to avoid alienating the *zoku* elders whose role in the agency's key personnel decisions is more than marginal.[15]

Career officials have been taken off their upward mobility ladders and even ousted from the agencies for refusing to cooperate with the party. This fate has befallen even such partisan agencies as the MOE, where socialization of career officials places a premium on deference to and cooperation with the party. Yasujima Hisashi, then director of the MOE's senior bureau (Elementary-Secondary Education or BESE), when "struck" by the LDP *Bunkyōzoku* just before his widely expected move up to the post of AVM, had reportedly offended the party dietmen by dragging his feet on a party-initiated policy of installing additional high schools in metropolitan regions. Imamura Taketoshi, also BESE director when he was demoted, had angered the party *Bunkyōzoku* over the JTU. Like his predecessor, Imamura had been widely slated to become AVM.[16] Cases such as these (both occurred in the mid-1970s) are bound to have major impacts upon the attitudes of career-conscious bureaucrats toward the party in power.

---

[15] *Imai Kazuo-shi danwa sokkiroku,* no. 14, p. 93, and no. 15, p. 166. Several interviewed MOF, MOE, and MHA officials (former and incumbent) concurred with Imai's generalizations.

[16] Kanryō kikō kenkyūkai, ed. *Mombushō zankoku monogatari* [The Ministry of Education inside out] (Tokyo: Ēru shuppansha, 1978), pp. 26–31.

A *zoku* minister is already well acquainted with the policy of orientations of his colleagues and can easily anticipate their probable reactions to his agency's policy recommendations. If a junior *zoku* member, he is most unlikely to go against his senior colleagues. If a *zoku gosanke* dietman, the minister would of course be in a stronger position vis-à-vis not only the ministry but also his *zoku* colleagues because of his senior status among the *zoku* members. Still, he will refrain from supporting ministry actions that run squarely counter to the consensus of his party *zoku*. For policy proposals advocated by his *zoku* colleagues, he will most likely take it upon himself to promote them and to mobilize intraagency and cabinet support for them. If the policy proposal happens to be one he himself championed prior to his cabinet appointment, "he will have no choice but to [go along with his *zoku* colleagues and] support and push the party policy," although it may be opposed by the agency's career officials.[17]

An illustration of these generalizations can be found in the MOE's changing policy toward private education and Education Minister Sakata's role in it. Notwithstanding the growing clamor for government action to alleviate the sorry plight of private education, which had become pronounced by the late 1960s, the MOE hesitated to go beyond its traditional policy of giving small subsidies and loans for improvement of facilities and for select research projects at private institutions. It argued that a comprehensive review of the entire school system was in order before any plan could be devised for large-scale aid to private institutions to help defray their operating costs.[18] This approach, foot-dragging as it then seemed, was understandable because of the agency's pro–public education bias and the anticipated difficulties of obtaining, under the increasing fiscal structures, the massive funding that the suggested aid program required.

The activist core of the party *Bunkyōzoku*, which included several graduates of Waseda University (a top private university and the leading producer of the so-called pure party politicians of the LDP), did not share the MOE's caution. Sympathetic and responding to the pleas from private institutions and their lobbying groups, the *Bunkyōzoku* advocated immediate action. Prompted by the campus disturbance of 1968–69, and in a manner characteristic of the *Bunkyōzoku*'s *Kantōgun* (Kantō Army) approach, the PARC Education Division, chaired by Yagi Tetsuo, took the lead and came up with a comprehensive plan known as the Yagi

---

[17] Interview with Yasujima Hisashi, February 29, 1980.
[18] Interviews with Nishioka Takeo, February 19, 1980, and Taki Yoshie, April 25, 1980.

Plan for Aid to Private Education.

The party plan, widely deemed revolutionary because of its dramatic deviation from the government's hands-off policy on private education, called for (1) serious governmental commitment to qualitative improvement and promotion of the fiscal stability of private institutions; (2) one half of all operating expenses (including salaries for teachers) of private institutions to be subsidized by the state's treasury; and (3) the above objectives to be achieved over a five-year period commencing in 1970.

In November 1968, at the peak of the nationwide campus crisis, Prime Minister Satō chose as his education minister Sakata Michita, a key *Bunkyōzoku* member whose interest and expertise in private education were widely recognized.[19] Bolstered by the initiative taken by his colleagues in the party *Bunkyōzoku,* Education Minister Sakata not only quelled the agency's opponents and skeptics but also succeeded in incorporating into the agency's proposed budget a massive allocation to meet the goals of the Yagi Plan. Aided by the sense of urgency and reformism that the campus disturbance generated, Sakata and his *Bunkyōzoku* cohort successfully extracted a governmental subsidy that amounted to 7 percent of the operating cost of private colleges for 1970–71, to increase gradually to approximately 32 percent by 1979.[20]

Commenting on the politics of the 1950s, Ardath Burks singled out as a major characteristic "a growing trend...tied to the new legal position of the Diet, wherein the bureaucracy has come to bypass even the cabinet in order to link its technical knowhow with the growing political prestige of the parties." To Burks this was a product of the tendency of the majority party, and particularly the factions within the party, "to overshadow both the bureaucracy and the cabinet."[21] In a case study of the Japanese foreign policy-making process of the 1950s—one involving the signing of the Japanese-Soviet peace agreement of 1956—Donald Hellmann concluded that in the Soviet negotiations the factions of the conservative party replaced the "ruling oligarchy of the military, the Court officials, the *Gaimushō* (the Foreign Ministry), and the party

---

[19] Interview with Kida Hiroshi, April 15, 1980.

[20] Nishioka Takeo, "Shigaku shinkō joseihō no mezasumono" [Aims of the law to promote and encourage private education], *Kikan kyōikuhō,* no. 17 (Fall 1975), pp. 114–118. See also Kuroha Ryōichi, "Gyōsei to setten ni miru shidai no sanjūnen" [Thirty years of private higher education as seen from the point of contact with the administration], *IDE,* no. 199 (May 1979), pp. 31–42.

[21] Ardath W. Burks, *The Government of Japan,* 2d ed. (New York: Thomas Y. Crowell, 1964), p. 148.

leaders" that had dominated foreign policy-making in the prewar years.[22]

This centrality of the factions in Japanese politics has not changed significantly to this date. Not only is the factions' pivotal role widely recognized in the party's presidential elections and the distribution of the party, government, and legislative posts but also the intraparty groupings are powerful in all facets of policy-making, both in the party and in the government. Equipped with the ultimate powers of decision making and conflict resolution over important, controversial matters that defy handling by other, lower-level actors, the chieftains of the factions undoubtedly constitute the locus of governmental and even political power in the contemporary Japanese political system. Although these other, lower-level actors are also factionally chosen party and governmental individuals, and minor, smaller factions cannot be ruled out in the faction-ridden politics of contemporary Japan, the lion's share of power is clearly held by powerful "mainstream" factions.

Most LDP dietmen are affiliated with intraparty factions, which provide them with vital services including electoral and financial support[23] and opportunities for upward mobility (inasmuch as party, Diet, and government appointments are largely determined by factional considerations).[24] In return, the members must perform functions pivotal to their factions' strength and prosperity, which include contributions to the groups' coffers and recruitment of the "able members" as factional colleagues. Not surprisingly, all dietmen take their factional obligations seriously. For the factional minister this means that while in office he must not only protect but also promote his faction's interests. This is indeed a foremost duty he is expected to fulfill, a powerful impetus to his intraagency activism.

Notwithstanding their claims to political and factional neutrality, the contemporary ministries are involved with and partial toward LDP factions and influentials. This partiality has stemmed from a multitude of factors. It is a function of former bureaucrats' presence in the party. A faction with a large contingent of graduates of a particular ministry is bound to be close to that ministry because of this contingent's sense of

---

[22] Hellmann, *Japanese Foreign Policy and Domestic Politics*, p. 157.

[23] One study showed that only 20 percent of LDP dietmen's campaign expenses were covered by funds provided by the party itself, meaning that their factional contributions and private funds made up the rest. Haruhiro Fukui, *Party in Power: The Japanese Liberal-Democrats and Policy-making* (Berkeley and Los Angeles: University of California Press, 1970), p. 130.

[24] For discussion of the benefits that LDP dietmen draw from their factional affiliations, see *Jimintō: hoshu kenryoku no kōzō,* pp. 287–325.

attachment to the agency and the importance of *senpai-kōhai* (senior-junior) and *oyabun-kobun* (leader-follower) relationships. Likewise, a faction led by a bureaucrat-turned-dietman has intimate ties with his parental agency. Also important in faction-ministry relations is a growing bureaucratic dependence on party factions for political and legislative support in this age of increasing budgetary constraints. It is not uncommon for bureaus and ministries to turn to powerful factions and their leaders for support in their efforts to seek legislative authorization and appropriation for their controversial or costly programs. This is true with all ministries, including the powerful MOF and MITI. Then there is an intense drive by all factions to establish and maintain their footholds or "colonies" within the bureaucracy, and especially the agencies charged with distributive, regulative, and extractive tasks, such as Finance, Construction, Transportation, and MITI. Mentor-protégé relationships are established with promising and ranking officials of the agencies. In some ministries, for example, the MOF, the faction's co-optation, *"jinmyaku-*building," not only is aimed at division chiefs but even starts with lower officials such as "investigators" (*shusa*) and deputy division chiefs (*kachō hosa*) in the MOF's pivotal Budget Bureau. Factional ministers and *zoku* members see to it that their protégés remain on the elite tracks of promotion and are placed in strategic positions where they can render desired services to the factions. When they retire from governmental service, they are encouraged to seek Diet seats with the backing of the sponsoring factions, and upon election they become bona fide members of the factions' Diet phalanxes. Needless to say, these former officials become key conduits between their parental agencies and the factions.[25]

As elite bureaucrats move up their promotional ladders, their contacts with the LDP and the Diet not only become frequent but also widen to include both formal organs (e.g., PARC divisions and Diet standing committees) and "informal" groupings such as factions and cross-factional "policy-study groups" within the LDP.[26] In the course of these interactions with the party, the bureaucrats sooner or later make, either consciously or unconsciously, commitments to and ties with powerful factions and their elder members. Aspiring bureaucrats in the

---

[25] "Elīto kanryō ga 'tanakaha' ni naru 'henbō' no purosesu" [The process by which elite bureaucrats are "transformed" into members of the Tanaka faction], *Shūkan shinchō* 27, no. 15 (April 14, 1982): 46.

[26] For descriptions of these intraparty groupings by a *Mainichi* political reporter, see Inoue, *Habatsu to seisaku shudan*.

agencies heavily "colonized" by the factions are quickly educated in the role of the factions in agency affairs—not only in substantive policy but also in personnel matters. They behave accordingly. Although shunning overt attempts to curry favor with factions, career officials discreetly seek special relationships with prominent members of a powerful faction and perform a wide range of activities for them. As one recent Japanese study drawing on interviews with bureaucrats concluded, "The central bureaucrats, even at the division chief level, begin to cultivate friendly ties with LDP factions."[27] The former MAFF elite bureaucrat Tekeuchi Naokazu offers his assessment of the situation:

> At the high levels of the contemporary bureaucracy we invariably find factions, each centering on a political boss. They naturally come into being, even though there is no faction to be countered. It is through the faction that the bureaucrat seeks peace and security for himself. When he reaches the division chief level, he picks out a political boss and joins his faction "in anticipation of future gains." Before joining he must carefully determine which faction is most advantageous and offers most security to him. In short, at this point (of his career) he is taking one of his greatest risks as an elite bureaucrat. When he moves up to the bureau director class, he gets frantic; he must squash his rivals before he is thinned out. To achieve this, he must borrow the power of his political boss.[28]

Speaking of how this system of factional-bureaucratic linkage worked with the all-powerful Kōno faction in the agency he served in, Takeuchi notes:

> The elite bureaucrats who pledged their allegiance to Mr. Kōno and Mr. Yasuda [Sen'ichirō, who was Kōno's handpicked director of the Minister's Secretariat] were allowed to attend the periodical meetings of the *Shunjūkai* [the Kōno faction's organization] and to plight themselves to the politicians. Even the freshmen division chiefs, when spotted and favored, would rush to the factional gatherings, wagging their tails.[29]

Bureaucratic fraternization with the party factions is not confined to the ministries reputed to be partisanized agencies, such as the MAFF, the MOC, and the MOT. What the former MOF bureau director Imai Kazuo referred to as "the bureaucrats' tail-wagging to politicians" has afflicted the foremost economic agency as well,[30] for as one interviewed

---

27 Muramatsu, *Sengo Nihon,* p. 58.
28 Takeuchi, *Konna kanryō,* p. 38.
29 Ibid., p. 14.
30 *Imai Kazuo-shi danwa sokkiroku,* no. 14, p. 93.

MOF division chief put it, "To be promoted beyond the division chief level, a career official needs to be backed by a powerful dietman of a faction influential in his agency." Most ministries, except for a few "apolitical" ministries (e.g., the EPA, the MOJ, and the AMA), have been seriously affected by factional politics and have developed varying degrees of affinity with the factions.

For the first half of the 1950s the MFA was dominated by the protégés of the then prime minister, Yoshida Shigeru, who, a distinguished graduate of the prewar Foreign Office, held firm control over government foreign policy-making and the affairs of the Foreign Affairs Ministry, including personnel decisions. In all key ministries, and especially the MFA, he unreservedly exercised the power of appointment and removal by demoting or even firing uncooperative officials and by "favoring those close to him" (*sokkin jinji*). Widely practiced, Yoshida's "ruthless beheading" quickly earned the sobriquet *Y-kō pāji* (Column Y purge); Y, the initial of Yoshida's name, was derived from SCAP's ranking of purged Japanese officials—"Group A" to include top war criminals, "Group B," army and navy officers, and so forth.[31] In the first half of the 1960s, during the premiership of Ikeda Hayato (a product of the MOF bureaucracy), the MOF was considered to be in the sphere of influence of the prime minister and his faction.[32] The MAFF of the 1950s and 1960s, as previously noted, had many ranking officials closely linked with Kōno Ichirō and his faction.[33] In the 1970s the agency developed intimate ties with the right-wing activist group *Seirankai,* then led by Nakagawa Ichirō, which supplied a string of MAFF ministers and PVMs.[34] The highly lucrative MOC post has in recent years been occupied by members of the mainstream factions, and especially the prime minister's faction. For example, during the Satō government (1964–72) the portfolio was monopolized by veteran members of the Satō faction, who included Hashimoto Tomisaburō, Nishimura Eiichi, and Hori Shigeru. The only "outsider" to head the agency during this period was Setoyama Mitsuo. He, however, was a dietman close to Kishi Nobusuke, Satō's elder brother. The three occupants of the MOC post during the Tanaka government (1972–174)—Kimura Takeo, Kanemaru Shin, and Kameoka Takao—were all Tanaka loyalists.[35] In the MPT, also widely

---

[31] Yomiuri shimbun seijibu, *Sōri daijin,* pp. 66–67.

[32] For discussion of several agencies including the MAFF, MITI, the MOF, the MOC, and the MOT and of their relations with the LDP factions, see Tokyo shimbun-sha, ed., *Kanchō monogatari* [Tales of government offices] (Tokyo: Chōbunsha, 1962), pp. 25–93.

[33] Takeuchi, *Konna kanryō,* pp. 12–16 and 52–58.

[34] Tahara, *Nihon no kanryō,* pp. 234–236.

[35] Ibid., p. 370; and Kanryō kikō kenkyūkai, *Kensetsushō,* p. 90.

considered a Tanaka stronghold,[36] at least one or two, at times all of the three, top political and career posts (minister, PVM, and AVM) between 1957 (when Tanaka held his first cabinet post in the MPT) and 1979 were consistently held by Tanaka's confidants.[37]

These powerful party factions are intimately involved in the personnel and policy decision making of the agencies they have developed close ties with. This function of factional representation in agency affairs is performed by various members of the faction. Senior members who hold key government and party positions (e.g., the PARC chairman, who plays a powerful role in budgetary decisions for the agency) are of course effective input-makers. Factional members of the appropriate *zoku* and PARC divisions are also key actors;[38] so are the members of the faction who are former ranking officials of the agency. Naturally, key incumbent officials of the agency allied with and often handpicked by the faction are major conduits for factional influence in the agency.[39] The ministers and, to a lesser degree, the PVMs from the ranks of the faction are also powerful agents of factional interest representation.

Some informed observers go as far as to characterize the minister's intraagency role solely in terms of activities beneficial to him and his faction. In the words of a former MAFF official, "The minister's only concern during his tenure is to make full use of his official powers to further his faction's interests as well as his own."[40] Naturally, a minister holds a special position in the agency "colonized" by his faction and commands a deference and power often denied to the ministers from other factions.

Inasmuch as the ministries are heterogeneous entities, divided by not only formal functions (bureaus and divisions) but also informal factors (e.g., factional allegiances, educations, hometowns, types of civil service examinations passed, and years the officials joined the ministries), they defy effective and long-term "colonization" by single factions, however powerful they may be.[41] Hence, a realistic statement about faction-

---

[36] Tahara, *Nihon no kanryō,* pp. 450–452. Some observers go as far as to characterize the MPT as the "Kakuei kingdom." See Manabe, Chiba, and Nakayama, "Abaku Kakuei ōkoku," pp. 209–234.

[37] Manabe, Chiba, and Nakayama, "Abaku Kakuei ōkoku," p. 222.

[38] For discussion of the Tanaka faction's highly "productive" activities, see Sasaki Takeshi, "'Jimoto minshu shugi' o koete" [Beyond "grass-roots democracy"], *Sekai,* no. 458 (January 1984), pp. 23–34.

[39] "Elito kanryō ga 'Tanakaha' ni naru 'henbō' no purosesu," pp. 42–46.

[40] Takeuchi, *Konna kanryō,* p. 42. For discussion by a former MHA official of the articulative role performed by Tanaka-faction ministers and officials for the so-called Mejiro Palace, see Katō, "Toshi no fukushū."

[41] For discussion by a former MOF official of bureaucratic fragmentation and sectionalism, see Imai, *Kanryō,* pp. 140–143.

ministry relations has to highlight the competitive involvement of powerful factions in ministries, although one of them can assert dominant status, as did the Satō faction in the MOT and the SDA in the 1960s.[42]

Also, the notion of faction-bureau linkage, rather than that stressing the centrality of faction-ministry relations, might be argued to capture better the contemporary reality of factional relations with some agencies. In view of the traditional interbureau autonomy found in many ministries and the marked tendency of LDP dietmen policy specialization, this notion is not farfetched at all; much of the factional maneuvering found in MITI, the MOT, and the MOF can be explained by it.

In an agency fragmented into "factional networks of personalities" (*habatsu jinmyaku*), therefore, the minister faces an additional restraint upon his powers. As agency decision-maker and in his relations with the career officials, he must take into account other factions, and especially those that have powerful claims on the agency through their *jinmyaku*. For example, in contemplating actions against a high-ranking official whom he considers persona non grata, the minister must carefully calculate the probable reactions of the official's factional mentors in the party. The MAFF provides a case in point. In the 1950s and 1960s, during which Kōno Ichirō "reigned" over the agency, its key officials, loyal to and supported by him, could effectively deter a non-Kōno faction minister from taking actions—both policy and personnel—considered detrimental to their "agency interests."[43] Similarly, in the 1970s the *Seirankai,* the foremost LDP guardian of the MAFF, could easily frustrate the attempts of a non-*Seirankai* minister to institute policy or personnel changes that the agency deemed undesirable.[44]

The minister is appointed by and accountable to the prime minister. He is also a member of the cabinet headed by the prime minister. As such he is expected to articulate in his agency the policies of the prime minister and his cabinet. Although pluralistic politics and LDP factionalism, among other factors, limit the formal powers of the prime

---

[42] Factional competition is particularly serious in the MOF, MITI, and the MAFF where many high-level officials can be grouped into several factional *jinmyaku*. This is a contrast to the MOC, which is controlled by the Tanaka *jinmyaku*. A 1982 press source says: "When an MOC official, whether AVM or director of the Minister's Secretariat, is told by Takeshita Noboru or other top [Tanaka faction] elders, 'Hey you, you should run for a Diet seat,' he obliges. But this is not the case with such agencies as the MOF, MITI, and the MAFF where different factions have formed their own *jinmyaku*." See "Elīto kanryō 'Tanakaha' ninaru 'henbo' no purosesu," p. 46.

[43] *Asahi,* May 24, 1979.

[44] Kanryō kikō kenkyūkai, *Nōrinshō,* p. 109.

minister and his cabinet, their policy-making role is nevertheless formidable. Especially pronounced is their role in important, controversial matters and especially those defying policy coordination at lower levels of government and party hierarchies. It is quite typical for government leaders to make, usually in concert with top party executives, final authoritative decisions on these matters, with bureaucrats playing secondary roles.[45] In this situation of "top-down" policy making the minister's support and effective intraagency articulation are essential to the success of the policy decision involved. Indeed, one of the foremost ministerial roles as perceived by interviewed former ministers is to see that top-down policies are developed, elaborated and carried out by agency officials.

The prime minister's major role in key foreign policy decisions has already been mentioned in the preceding chapter. In recent years this role has been further bolstered by developments of Japan's economic relations with other nations and especially the United States. They include: (1) the inability or reluctance of "vertical" (*tatewari*) subgovernments (LDP, bureaucratic, and interest group actors) to deal with weighty issues of Japanese-U.S. textile, steel, automobile, agricultural products (beef and citrus), telecommunication, and so forth; and (2) the resultant politicization of these issues.[46]

For illustration, let us look at the politics involved in one particular case, the issue of Japanese-American textile trade which, along with the Okinawa and China issues, occupied much of the Satō government's attention in its waning years.

In his bid for the presidency, Richard Nixon had promised to support American textile manufacturers, who felt threatened by imported Japanese goods. Once in office, he proceeded to make good on his pledge by seeking controls on imports of Japanese products, just as the two powers were nearing the end of their negotiations on the reversion of

---

[45] For an interesting account by a former MHA AVM of one such case involving the MOF and the MHA, see Okuno Seisuke, "Kitaishitai fuken seido no kaikaku to honenoaru kankai" [The desired reform of the urban prefectural and rural prefectural system, and backboned officialdom], in Jichishō, ed., *Jichishō jūnen no ayumi* [A ten-year history of the Ministry of Home Affairs] (Tokyo: Jichishō, 1971), pp. 18–20.

[46] For discussion of these issues, see I. M. Destler and Hideo Satō, eds., *Coping with U.S.-Japanese Economic Conflicts* (Lexington, Mass.: D. C. Heath and Co., 1982). For discussion by former high-ranking economic officials of the politicization of international economic issues and its implications, see Ōkita, *Nihon kanryō jijō*, pp. 180–194. My thinking about top-down decision making on international economic issues benefited greatly from interviews with economic officials including LDP Dietman Omi Kōji, formerly a MITI official, and Sakata Hatsumi of MITI.

Okinawa to Japan.

After briefly working through administrative channels which he found unproductive, Nixon in late 1968 raised the textile issue with the visiting prime minister, Satō Eisaku. Pleased with Nixon's consent to Okinawa reversion without nuclear weapons on the U.S. base there, Satō obviously promised positive actions on the textile issue. In this forward-looking posture he was supported by the minister (Aichi Kiichi) and officials of the MFA who, like Satō, felt that a textile concession was an unavoidable price for achieving the nation's historic goal of regaining the lost territory. The Japanese textile industry and its governmental ally MITI, however, refused to go along. This position was backed by Ōhira Masayoshi, then MITI minister and a senior member of the Maeo faction (one of Satō's rival groups).

Using a cabinet reshuffle, Satō replaced Ōhira with Miyazawa Kiichi, a rising star of the party known for his pro-American views and advocacy of "free trade." Asked by Satō to bring about a speedy settlement of the issue, the new minister proceeded to tackle it along lines close to the American position. Though unhappy about hurting the very industry they had helped build up, MITI's Textile Bureau dutifully performed supportive, elaborative, and information-providing tasks for the minister. Because of MITI's supportive performance, Miayazawa saw "no need to set up an independent LDP staff" or his own "personal braintrust."[47] As a ranking MITI official put it, "The textile issue is far from being an economic issue. Once politics has decided to go for an agreement, we cannot rebel against it."[48]

Seeing that Miyazawa was making no significant headway in dealing with the recalcitrant industry, the prime minister let him go in July 1971 and chose as his successor Tanaka Kakuei, Satō's key lieutenant, eager to impress "big business" with his problem-solving and leadership abilities. Satō had apparently concluded that Washington's growing impatience with Tokyo threatened the success of what he saw as his administration's major diplomatic achievement, Okinawa reversion. Moreover, both government and *zaikai* leaders were "now preoccupied with larger economic concerns, and saw acceptance of an unpleasant textile agreement as necessary to help salvage the larger U.S.-Japan relationship."[49]

---

[47] Ōtake Hideo, *Gendai Nihon no seiji kenryoku keizai kenryoku* [Political power and economic power in contemporary Japan] (Tokyo: San'ichi shobō, 1980), p. 85.

[48] *Yomiuri*, October 16, 1971, as quoted in Ōtake, *Gendai Nihon*, p. 156.

[49] I. M. Destler et al., *Managing an Alliance: The Politics of U.S.-Japanese Relations* (Washington, D.C. Brookings Institution, 1976), p. 44.

Under the new minister's strict order of secrecy, which limited MITI-industry contacts, top Textile Bureau officials (director and deputy director) worked out the specifics of the Japanese position; even division chiefs responsible for textile affairs were excluded from the drafting process. Tanaka then "forced" the terms of a U.S.-Japanese textile memorandum on the industry, thus ending the three-year-old controversy.[50] Last-minute attempts by LDP "textile dietmen" (*sen'izoku*) to keep Tanaka from yielding too much to the American demands did not go very far.[51]

The government handling of the textile industry was not based only on its authority and legitimacy; it also had to dole out "carrots" in the form of monetary compensations. The pattern involved in the authorization of compensatory measures was also a top-down process in which ministers and party officials assumed the dominant role.

When industry leaders sought compensatory grants, loans, and tax exemptions in return for their voluntary control of exports to the United States, the MOF Budget Bureau promptly turned them down while suggesting possible loans for the factories severely hit by the voluntary restraints. In this position the budget office was supported, at least initially, by its minister Fukuda Takeo, a key member of the Satō government. Other party influentials, however, were more sympathetic to the plight of the industry. Tanaka Kakuei, for example, then secretary general, promised his party's support. When industry leaders later formally requested government aid totaling well over 120 billion yen, the LDP PARC committees on commerce and textiles expressed a willingness to endorse up to 80 billion. This figure was quickly seconded by MITI minister Miyazawa. Against this backdrop the party committees and MITI officials agreed on a sum of 77 billion for the aggrieved industry. Of this, however, the MOF approved only 54 billion, which MITI promptly urged the budget officials to reconsider. The MOF consented but stated that the compromise figure would have to stay under 60 billion.[52]

At this point, however, decision making regarding aid was shifted from the economic bureaucrats to a small circle of party and government leaders: Finance Minister Fukuda, MITI Minister Miyazawa, Foreign Minister Aichi, Chief Cabinet Secretary Hori Shigeru, and Chairman of

---

[50] Ōtake, *Gendai Nihon*, pp. 124–125.

[51] For discussion of the textile industry's weak intraparty clout, see Asahi shimbunsha, *Jimintō*, pp. 170–173. According to Fukuda Hajime, leader of the LDP textile *zoku*, the industry had neglected support-building (e.g., giving political funds) within the party. Ibid., p. 172.

[52] Ōtake, *Gendai Nihon*, p. 127.

the LDP Committee on Textile Problems Fukuda Hajime. This group of government and party executives made the final decision approximating the PARC committee's original proposal. It was later approved by the cabinet.[53]

As Japan and the United States moved closer to a textile agreement, the Tokyo government felt compelled to authorize additional compensations to appease the industry. Decision making involved in this stage was also dominated by key party elders in the government—Prime Minister Satō, MITI Minister Tanaka, and Finance Minister Fukuda, with MITI officials performing a supportive, elaborative role. Of special note is the central role assumed by MITI Minister Tanaka in this process and in persuading the textile industry and its LDP allies. Significantly, MOF officials were virtually excluded from the budgetary decision making. Also important is the behavior of two MOF ministers involved: Fukuda and later Mizuta Mikio. On the whole, they were supportive of the "political decisions" of the Satō government and rendered valuable services in calming their agency officials who had misgivings about the government's "generosity" toward the textile industry.[54]

The foregoing discussions have focused on the contemporary minister's articulative role for his party, cabinet, and prime minister. He is also a key interest articulator for extraparty constituencies—corporate and interest groups—that in their lobbying strategies concentrate more on LDP organs and legislators (especially *zoku* members and cabinet ministers) than on career bureaucrats. These constituencies include not only such powerful clientele groups as *Nōkyō* and *zaikai* organizations, which enjoy exalted status in the party because of their electoral and financial support, but also less powerful organized interests of all types, and especially those of conservative persuasions that can count on sympathetic hearings in the party.[55]

This "political" pattern of contemporary interest group operations differs from the widely held "bureaucratic dominance" thesis, which views the bureaucracy as the primary decision-maker and thus the target of all lobbying efforts by organized interests. Groups' reliance on the political sector, however, is not surprising in view of the growing policy role of the party—its dietmen and ministers—and the finely tuned sense

---

[53] Ibid., 126–127.

[54] Ibid., pp. 128–146.

[55] This observation, repeated by various individuals interviewed in Japan, fully concurs with a conclusion reached by a team of Japanese political scientists (including Muramatsu Michio of Kyoto University) from their surveys of interest group representatives. Interview with Muramatsu, February 26, 1980.

that groups have of the shifting balance of power between the party and the bureaucracy in contemporary Japanese policy-making.

According to interviewed representatives of interest groups,[56] all groups make a careful distinction between matters that can be dealt with "administratively" (*jimutekini* or *jimukyoku ni yotte*), on the one hand, and important and controversial matters that require "high-level governmental and party judgment" (*seifu yotō no kōdoteki seiji handan*) and legislative approval, on the other. The former, normally minor and "secondary" ("operational") policy matters, are addressed to the middle-level officials of the appropriate ministries, where they can be handled without consultation with higher agency and party authorities. Controversial and important matters that require large-scale governmental spending and Diet assent are taken to not only the appropriate offices of the agencies but also the party organs and ministers in charge. Naturally, greater effort is directed to the political sector. The National Association of High-School Principals (*Zenkoku kōtōgakkōchō kyōkai*), for example, takes requests and petitions concerning administrative policy to the chiefs of the relevant MOE divisions, but important matters are "directed by either the national council or regional associations to LDP organs, dietmen, and the education minister."[57]

Take another educational interest group, of conservative (pro-LDP) persuasion, the National Association of Public School Superintendents of Instruction (*Zenkoku kōritsu gakkō kyōtōkai,* or NAPSSI); this group also adheres to the "political" pattern of interest group operations—one increasingly followed by groups not only in the education-policy system, in which the primacy of LDP policymakers has long been undisputed, but also in areas where the bureaucrats have traditionally played an assertive role. A nationally organized group of deputy principals in charge of school instruction, the NAPSSI vigorously and successfully fought for a 1974 Diet law granting them legal status as *kyōtō* (superintendents of instruction)—a measure vehemently condemned by the JTU as being aimed at establishing an elaborate system of hierarchy at every school,

---

[56] Interviewed interest group officials include those representing local government interests, the national universities' association, organizations of private institutions, federations of elementary and high-school associations, transportation and road organizations, dental and medical associations, and fisheries and agricultural organizations.

[57] Interviews with Mori Takeo and Kobayashi Masanao, respectively president and staff director for the National Association of High-School Principals, July 25, 1976. I am deeply grateful to Kobayashi, the educator-turned-lobbyist for the association, for enlightening me on the dynamics of interest groups. The three interviews with him took no less than eight hours.

thus weakening the union's solidarity. The NAPSSI leadership decided early in its legislative campaign that the proposed legislation, in view of its controversial nature and the political and legislative endorsement it required for successful implementation, was a measure well outside the realm of minor, administrative matters under the bureaucracy's jurisdiction. The NAPSSI's legislative strategy, therefore, centered largely on persuading and mobilizing the key actors in the LDP, including the education minister. In the words of a prominent Japanese scholar of education politics:

> Starting with Education Minister Araki [Masuo] [1960–63], NAPSSI representatives have met with every education minister to solicit support of proposed legislation. Since 1968 the NAPSSI has invited education-related dietmen (*Bunkyōzoku*) to its yearly plethora of rallies, conventions, and workshops. Whenever a bill is introduced in the Diet, NAPSSI members launch an intense campaign of writing letters to their dietmen, asking them to support the proposed measure. At every election time they send similar messages to their dietmen.[58]

In responding to urgings and pressures from outside groups, the minister of course "pays special attention to" (*daijinisuru*) those emanating from groups closely allied with or deemed important to his faction because all factions are dependent upon organized interests for political and financial support and cannot afford to alienate their support groups. A minister's deaf ear to a clientele group's plea will not only cool its support for him but also prompt a serious chiding by his faction's leaders.

Interest group politics, however, do not always run along factional lines. Rather, on most issues of public policy, interest group activities to influence LDP policy-making tend to be more cross-factional than factional. The reason is that in any given policy area the key party dietmen and government leaders represent a number of factions of the party.

This was typified in the LDP government's education policy subsystem during Ōhira's premiership. The Education portfolio was held by Tanigaki Sen'ichi, a senior member of the prime minister's faction, but he was surrounded by other members of the education subsystem coming from antimainstream, anti-Ōhira factions—the Fukuda, Miki, and Nakasone factions.[59] The MOE PVM post was occupied by Mitsuzuka

---

[58] Kumagai Kazunori, "Kyōiku seisaku no rippō katei ni kansuru shakaigakuteki kenkyū" [Legislative process involving education policy: a sociological analysis], *Bungaku ronshū* [Faculty of Literature Occasional Papers] of Sōka University, vol. 3, no. 1 (PDU), p. 122.

[59] *Asahi*, November 26, 1979.

Hiroshi, a key *Bunkyōzoku* member of the Fukuda faction; the PARC Education Division was chaired by another Fukuda faction loyalist and *Bunkyōzoku* member, Mori Yoshirō; the lower-house Education Standing Committee was headed by Tanikawa Kazuo, a member of the Miki faction and a *Bunkyōzoku* activist. The PARC ICES was chaired by Okuno Seisuke, who, though close to Tanaka Kakuei, was an independent not affiliated with a faction.

This pattern of factional representation is quite the norm in all other policy areas. Moreover, the appropriate *zoku* in the party is equally multifactional in its makeup and is thus not controlled by any particular faction. A major policy decision, therefore, must rest on a consensus among these key "official" actors as well as other non-office-holding members of the multifactional policy subsystem.

Because of the cross-factional basis of the policy subsystem, it is imperative for interest groups to direct their lobbying to all major factions represented in the subsystem. Commenting on business-faction linkage in contemporary Japanese politics, Hatakeyama Takeshi, a veteran *Asahi* political reporter, notes that "business enterprises have now come to uniformly distribute their monies to all factions rather than single out specific factions [for special favors]."[60]

Several factors account for this development. One is of course the heterogeneous makeup of policy subsystems, as pointed out above. Another reason is the changing nature of enterprises' internal power structures. Nowadays there are fewer firms run by authoritarian, "one-man (*wanman-teki*) entrepreneurs who have the power of dispensing money to politicians and factions" of their liking. The contemporary norm is for "salarymen-managers," who lack this kind of freedom, to manage the firms in a less authoritarian manner. Moreover, corporate leadership cannot escape the watchful eyes of such intracompany organizations as labor unions, which may well be affiliated with national organizations markedly anti-LDP in their orientations. Furthermore, from a company's perspective, an "intimate relationship" with a particular faction may boomerang; it may alienate and anger the other factions not favored with enterprise supports.[61]

Admittedly, these considerations are important factors militating against special ties between factions and extraparty interests. They are, however, by no means the only factors governing interest groups' poltical

---

[60] Hatakeyama Takeshi, *Habatsu no uchimaku* [Factions inside out] (Tokyo: Tachikaze shobō, 1976), p. 112.

[61] Ibid.

lobbying. In no policy area is the decision-making power equally shared by all factions. Some are more powerful than others, as are their leaders. This is well reflected in party and government policy-making, notwithstanding Japan's traditional penchant for decision making by consensus and emphasis upon "fair share." Mainstream factions, holding the largest shares of key party and government posts, are bound to play larger roles in policy-making. Thus, it is not surprising at all that interest groups gravitate toward the foremost of all mainstream factions—the one led by the prime minister, who often is the most powerful of the LDP faction leaders. For this reason, among others, mainstream factions, and especially the prime minister's faction, fare better in fund-raising.[62] An interest group may also be attracted to a particular faction because it is the home of key *zoku* dietmen in the group's area of interest. This explains, at least in part, close ties between some education-related groups and the Miki and Nakasone factions, which have large shares of *Bunkyōzoku* members. Likewise, the Tanaka faction, which contains a large contingent of "public works" *zoku* dietmen, is popular among "public works" interest groups.[63] Moreover, the career backgrounds and family ties of faction leaders also play important roles in bringing factions and special interests together. For example, Miki Takeo has been backed by several firms linked with his wife's family. It was only natural that the Kishi faction, because of his affiliation with the prewar Industry-Commerce Ministry, had a special relationship with the heavy industry sector of big business.[64] Similarly, the Ikeda faction had intimate ties with the financial and security institutions, the constituencies that he had served as a career official. The Satō faction's close link with the transportation industry stemmed from his long career in the MOT. The Kōno faction's special ties with farm groups and construction firms was attributable to his cabinet posts involving the MAFF and the MOC.

Similar patterns of clientele relationships can be found between present-day factions and economic interests: the Tanaka faction and construction; the Fukuda faction and petroleum interests; the Ōhira faction and financial, security, and other clientele interests under MOF jurisdiction; the Nakasone faction and fishery interests; and the Miki fac-

---

[62] Yomiuri shimbun seijibu, *Sōri daijin*, pp. 142–145. See also Frank Langdon, "Political Contributions of Big Business in Japan," *Asian Survey* 3:10 (October 1963), 469.

[63] Takabatake Michitoshi, "Etsuzankai no tsuyoki to yowaki" [The bullishness and timidity of the Etsuzankai], *Ushio*, no. 296 (December 1983), p. 84. See also Kanryō kikō kenkyūkai, *Kensetsushō*, pp. 90–96; and Nihon keizai shimbunsha, *Jimintō seichōkai*, pp. 120–124.

[64] Tokyo shimbunsha, *Kanchō monogatari*, pp. 34–35.

tion and *Nihon yakin* (Japan Metallurgy) and *Shōwa denkō* (Shōwa Electric and Industrial) companies, closely tied with the family of Miki's wife. The close relationships the factions have with their clientele groups are well evidenced by the generous financial support they receive from business groups.[65]

Interest groups' factional preferences are governed by other factors. One such is the ideological and policy orientation of a faction and its leaders. True, LDP factions are not distinguished by ideological and policy differences, unlike the factions in the Japan Socialist party, which run along ideological lines. On many policy issues, domestic or foreign policy, the LDP factions are internally divided. For example, on normalizing Sino-Japanese relations in the 1960s and 1970s, the intraparty division was cross-factional, and both opponents and supporters of Peking's terms for normalization were found in all factions. At the same time, the pro-Peking position enjoyed a larger backing in the Kōno, Matsumura, Ōno, Miki, and Fujiyama factions than in the others. In the 1970s Miki and Nakasone were the first major faction leaders—followed by Ōhira and Maeo Shigesaburō—to challenge the wisdom of the Satō government's pro-Taipei orientation.[66] The "Nakagawa group," active in the 1970s and headed by the late Nakagawa Ichirō, was staunchly anti-Communist on foreign- and domestic-policy issues; the Nakasone faction is markedly pro-American on the controversial issue of Japan's defense buildup.

What the preceding discussions suggest is the variation found among the intraparty groupings and their leaders in their policy preferences and inclinations. The interfactional differences are recognized by outside interests, which formulate their lobbying strategies accordingly. Although pursuing an "omnidirectional" policy (i.e., eschewing the overt ties with a faction or factions that would alienate the others), interest groups focus their efforts on the powerful and potentially sympathetic factions and their leaders who are most likely to "deliver the goods." Hence, covert deals and arrangements are often made, and close relations established, with powerful factions and politicians. Naturally, the factional ministers in the appropriate agencies become key vehicles for articulating and legislating policies promoted by their clientele groups. It

---

[65] Hatakeyama, *Habatsu,* p. 112.

[66] Yung Park, "The Roots of Sino-Japanese Detente" and "The Tanaka Government and the Mechanics of the China Decision," in *China and Japan: A Search for Balance Since World War I,* ed. Alvin Coox and Hilary Conroy (Santa Barbara: ABC-Clio, 1978), pp. 354–384 and 387–397.

is in this context of faction-group linkage that the *Asahi shimbun* made the following commentary on health-welfare policy-making: "The extent of change in the tone of health-welfare administration brought about by past ministers of health-welfare has depended largely on the level of intimacy of the relationships between their factions and the JMA."[67]

In view of the minister's articulative role for organized interests, and especially those closely allied with his faction, it is not surprising that in recent years the major bribery scandals of regulative-distributive agencies (e.g., Post-Telecommunications, Self-Defense, and Transportation) have involved primarily the agencies' political appointees (ministers and PVMs) and their factions.[68] These incidents suggest the manner in which the agencies process decisions "dictated" by powerful external interests—the minister assumes the initiating role (often acting under instructions from his faction or a key faction member) with little substantive input from the career bureaucrats, who tend to go along with the minister's directive, either willingly or reluctantly, and at best perform an elaborative role.

The MOT provides a telling illustration of the foregoing generalizations. Under the agency's "jurisdiction" are a multitude of interest groups and corporate entities. A glance at the agency's organizational chart will show the diversity of these groups whose interests are affected by the agency's powers of policy-making, administrative guidance, and licensing and permit issuance. They include shipping, maritime insurance, shipbuilding, ports and their facilities, warehouses, railways (both state run and private), automobiles, auto insurance, taxis, transit systems, freight industry, aviation, and airports. Well endowed and usually with excellent access to the political sector, these groups have the habit of rushing to LDP influentials, the MOT minister and PVM, and transportation dietmen (*Un'yuzoku*) who are placed in the key decision-making organs of the party and the Diet and are in a position to influence MOT policy decisions. This tendency is pronounced in the group's efforts to influence not only policy matters of importance that require party, cabinet, and Diet approval but also minute items of permits and licenses.

---

[67] *Asahi*, September 4, 1959.

[68] This does not mean that the career officials of central bureaucracy are immune from corruption and bribery scandals. The MOT and the MOC among others have had their shares of scandals involving licensing and permits. See Tahara, *Nihon no kanryō*, pp. 105–138 and 369–396.

A source close to the MOT likens contemporary transportation policy-making to a play staged by two actors—LDP politicians, including the minister and PVM, and corporate and interest groups. The role assigned to the MOT bureaucrat is merely that of a custodian looking after the playhouse and technical details of dramatic productions. He has no substantive power over what happens on the stage.[69] Fujimoto Tadashi, a former senior executive of the Tōa Air Lines and later a ranking official of the All-Japan Aviation Federation (the lobbying group for the aviation industry), concurs with this characterization as it applies to aviation policy-making. As he put it: "It is not that they [MOT bureaucrats] don't wish to get involved in dark aerial combats performed by politicians and enterprises. Rather, they cannot; they are not allowed to participate."[70] In a similar vein, a member of the *Un'yuzoku* compares the MOT to "a messenger boy" driven by LDP politicians, Japan's three airlines (Japan, All-Nippon, and Tōa), and the Ministry of Finance.[71] These colorful characterizations, extravagant as they may seem, are fitting descriptions of the reality of contemporary transportation (especially aviation) policy-making. A case in point involves the MOT minister of 1970-71, Hashimoto Tomisaburō, who was a leading member of the Satō faction and later the Tanaka faction and was implicated in the Lockheed scandal.

The testimonies of the then officials of the MOT's Aviation Bureau, including Sumita Shōji, director of the Aviation Management Department (*Kōkū kanri-bu*), provide the following picture of the making of a major decision on Japan Air Lines (JAL)—one of the many subdecisions involved in the Lockheed scandal. Under the Civil Aviation Law, the operational plans of all airlines, both the semigovernmental JAL and private lines, must be approved by the MOT, and acquisition of new aircraft by an airline constitutes a change in its business plan and is hence subject to approval by the MOT (i.e., transportation minister).[72] In late 1970 the MOT approved a JAL request for purchase of four super-sized Boeing passenger planes as part of the airline's full-scale modernization program to commence in 1972. The scheduled purchase was later given cabinet approval. In February 1971, only two months after the initial go signal, however, Sumita issued a new directive instructing JAL to postpone the introduction of the jumbo planes.

[69] Kanryō kikō kenkyūkai, *Un'yushō*, p. 88.
[70] Tahara, *Nihon no kanryō*, p. 118.
[71] Ibid., p. 19.
[72] *Japan Times Weekly,* October 15, 1983, p. 2.

What accounts for this volte face? In early February 1971 Minister Hashimoto had instructed AVM Machida Tadashi to proceed with the planned acquisition of the planes "after careful consideration has been given to every aspect of their safety." The delay was obviously intended to give an edge to JAL's rival, All-Nippon Airways, which later purchased a fleet of Lockheed's big TriStar planes. Machida conveyed the minister's directive to his subordinates, including Sumita, who in turn communicated the policy change to JAL. Sumita later admitted that the minister's "safety directive" had formed the basis of the new MOT administrative guidance instructing JAL to delay the introduction of the jumbo planes. Sumita added, however, that "the minister had never specified that the purchase plan should be delayed."[73]

The typical dietman-minister is an established member, if not an elder, of a *zoku* or two. He is often given the cabinet post in his *zoku*'s "sphere of influence." Once in the agency under the *zoku*'s jurisdiction, his *zoku* membership requires him to assume an activist role in advancing the interests of the *zoku*'s clientele groups in ministry policy-making, as several interviewed Diet staff members noted. This is especially the case with a junior *zoku* minister who needs to impress the clientele groups with his growing "delivery power." A member of the *Un'yuzoku* in the post of transportation minister will take seriously his representational role for transportation interests, just as a *Kensetsuzoku* (construction tribe) minister of construction will feel obligated to speak for the construction industry. This relationship between the *zoku* minister and the *zoku*'s clientele interests can roughly be compared to that between a Jesse Helms as the American secretary of agriculture and the agriculture-tobacco sectors of the economy. Other similar analogies can be made—a Russell Long (as either interior or energy secretary) and the oil industry, a John Tower (as defense secretary) and the defense industry, a John Dingell (as transportation or commerce secretary) and the auto industry, and so forth.

The close relationship between his *zoku* and the clientele groups is indeed a major factor governing the *zoku* minister's performance. Take education policy for illustration. Many existing programs of education policy, such as school lunches, physical education, aid to private education, and free texts, are firmly rooted in the symbiotic relationship between the *Bunkyōzoku*, on the one hand, and educational interest

---

[73] *Asahi*, December 4, 1979. The prosecution's indictment against Hashimoto charged that he had been bribed by All-Nippon airways into issuing the controversial administrative guidance to its archrival, JAL.

groups and enterprises (e.g., publishers), on the other. As an education specialist on the Diet staff put it, "No *Bunkyôku* minister of education can afford to ignore this reality if he wants to remain a full-fledged member of the *Bunkyôzoku* in the eyes of the support [clientele] groups."

Not only in education but also in other areas of public policy, the *zoku*'s clientele groups have a major influence upon the *zoku* minister's policy performance. As a Diet staff member stated, "On a policy proposal initiated by his *zoku*'s clientele groups and backed by his *zoku* elders, the minister must see that the proposal is converted into an agency policy or bill." A poor showing in the *zoku* minister's articulative performance during his tenure in office is sure to diminish his standing in the eyes of the clientele groups and thus weaken his ties with them. This means, among other things, declining monetary and electoral support for him from the groups; they will shift such support to the *zoku* actors more responsive to their demands.

On the whole, the *zoku* minister finds his bureaucracy more compliant than defiant toward policy proposals initiated by powerful clientele groups and promoted by him. This is so not only because he enjoys the inherent powers of a *zoku* minister vis-à-vis the agency under the *zoku*'s jurisdiction but also because the groups may well have special relationships with the agency bureaucrats as well. However, groups without such relationships with the bureaucracy or faced with its resistance must turn to their LDP *zoku* allies (including the *zoku* minister) who are far more sympathetic. Prodded by the clientele groups, either directly or indirectly (e.g., through his party, his faction, and an influential member of the *zoku gosanke*), the *zoku* minister usually assumes an activist role in the efforts to legislate the policies desired by the clientele groups. Armed with the *zoku*'s support, his ministerial authority, and the necessary data supplied by the groups (thus, he may have more specialized technical information about the issues than the responsible agency officials), he is indeed in a powerful position to play a initiating and directive role in agency policy-making.

The utility of the "minister-group linkage model" is powerfully brought home in the turbulent politics of health-welfare policy, in which the powerful JMA has worked through a multitude of "access points," including health-welfare ministers of *Kôseizoku* (health-welfare group) backgrounds. For illustration, let us look at a 1958 case involving the MHW and the JMA.

In that year the ministry was in a serious controversy with the JMA, then headed by the influential Takemi Tarō, over fee rates for doctors and hospitals. The JMA demanded an increase in the fees the doctors could collect; the MHW proposed a complex "unit fee system" that in the JMA's view not only meant rejection of the JMA's demand but also failed to take inflation into account. The deadlock dragged on, and as a way out, the MHW came up with a system of two fee-lists—List A applying to government-run hospitals, and List B to private clinics and their practitioners. To the JMA's disappointment, List B was to be based on the old fees that the doctors had been trying to raise. Naturally, the JMA rejected what the MHW officials viewed as an important compromise. The then MHW minister, Horiki Kenzō, was fully supportive of the agency's position and adamantly refused to retreat from it in his meetings with the JMA president.

Subsequently, in a cabinet reshuffle of June 1958, Horiki was replaced by Hashimoto Ryōgo, a veteran member of the party's *Kōseizoku* who had previously headed the health ministry. A bureaucrat-turned-politician of strong personality, widely considered sympathetic to the JMA,[74] the new minister agreed to reconsider the agency proposal. He held a series of meetings with Takemi, some without the participation of agency bureaucrats; out of these sessions came a new compromise that, when revealed, stunned the agency officials in charge. Although accepting the MHW's two-list formula in principle, the Hashimoto-Takemi compromise plan designated List B as flexible and subject to inflationary changes determined by the economic index. Below is a reminiscence by Takemi of what subsequently happened to the compromise plan, which was undoubtedly a boon to the JMA:

> [At the end of our meeting] Hashimoto said: "Well, our negotiations are finally over. I will make sure that the new agency guidelines reflect our compromise agreement." Then he called in AVM Tanabe Shigeo and Health Bureau Director Takada Masami. He told them: "This is the decision the JMA president and I have arrived at. Please see to it that the decision is carried out." Shocked and pale, Bureau Director Takada went at his minister, saying: "Minister, you have promised something outrageous. It would frustrate the ministry's plan for the next ten years." Turning to me, the bureau director said in all seriousness, "President, I would like to see this agreement nullified." I angrily retorted: "This is what your minister and I have agreed to. You have no right to intervene." I then told Hashimoto, "You should get rid of these guys who won't listen to you." I left them, saying: "I am leaving. You had better settle this among yourselves."[75]

---

74 *Asahi*, September 4, 1959.

According to a later account by the then deputy chief of the MHW Division of Medical Affairs, "The List B eventually adopted by the MHW was not based on the agency's position but on the revisions put forward by the JMA."[76]

Even a non-*zoku* minister (i.e., a newcomer to policy matters under the agency's jurisdiction) cannot be indifferent to the interests and needs of the *zoku*'s clientele groups. After all, he also is a primary target of group lobbying, as noted earlier. By assuming the highest post of the agency with appropriate jurisdiction over the groups, he has already gained an entrée to the party *zoku*, and when his ministerial term is over he will in all likelihood be a member of and even take important positions in intraparty groups (PARC divisions and investigative committees) that a legitimate *zoku* member is expected to join. Cognizant of the electoral and financial support that his embryonic relationships with the clientele groups bring to him, the non-*zoku* minister will try to impress the clientele leaders with his intraagency interventionist, articulative, and input-making abilities for them.

Even the non-*zoku* minister who has no desire to pursue an activist role in the ministry's corresponding *zoku* following his ministerial tenure may find it difficult to completely ignore the interests of the *zoku*'s clientele groups. As previously indicated, these groups typically have two-pronged political tactics—mobilizing the ministry's political contingent, on the one hand, and the leaders of the appropriate *zoku* and party leaders, on the other. Once the *zoku* elders are successfully mobilized by the groups, even the uncooperative non-*zoku* minister finds it judicious to go along. Such cooperation with the party *zoku* is necessary to secure party support of important agency programs, a major role expected of him.

All dietmen-ministers, inasmuch as they are elected officials, attempt to use their ministerial and agency powers in building and "nursing" their political constituencies—activities they cannot successfully undertake without ability to influence agency policy-making. Many succeed in these efforts. For *jitsuryokusha* dietmen with an eye on the party presidency (and premiership), constituency cultivation assumes special importance with regard to big business (*zaikai*) closely allied with the party. This is so because of the influential position *zaikai* holds in Japanese politics.

---

[75] Takemi Tarō, "Ishikaichō nijūgonen," April 9, 1982.

[76] Ibid.

The nature and extent of *zaikai*'s political power has been extensively debated. Some say that big business is so powerful that it has the controlling vote in Japanese policy-making—an opinion by no means confined to Marxian interpreters of Japanese society. Chitoshi Yanaga goes as far as to liken Japanese politics to "a dramatic production" in which big business is "the playwright as well as the financier."[77] Another scholar notes that *"zaikai* literally presides over Japanese society" and holds "the power of life and death" over *all* aspects of society.[78] Recent studies of *zaikai,* however, have shown that its power has been grossly overstated and, though large, is in reality quite limited and specialized, not generalized.[79] The issues of public policy in which *zaikai*'s influence is most pronounced are naturally economic (both domestic and international); even in these sectors its power is held in check by the pluralism of the contemporary Japanese polity.

Nevertheless, no serious student and practitioner of Japanese politics can overlook the strategic importance big business holds in key areas of economic and foreign (because of the economic basis of Japan's contemporary foreign policy) policy-making. Although the selection of the LDP president is an intraparty affair over which *zaikai* has no direct power, political and financial support from *zaikai* and corporate sources plays an important role in the process and thus is highly valued by all presidential aspirants, both actual and potential. Because the two key economic agencies (the MOF and MITI) are responsible for regulative, extractive, and distributive decisions vital to the business sectors, it makes sense that serious LDP presidential hopefuls covet the cabinet posts for these two agencies and that once in office they would want to demonstrate to *zaikai* elders that they are not *banshoku daijin* (figurehead ministers) who simply wear the ministry's hat. Rather, they must try to impress upon *zaikai* leaders their economic credentials, understanding posture toward business, and leadership over the reputedly assertive economic bureaucrats.

Cultivation of *zaikai* support takes on added importance for *jitsuryokusha* politicians without proper economic qualifications. Take

---

[77] Yanaga, *Big Business in Japanese Politics,* p. 29.

[78] Andō Yoshio, "Zaikai no chii to yakuwari" [The status and role of big business], *Ekonomisuto* 35, no. 1 (December 21, 1957): 16.

[79] Yung Park, "The Central Council for Education, Organized Business, and the Politics of Education Policy-making in Japan," *Comparative Education Review,* no. 19 (June 1975), pp. 296–311; Yung Park, "'Big Business' and Education Policy in Japan," *Asian Survey* 22, no. 3 (March 1982): 315–336; and Gerald Curtis, "Big Business and Political Influence," in *Modern Japanese Organization and Decision-making,* Vogel, pp. 33–70.

Tanaka Kakuei, who, unlike such former economic bureaucrats as Satō Eisaku and Fukuda Takeo, lacked strong economic credentials and solid linkage with the leadership of big business. During the days of his MOF and MITI portfolios he was able to cement his ties with *zaikai* elders. As the veteran *Yomiuri* political reporter Fukutomi Tōru put it, "Tanaka's decisiveness and political power [as demonstrated during his MITI tenure] strongly impressed not only MITI bureaucrats but also the mainstream *zaikai* elements." On textile trade with the United States, a thorny issue settled to *zaikai*'s satisfaction during Tanaka's tenure, "*Keidanren* president Uemura Kogorō, *Nisshō* chairman Nagano Shigeo, *Keizai dōyūkai* president Kikawada Kazutaka, and other *zaikai* leaders continually met with Minister Tanaka at MITI, and these interactions significantly strengthened his connections with the mainstream of *zaikai*." It is true that "Tanaka had lacked the kind of powerful support among *zaikai* leaders that Fukuda Takeo enjoyed, but from Tanaka's handling of Japanese-American textile and yen issues, *zaikai* leaders learned a great deal about his personality and way of thinking and must have arriveed at the conclusion that 'Tanaka should be able to handle the premier's job without any difficulty.'"[80]

A similar problem was faced by Nakasone Yasuhiro, who was also without the economic credentials of Kishi, Satō, Fukuda, and Ōhira, all products of the economic bureaucracy. Thus, much of the constituency building Nakasone practiced in his long and successful pursuit of the prime minister's post was directed at *zaikai* and carefully emulated the strategy brilliantly executed by Tanaka.[81] One important political axiom carefully adhered to by all prime ministerial hopefuls of today is constituency building in the community of powerful business elders and organizations; this requires demonstrated leadership vis-à-vis the key economic agencies.

The post of foreign minister, one of the top three cabinet posts (with the two economic offices), is also highly coveted by upwardly mobile dietmen, including prime ministerial hopefuls. This important platform certainly gives the occupant high public visibility and excellent opportunities to enhance his stature among voters and party members.

---

[80] Fukutomi, *Daijin*, pp. 108–109. Tanaka's successful courtship of *zaikai* during his MOF and MITI tenures is well described in ibid., pp. 88–112. One of the axioms widely subscribed to by prime ministerial hopefuls is "The man aiming at the premiership must first go after the post of MITI minister." See "Shinkeizai kakuryō no jitsuryoku: Esaki Masumi" [Power of new economic ministers: Esaki Masumi], *Chūō kōron* 94, no. 2 (February 1979): 52–53.

[81] Ibid., pp. 119–125.

For many LDP dietmen this post has served as a stepping-stone to the premiership (e.g., Miki, Fukuda, and Ōhira) or candidacy for the top post (e.g., Fujiyama Aiichirō). Abe Shintarō, considered a serious contender for the premiership, and foreign minister in the Nakasone cabinet, vigorously sought the foreign post to strengthen his credentials for the top party and government office. The foreign minister exercises supervisory powers over a key agency of foreign and economic policy whose actions affect Japan's economic and trade relations with other nations. For this reason the economic community has a particular interest, and its views are given consideration, in the selection of foreign ministers, as they are in the case of the top economic positions. Naturally, the minister's performance in the agency will be carefully watched and judged by *zaikai* elders.

In his lucid account of the LDP, Nathaniel Thayer argues that Japanese cabinets have had their shares of "chapeau ministers" (figurehead ministers). "Minor men are appointed to minor posts," as he puts it. "But the observer would be hard put to find a 'chapeau minister' among the foreign and top economic posts, and they are at the heart of the government." On major reason for this is the prime minister's considerable freedom to "select the right man for the right post" and to base his decisions on ability, not just on faction, as Thayer correctly points out.[82] This selection process, together with the need of ambitious economic and foreign ministers to impress the powerful business community, has certainly contributed to making ministers important actors of agency policy-making in both the economic and foreign-policy realms.

Finally, we come to the minister's role as an interest articulator for his constituency. Needless to say, for an elected dietman it is imperative to look after his constituents and their dominant interests. Many say that this is the role expected of him that outweighs all other considerations. If he is from a "marginal district," he is bound to be far more sensitive and responsive to his constituents' needs and interests. Under the competitive election system of contemporary Japan, even "political durables" or "heavyweights" cannot afford to be delinquent in attending to their constituents' requirements.

In the 1983 general election several senior and influential members of the party, unable to build sufficient voter support, failed in their reelection attempts. They included Kosaka Zentarō, a fifteen-term dietman who had held key cabinet and party posts including the foreign ministership and LDP PARC chairmanship; Kunō Chūji, a thirteen-term legislator who had held the MPT portfolio and was considered a leading

---

[82] Thayer, *How the Conservatives Rule Japan,* p. 206.

LDP expert on election laws; Tokai Motosaburō, a senior member of the Fukuda faction who had served as MOC and MHA minister; and Nishioka Takeo, then senior vice-chairman of the LDP PARC and one of the most influential members of the party *Bunkyōzoku.*

When, as a freshman dietman, Kaifu Toshiki, now a powerful elder of the Kōmoto faction, joined Diet and party organs handling commerce and industry, he had very much in mind what he calls the "overwhelming" interest of his district—small and medium-sized enterprises. It is not surprising that his primary policy efforts have been in matters that affect these interests,[83] although his range of interest and expertise has progressively widened with his rising political ambition (he is widely mentioned as one of the probable contenders for the party presidency in the late 1980s). Nor is it strange that the core of the League of Big City Dietmen (*Daitoshiken giin renmei*), a Diet group formed in 1979 to promote the interests of big cities, consists of such urban LDP dietmen as Harada Ken (Ōsaka) and Yasui Ken (Tokyo). That nearly 80 percent of LDP dietmen come from rural districts and belong to party organs on agricultural policy bears testimony to the legislators' sensitivity to constituency considerations.

All LDP dietmen covet seats in the cabinet, although not everyone will fulfill his ministerial ambition. The cabinet post is sought because it means, among other things, an increase of votes and a virtual guarantee of reelection. It gives the dietman-minister greater media visibility, increased opportunities for fund-raising, greater interest group support, and the ability to articulate constituency interests in agency policy-making and resource allocation. To effectively perform his articulative role, the minister needs to be much more than a chapeau minister; he must be an activist and interventionist minister. Indeed, all ministers use their new posts and powers to make friends at home, usually with considerable success. Former transportation minister Arafune Seijūrō's "infamous" decision to designate Fukaya as a new express train stop, as previously mentioned, is a telling demonstration of how far a minister can go to impress his constituents by exercising his ministerial authority.

The MAFF provides an interestig illustration of the minister's constituency nursing. One of the major distributive agencies, the MAFF is responsible for various subsidies, which constitute more than 14 percent of the total of all governmental subsidies to local government and private entities.[84] In 1979 the MAFF adopted, notwithstanding the budgetary

---

[83] "Bū-chan no seiji dōjō," p. 181.

[84] The following accounts draw heavily on excellent analyses by *Asahi shimbun*'s Hirose Michisada. See his *Hojokin to seikentō* [Government subsidies and the party in power]

constraints placed on it, a new subsidy program, Projects as Promotional Measures for Agricultural and Fishing Villages (*Nōrin gyogyō sonraku shinkō taisaku jigyō*), which was intended to "promote a sense of community among village residents." Created under the prompting of Minister Watanabe Michio, the new subsidies were for the construction of a variety of community projects, ranging from village halls to volleyball courts.

The new program was an instant hit; a large number of prefectures rushed their grant applications to the MAFF, which was to select local recipients in accordance with its supposedly objective criteria, including "broad geographic distribution of grantees." The final list of recipients announced by the MAFF, however, showed that the objective factors of interregional balance and fair share had obviously taken a back seat to political considerations, at least in some cases. One election district, the First Tochigi district, had no fewer than five rural communities awarded new MAFF grants, although no funding was allocated for some districts in Fukushima and Gifu prefectures.

Not surprisingly, the district in Tochigi blessed with the largest number of recipients was none other than Watanabe's own constituency. According to a Tochigi prefectural official in charge, the MAFF had indicated to the prefecture how many community grants it could have—the number that he thought was "quite high compared to other prefectures."[85] Five other prefectural districts, each blessed with four community grants, were also represented by influential agricultural dietmen. Satō Takashi of Niigata, a former MAFF PVM and a leading member of the LDP agricultural-policy group, was one of them; he then chaired the lower-house Committee on Agriculture, Forestry, and Fisheries. In view of Watanabe's successful support-building, it should not come as a surprise that in the 1980 elections he received the largest share of votes of the five legislators chosen in his district; in 1983 he got an even larger number of votes.

In 1980 Watanabe's subsidy program was given a "face-lifting" and a new name, and Mutō Kabun, Watanabe's immediate successor and then MAFF minister, became one of the beneficiaries of the new subsidy program. In 1979 Mutō's Gifu district had been one of the regions denied MAFF funding under Watanabe's program.[86]

---

(Tokyo: Asahi shimbun-sha, 1981), pp. 93–107 and 144–153.

  [85] Ibid., p. 146.

  [86] Ibid., p. 148.

Watanabe and Mutō are by no means atypical; such cases are found in other distributive agencies. Not only are new subsidy programs often instituted by new ministers that would favor their constituent interests but also, according to Hirose Michisada's meticulous analysis of the MAFF, the level of agency support under the existing subsidy programs goes up markedly for new ministers' districts.[87] The increased agency favoritism for the new minister may be attributable, at least in part, to the agency officials' "eager" desire to please their new chief; it may not involve his vigorous intervention in agency policy-making. New programs and any major changes in the ministry's existing allocation practices, however, may come about in a less voluntary manner; they may involve the minister's activism in agency policy-making and resource allocation.

---

[87] Ibid., pp. 149–151.

# VIII

# Conclusion

The portrayal of the contemporary Japanese cabinet minister presented in the preceding chapters deviates considerably from the popular assumption that places him in a subordinate position to the agency he heads. This notion of ministerial impotency may have been relevant to many of his predecessors of the 1950s who, new to their governing role, had to deal with the bureaucracy that had been "pampered" by SCAP rulers. The bureaucratic dominance thesis, however, overlooks the powerful activist ministers who, often helped by their political and bureaucratic experiences and using the opportunities afforded by the turbulent decade of the 1950s, reigned in various agencies of central officialdom. Moreover, when applied to the minister of today, the thesis fails to take into account the various factors that put him in a very powerful position vis-à-vis the bureaucracy.

The bureaucratic milieu within which the contemporary minister operates is more authoritarian, centralistic, and deferential than that of the 1950s. This trend, as widely suggested by interviewed officials, started after the conservatives merged to form the majority LDP in 1955; in this way the bureaucracy internally responded and adapted to the norms of "party government." After 1967 it accelerated, prompted by the party's declining base of popular support. In that year, the LDP's popular electoral showing dipped below 50 percent for the first time since its founding. The sense of urgency among the party dietmen required undivided loyalty from the bureaucracy; this in turn hastened the attitudinal changes within the bureaucracy that were well under way after 1955.

This development in organizational culture, perhaps inevitable because of the supreme status granted to the Diet (and its majority party) under the postwar constitution, has taken place while the larger political system, of which the bureaucracy is a part, has become increasingly pluralistic, competitive, and conflictual. Naturally, the organizational authoritarianism and centralism have had a dampening effect on the career officials' sense of policy-making efficacy, making them noticeably deferential toward their superiors and, especially, the political authorities. Organizational decision-making power has been progressively pushed upward, with lower- and middle-level officials relegated largely to supportive and elaborative roles for their more partisanized bureau directors and the AVM.

The authoritarian, centralistic, and deferential influences are so widespread throughout the officialdom that they have even affected such agencies as MITI and the MOF's Taxation Agency, noted for their traditions of assertiveness and *gekokujō;* seldom heard are the spirited policy debates by junior officials that frequently filled the corridors and offices of these economic agencies. In the meantime, the LDP dietmen, endowed with their legitimate authority as members of the "semipermanent" government party and socialized in their party's growing power vis-à-vis the bureaucracy, have increasingly come to see themselves as political suzerains standing above the career officials, expecting and receiving appropriate deference from them. "Prestigious" (*erai*), "haughty" (*kōman'na*), and "uppity" (*takabutta*), adjectives often used by interviewed bureaucrats to describe the "honorable dietmen" (*giin sensei*), are fitting allusions to the sense of weakness and inadequacy that the contemporary bureaucrats have in relation to the LDP dietmen.

It is not surprising, therefore, that a growing number of ambitious bureaucrats abandon their ministerial careers at midpoint to enter the "all-powerful" political sector (the LDP Diet contingent) rather than try to reach the pinnacle of the bureaucratic hierarchy (the post of AVM), only to toil under *erai* and often much younger LDP ministers. Unlike some of his predecessors of the 1950s who were often reticent about exercising their ministerial authority and prerogatives, the contemporary minister, with his "haughty" and assertive attitude toward the bureaucrats, finds the organizational culture of his agency most congenial.

The contemporary minister is not a political amateur without any governing or substantive policy experience. More often than not, he is a veteran dietman of at least twelve years with relevant experience in not only legislative and party but also bureaucratic sectors. Most LDP dietmen can justifiably claim a considerable level of expertise in a policy area or two. In other words, they are *zoku* dietmen. They are often appointed to the agencies under their *zoku*'s jurisdiction.

A *zoku* minister has some important advantages. He is already well acquainted with the agency's top personnel and policy orientations; his long association with the agency as a *zoku* member has made him "an agency insider." His extensive contacts with the *zoku*'s clientele groups have further contributed to his policy expertise. The bureaucrat–turned–*zoku* dietman at the helm of his parental agency has added advantages. He not only is intimately familiar with agency affairs but also is an *erai senpai* (successful senior) who has "made it" in politics and can command deference from his agency *kōhai* (juniors).

While looking after the interests of his old agency, which nurtured him, the dietman-minister must cater to other constituencies (e.g., his party, faction, voters, and clientele and support groups) that do not always see eye to eye with the agency. In his interactions with these political sectors over a long period, he is subjected to politicizing and partisanizing influences that modify his earlier policy perspectives shaped during his bureaucratic years—perspectives still held by his agency *kōhai*. In most cases a lower-house LDP dietman must have served in the Diet a minimum of twelve years or even longer before he can be considered for a cabinet appointment. Because of his extraagency commitments and his politicized, partisanized orientations, his policy views are not always congruent with those of his agency subordinates. He is by no means a mere cheerleader for his agency, dutifully adhering to the norms of *gekokujō*. Rather, he is a person of authority and power, experienced and versed in agency affairs, who is taken seriously by his *kōhai* subordinates.

The minister's intraagency power comes from not only his relevant experience and expertise but also his control over agency personnel matters. Undoubtedly, merit-related, intrabureaucratic factors are among the major criteria for most personnel decisions in all agencies. It is also true that the minister is endowed with the ultimate authority for all agency personnel decisions. The only intragovernmental check on this authority can come from the prime minister and his cabinet, whose approval legitimates all high-level personnel decisions. Their active intervention, however, is viewed as a deviation from the norm and is thus unlikely.

The minister's personnel authority gives him an ability not only to reward cooperative officials but also to punish those who oppose him and his policy priorities. He has formidable veto power over personnel recommendations from below that fail to reflect his strongly held views. Many a minister has exercised these powers, though ministers are occasionally subjected to extraagency limitations emanating from the LDP (e.g., factional and *zoku* considerations) and the agency's distinguished graduates. As the outspoken Kimura Takeo, twice a cabinet minister, put it, "The minister can do anything [in personnel matters] if he is so determined."[1] Career-conscious officials and especially partisanized

---

[1] Kimura, *Nihon o ayamaru kanryō*, p. 24.

higher officials are well aware of this and behave accordingly.

In the competitive, pluralistic setting of contemporary Japanese politics, the ministry must overcome a multitude of obstacles both within and without the government to obtain the necessary authorization, appropriation, and acceptance for its program. Agency efforts to enlist outside support and adjust conflicts with other sectors of the policy system take much of the agency's time and energy. Undoubtedly, agency bureaucrats play a major role in the mobilizational and coordinative efforts, but the widely touted notion of "bureaucratic centrality" obscures the participation of the dietman-minister and the relevant LDP PARC committees and *zoku*.

For controversial and costly programs, the minister's role is often pivotal. Often his successful mobilizational campaign drums up the necessary support and funding for the programs. His ability to articulate agency interests and mobilize external support readily translates into his intraagency power. As mentioned before, to be able to defend and promote an agency program to the party, MOF, Diet, and interest groups, he must perceive it as defensible; he must believe in it.

The contemporary minister, a popularly elected dietman of the ruling majority, has a variety of political constituencies and groups he must please and look after. They include his party, faction, intraparty *zoku,* clientele groups, and voters and their dominant interests. As an LDP member he must be responsive to party views and see to it that they are incorporated into agency policy. Of course, he is not the only actor representing party policy, but he is one of the key articulators. As a partisan advocate he can count on his party's backing. If supported by a strong intraparty consensus, the policy proposal he is promoting is seldom rejected by the agency officials unless they are backed by the prime minister—and the party president rarely defies his party's opinion consensus.

The minister's standing in the agency is also enhanced by his affiliation with an LDP faction whose interests and clientele groups must be protected and promoted. This is especially so if his faction happens to be one of the powerful "mainstream" groups. If appointed to a ministry closely tied to his faction (i.e., an agency that is heavily penetrated or "colonized" by his faction and has supplied a large contingent of its graduates to the faction), he is in a much more formidable position vis-à-vis the agency officials.

The minister's intraagency power is further bolstered if he comes from the PARC committees overseeing the agency and especially if he is one of the influential members of the appropriate *zoku* (e.g., *zoku gosanke*). Intimate, symbiotic relationships exist between his *zoku* and a multitude of special interest groups that are affected by agency decisions. To remain a legitimate *zoku* member and move upward in the groups' ratings of *zoku* members (on their ability to influence agency decision making; as their influence grows, the benefits accruing to them from the groups naturally increase), the *zoku* minister must see that the clientele groups' interests are protected. Armed with specialized information and political backing provided by these groups, the minister is often in a most advantageous position in dealing with agency officials. And while performing his promotional role for the clientele groups, he is powerfully backed by his *zoku* and its elders.

Interest groups under the ministry's jurisdiction tend to direct lobbying efforts more to even a non-*zoku* minister than to agency officials, although the latter are more involved in routine policy matters. The reason for this behavior is simple: the politician minister, who has the ultimate decision-making power for the agency, is more sympathetic to groups able to contribute to his political success. After all, when he leaves the minister's post he becomes, almost invariably, an influential member of the ministry's counterpart *zoku,* and an accommodative attitude toward the clientele groups during his incumbency is therefore politically advisable.

True, the tenure in office for a majority of cabinet ministers is about one year, hardly long enough to push through a major policy program. This brevity has been vigorously cited to lend credence to the notion of ministerial impotence. By belaboring the minister's short tenure, however, one obscures or overlooks some important facts about the contemporary minister. First of all, the one-year tenure is by no means a fixed rule adhered to by all ministers. Many ministers have served considerably longer terms, and every agency has had a sizable number of these "durables." Moreover, many ministers return to the same agencies for another term, even multiple terms.

Most significantly, under the Japanese parliamentary system, continuously dominated by the LDP, the cabinet minister, unlike many of his American counterparts, does not fade into obscurity when he leaves the agency. He retains his ties with the ministry. He not only will join (or return to) the appropriate PARC committees overseeing the ministry's activities but also will gain recognition as a member of the relevant party *zoku* whose blessings are required for all major ministry bills and whose support *chikara* is a sine qua non for obtaining budgetary allocations for major ministry programs. Although for many dietmen a ministerial portfolio constitutes the apex of a political career, many ministers do move up the mobility ladders, assuming progressively more important party and government posts that will allow them distinct advantages in dealing with the bureaucracy, including the ministries they headed. The end of ministerial tenure, therefore, by no means spells the end of influence over the agencies. For these reasons, the deception and lack of cooperation found in many bureaucracies are rare in Japan. Even after he leaves the agency, the minister can deal with those who sabotage his efforts. All these considerations deter politically astute and career-conscious officials from treating their ministers as transients who will go away in a year or so, never to bother them again.

Because of the assets and advantages he enjoys vis-à-vis the career bureaucracy, as discussed above, the contemporary minister is indeed in a powerful position. If he is determined to see his pet policy adopted and implemented, he will find his agency responsive and will be more likely to succeed than fail as long as his proposed policy is in accord with the agency's "organizational essence" and policy *nagare*. If his policy is a radical departure from these two powerful conservatizing forces, he will encounter a great deal of difficulty, not only because of intraagency opposition, but also because of extraagency groups supportive of the agency's organizational essence and policy *nagare*.

The foremost of these groups is, of course, the LDP—its leadership, faction leaders, *zoku* elders, and PARC and its committees. It is essential to recognize that not only the bureaucracy but also the ruling party has played a central role in the development of the agency's organizational essence and policy *nagare*. The organizational essence is defined, and policy *nagare* evolves, within this organizational essence *in concert with* the ruling party; at the least, these conservative constraints are tolerated and even embraced by the party because they are viewed as contributing to its electoral successes and as meeting other needs. A new mission can be added to or even imposed on the agency's organizational essence, to meet the changing needs of the government party. Likewise, the agency's policy direction can be altered to satisfy the new requirements of the party.

For illustration, let us take the MOE. The traditional scope of the MOE's organizational essence centers on the maintenance and promotion of the state (*kokuritsu*) and public (*kōritsu*) school systems.[2] This is attested to by the dominance within the agency of the two line bureaus in charge of the key sectors of public education, elementary-secondary and higher education. The agency's policy *nagare* in a large majority of

---

[2] Interview with Taki Yoshie, April 25, 1980.

areas under MOE jurisdiction (most of the agency's existing policy programs) is in line with this state and public education–oriented organizational essence of the ministry. This orientation has long been approved
and accepted by the party.

Since the 1960s, however, the MOE's mission has expanded, at the
urging of the party and its *Bunkyōzoku,* to include private education; as
a result the agency's policy toward private education has shifted from
"No governmental support, no control" to "Support and control."[3]
Again, it was largely at the prodding of the government party that in the
early 1950s the MOE's organizational essence took on a critical element,
"Fighting the Japan Teacher's Union"—the LDP's archenemy that one
MOE official described as occupying, in one way or another, "80 percent
of the attention" of the ministry.[4] Until 1952, when Okano Kiyotake, the
first dietman-minister of education, took over the MOE, the agency's relationship with the JTU was so cordial that it was depicted by the JTU
chairman Makieda Motofumi as "a relationship of cooperation."[5] Under
Okano, mandated to lead the MOE in the party-directed anti-JTU campaign, the MOE hastily but reluctantly shifted to its fateful anti-JTU posture, which has lasted to this date as a dominant component of its organizational essence.[6]

Not only in the MOE but also in other ministries, agency policy
directions and programs are prepared and established in anticipation of
the probable reactions of, and in consultation with, the LDP and its
PARC *zoku,* divisions, and committees. For all final programs, of
course, party approval is required.[7] Hence, Japan is no exception to the
dominant pattern of policy-making in Western European polities,
described by Joel D. Aberbach, Robert D. Putnam, and Bert A. Rockman in their pioneering study:

> Fundamentally, most descriptions of policymaking in Western na-
> tions concur that policy must be acceptable to the top political
> leadership, as embodied in the ruling party or parties.

---

[3] For discussions of the party's dominant role in the MOE's expanded organizational
essence, see Nishioka, "Shigaku shinkō," pp. 114–119. See also Kitamura Kazuyuki,
"Nihon ni okeru 'chūkōtō kyōiku' no seidoteki kōzō" [The structure of the post-secondary
education system in Japan], *Daigaku ronshū* [Essays in higher education] of Hiroshima
University, no. 7 (1979), pp. 23–37.

[4] Kusayanagi, *Kanryō ōkokuron,* pp. 176–177.

[5] Makieda Motofumi, *Kyōiku eno chokugen* [Speaking out on education] (Tokyo: Mainichi shimbunsha, 1972), pp. 144–153.

[6] Totsuka and Kio, *Mombushō,* pp. 210–215.

[7] Interview with Okuno Seisuke, April 23, 1979.

Policymaking is thus a kind of dialectic, in which the "law of anticipated reactions" normally governs the behavior of bureaucrats. Consequently, in broad political and ideological terms most major policies reflect the preferences of party and parliamentary majorities.[8]

One crucial difference, however, distinguishes Japan from the Western European nations. In most of the European polities the major political parties have held or shared governmental power on an alternating basis and thus have not enjoyed prolonged "monopoly" over the bureaucracy; the governing party in Japan has held power continuously since 1948 and thus has deeply penetrated the higher echelons of the bureaucracy far more extensively than have any of the Western European governing parties. The closest approximations of the Japanese case are (1) Italy, where the Christian Democrats led coalition governments for most of the postwar era and significantly partisanized the bureaucracy; and (2) the twenty-three-year reign of the French rightist-centrist groups (Gaullists and Giscardians), during which partisanization of the bureaucracy occurred on a large scale.[9]

Japan has gone further than either Italy or France in the partisanization of the bureaucracy, and its ruling party is far more involved in the governing process. In other words, the LDP, through its influentials and its PARC organs, has played an intimate role not only in the development of policy *nagare* but also in the making of secondary decisions supportive of policy *nagare*. It is in the context of this party-bureaucracy collaboration and symbiosis that one must respond to a recent Japanese characterization of the minister's role in economic policy-making: in most situations of policy-making, the minister seldom deviates from the path charted by his agency prior to his appointment.[10] To do so would be to go against not only the agency but also the party and its divisions (and *zoku*) involved in agency policy-making.

LDP involvement in the development of the agency's organizational essence and policy *nagare* and programs is well illustrated in the so-called administrative reform movement of the 1980s, initiated in 1981 with the creation of the Second Ad Hoc Commission on Administrative Reform. Intended to streamline the administrative structures and trim the programs that had raised the government's debt to an all-time high

---

[8] Joel D. Aberbach, Robert D. Putnam, and Bert A. Rockman, *Bureaucrats and Politicians in Western Democracies* (Cambridge: Harvard University Press, 1981), p. 248.

[9] Suleiman, *Politics,* pp. 358–371.

[10] Ōtake, *Gendai Nihon no seiji kenryoku keizai kenryoku,* pp. 84–85.

(by the end of 1983 the total sum of outstanding bonds had reached $479 billion),[11] the drive for "small government" was supported by several key sectors of Japanese politics.

First, big business, disturbed by the growing governmental debt and wastefulness, argued that the government should put its house in order. This urging was reasonable because business had proved its own efficiency by successfully weathering the "oil shock" and the international recession of the 1970s.[12] Also, the economy-minded MOF has consistently but unsuccessfully fought incessant claims on the shrinking national treasury. Both Suzuki Zenkō, then prime minister, and Nakasone Yasuhiro, his AMA minister, recognized the "political" logic behind "small government" as an alternative to taking the unpopular route of raising taxes to continue financing government programs. Suzuki felt that he would be able to consolidate his position by tackling the difficult task of administrative reform and spending reduction. With an eye on the coveted premiership, Nakasone also had a political motive for his reformist posture—his successful performance as head of the AMA (the agency responsible for reform of administration) would prove his leadership skills, improve his standing in the eyes of *zaikai* elders, and strengthen his ties with them.[13]

The administrative reform commission, composed of business elders, labor leaders, scholars, and former bureaucrats, was entrusted with the task of working out reform recommendations—a Sisyphean undertaking of not only reviewing all costly programs but also consensus building among all key groups and interests in support of ways to "rationalize" (*gōrika*) these programs. The commission's recommendations, however, were considerably different from the reformist hopes of the MOF bureaucrats and *zaikai* leaders. In the course of the commission's two-year work "ambitious plans for reform were cut down to size due to resistance" by institutions and groups having "a large stake in the status quo." The commission did identify various programs in need of rationalization, such as agricultural policy, social insurances, education, and taxation, but only one of the thirty-three wasteful subsidy programs cited by the commission was singled out for outright abolition.[14]

---

[11] *Japan Times Weekly,* March 19, 1983.

[12] For articles presenting *zaikai* positions in favor of administrative reform, see *Keidanren geppō* 29, no. 10 (October 1981); and Hirose Michisada, "Gyōsei kaikaku to jimintō" [Administrative reform and the Liberal-Democratic party], *Sekai,* no. 429 (August 1981), pp. 248–249.

[13] *Japan Times Weekly,* April 8, 1981. See also Yomiuri shimbun seijibu, *Dokyumento gyōsei,* pp. 12–28.

[14] *Japan Times Weekly,* March 19, 1983.

Over matters involving public corporations (*kōsha*), however, the reformist forces have made significant gains. In accordance with the recommendations of the administrative reform commission, the Diet in 1984 passed laws that broke up and privatized two mammoth public corporations: the Nippon Telegraph and Telephone Public Corporation (*Nihon denshin denwa kōsha*) and the Japan Tobacco and Salt Public Corporation (*Nihon senbai kōsha*). The laws went into effect in April 1985. The denationalization marks a major milestone in the Nakasone government's efforts to curb governmental spending and increase managerial efficiency and to respond to calls from other countries (especially the United States) to open its markets. The measure also attests to Prime Minister Nakasone's success in what E. E. Schattschneider calls the "socialization of conflict": arousing public opinion against antireform elements committed to the maintenance of the public corporation.[15] The chronically deficit-ridden JNR has also been affected by the reform movement, although its future is far from settled. The reform commission recommended that the JNR be dismembered into autonomous units, each placed under private management. The JNR and its LDP and government allies, however, have stated that they would accept this "radical" solution only as the last resort, after different measures have been tried to achieve necessary rationalization and efficiency in JNR management.[16]

In much of the literature on administrative reform, the bureaucracy—line agencies—is seen as the chief source of resistance to "small government," with other institutions, including the LDP and interest groups, performing a supportive and cheerleading role for the bureaucracy. For example, one scholar argues that the MOF-initiated proposal of terminating the government's free textbook policy was aborted largely by the MOE, which, like other ministries, is "almost all-powerful" in its area of jurisdiction—and that other groups, including the LDP, merely contributed to its defeat. It was only natural that the MOE, "the most powerful" actor, as he put it, in the education-policy system, played the pivotal role in emasculating the money-saving proposition.[17] Though pointing to the important role played by the MOE in

---

[15] For discussion of Schattschneider's concept, see his *The Semi-Sovereign People* (New York: Holt, Rinehart and Winston, 1960), pp. 1–19.

[16] For an excellent analysis of the conflict between reformist forces and the "railway subgovernment" opposed to radical reform of the JNR, see Takeshita Yuzuru, "Daini rinchō to gyōsei kaikaku" [The Second Ad Hoc Commission on Administrative Reform and the reform of administration], in Nakamura and Takeshita, *Nihon no seisaku katei,* pp. 250–289.

[17] Elliott, "The 1981 Administrative Reform," p. 771.

this particular episode of "small government" politics, the argument belittles the LDP's role—in fact, dominant—which was necessitated by what the party felt was at stake.

The controversial program, by no means cheap, was instituted in 1963 at the prodding of LDP dietmen, including Hasegawa Takashi and Araki Masuo (then respectively MOE PVM and minister in the Ikeda cabinet), who viewed it as fulfilling the constitutional provision that "compulsory education shall be free."[18] The program also "allows the [Liberal-Democratic] party to have a large voice in what goes into textbooks" and to reject values and ideas incongruent with the party's ideology.[19] Hence, the textbooks, approved by LDP-leaning MOE inspectors, can counter leftist views held by JTU card–carrying teachers. The free text policy, therefore, is very much in keeping with the party's policy of political socialization as well as its long-standing anti-JTU posture. Moreover, many LDP dietmen and especially *Bunkyōzoku* members have developed special ties with publishing and inspection interests.[20] Thus, it is understandable that the party was in the forefront of the battle against the reform commission's plan to phase out the free textbook program.

This program is one of the many governmental programs labeled "too costly" or "wasteful" by the MOF and the reform commission. Inasmuch as they are largely responsibilities added to the bureaucracy's original jurisdiction at the LDP's instigation and prodding, the antireform movement must be viewed more in terms of party interests and leadership than in terms of bureaucratic primacy. Thus, efforts to institute the much-heralded small government must be directed at not only the line agencies administering the costly programs but also the relevant party groups (e.g., *zoku*) and their clientele interests that are the primary beneficiaries of the programs. Larger efforts must be aimed at the party, which holds the key to the success of any reform attempt.

Miyazaki Teru, a business (*zaikai*) member of the reform commission and a veteran member of the Administrative Supervision Commission (*Gyōsei kanri iinkai*) (supposedly a watchdog agency over the bureaucracy), provides us with a rare insider's view of the difficulties his reform commission faced because of the party's opposition. Recalling

---

[18] Interviews with Hasegawa Takashi, September 17, 1981, and Mori Yoshiro, September 21, 1981. Hasegawa is widely viewed as the key individual responsible for the adoption of this program. This was confirmed by several interviewed former MOE officials, including Miyaji Shigeru.

[19] Yomiuri shimbun seijibu, *Dokyumento gyōsei,* pp. 66–67.

[20] Miyazaki, "Kigyō katsuryoku," p. 3.

his commission's encounter with party dietmen, Miyazaki said, "When we met with members of the LDP PARC, we were simply bombarded with a barrage of rebuttals on almost every issue of reform." The dietmen's position was that because they were "the very persons responsible for the formulation of the laws in question," they were "well acquainted with the circumstances" under which the laws were adopted, and that "we, without this knowledge, had no business to raise doubts" about the programs. "We all saw the logic of this position."

Miyazaki was particularly struck by the power of *zoku* members of the party. Speaking of one powerful *zoku*, the *Dōrozoku* (road dietmen), he noted, "We came to know how pertinacious (*shitsuyō*) the *Dōrozoku* is on matters regarding highways and roads." The reform commission originally entertained, as the MOF had hoped, the idea of "reviewing and revising" (*minaosu*) the existing vehicle weight tax (*jidōsha jūryōzei*) to create an additional base of tax revenue. The proposed recommendation was vehemently opposed by the *Dōrozoku,* and consequently the controversial *"minaosu"* was watered down simply to read "examine" (*kentō*)—a noncommittal wording that did not necessarily presage any change in the existing policy.[21]

The situation in Japan is not very different from what Morris P. Fiorina calls "the Washington establishment," whose "linchpin" is Congress, not the bureaucrats. As he sees it, congressmen, whose primary goal is reelection, seek "electoral credits" by fighting for and establishing various federal programs for their constituents. "The legislation

---

[21] Ibid. Miyazaki is not the only member of the reform commission attesting to the LDP's primary role in opposing the reform efforts. There are many others. Iijima Kiyoshi, a leading member of the commission, has suggested that the overall reform attempt consists of three components, the *foremost* of which is "political"—to "change the mentality of politicians." See "Kanryō seijika ni 'hoi' sareta rinchō no uchimaku" [Facts about the temporary commission surrounded by bureaucrats and politicians], a panel discussion by commission members, *Bungei shunjū* 60, no. 9 (August 1982): 375. In accounting for the government's policy status-quo-ism, Tanimura Hiroshi, a former MOF AVM, takes issue with the notion that bureaucrats are inherently conservative and lack flexibility. He says: "It is a problem involving those behind the administration." See Ōkita, *Nihon kanryō jijō,* pp. 171–172. For perceptive analyses by a senior *Asahi shimbun* researcher of the close relationship between the LDP's electoral strategy and the existing governmental programs, see Hirose, "Gyōsei kaikaku to jimintō," pp. 245–257; and by the same author, "Jimintō no rieki haibun shisutemu" [The LDP system of value distribution], *Seikai,* no. 437 (April 1982), pp. 43–50. Also useful is Hirose's recent article, " 'Rieki bunpai shisutemu' wa henkashitaka?" [Has the "system of value distribution" changed?], *Sekai,* no. 448 (March 1983), pp. 105–113. For an analysis by a former Home Affairs Ministry official of the LDP's dominant role in the government's rural programs, see Katō, "Toshi no fukushū," pp. 72–89.

is drafted in very general terms, so some agency, existing or newly established, must translate a vague policy mandate into a functioning program." This is "a process that necessitates the promulgation of numerous rules and regulations and, incidentally, the trampling of numerous toes." Then comes a stage in which "aggrieved constituents petition their congressmen to intervene in the complex decision processes of the bureaucracy." This cycle "closes when the congressman lends a sympathetic ear, piously denounces the evils of bureaucracy, intervenes in the latter's decision, and rides a grateful electorate to ever more impressive electoral showings. Congressmen take credit coming and going. They are the alpha and the omega." Therefore, the popular frustration with Washington's permanent bureaucracy, though "partly justified," is largely "misplaced resentment," for the basic problems are congressmen, not the bureaucrats. Fiorina goes on to note:

> The bureaucracy serves as a convenient lightning rod of public frustration and a convenient whipping boy for congressmen. But so long as the bureaucracy accommodates congressmen, the latter will oblige with ever larger budgets and grants of authority. Congress does not just react to big government—it creates it. All of Washington prospers. More and more bureaucrats promulgate more and more regulations and dispense more and more money. Fewer and fewer congressmen suffer electoral defeat.[22]

In this system of legislative-bureaucratic symbiosis, congressmen, like LDP dietmen in Japan, have a unique ability "to expedite and influence bureaucratic decisions." This ability "flows directly from congressional control over what bureaucrats value most"—higher budgets, reauthorization of old programs, and authorization of new programs. Most such decisions are perfunctory because of the close ties between the bureaucracy and its congressional counterpart (authorization and appropriation committees and subcommittees). In dealing with congressmen, the "bureaucrats do not forget the basis of their agencies' existence." When a congressman calls about an administrative regulation, the bureaucrats positively respond because they consider "his accommodation a small price to pay for the goodwill its cooperation will produce, particularly if he has any connection to the substantive committee or the appropriations subcommittee to which it reports."[23]

Like the United States Congress, the LDP and its influentials have been intimately involved in the development and evolution of the

---

[22] Morris P. Fiorina, *Congress* (New Haven: Yale University Press, 1977), p. 49.
[23] Ibid., p. 43.

bureaucracy's organizational essence and policy *nagare.* Hence, it is not quite accurate to assume that these conservatizing forces are purely bureaucratic limitations upon the minister; rather, they are party-bureaucracy restraints. For this reason they are all the more limiting, and the minister is reluctant to go against them. To push through a policy proposal viewed as a major departure from the organizational essence or policy *nagare,* he has to persuade not only the ministry's bureaucrats but also the party and especially its appropriate PARC *zoku,* without whose blessings no agency action can be undertaken. Thus, many a minister is simply averse to altering the policy *nagare* and, like many of his agency subordinates, settles for an incrementalist posture, even though intraagency persuasion and support mobilization are quite simple once he has secured blessings from the party.

# DATE DUE

| | | | |
|---|---|---|---|
| 10 1995 | | | |
| | | | |
| | | | |
| | | | |
| | | | |
| | | | |
| | | | |
| | | | |
| | | | |
| | | | |
| | | | |
| GAYLORD 234 | | | PRINTED IN U. S. A. |

## INSTITUTE OF EAST ASIAN STUDIES PUBLICATIONS SERIES

CHINA RESEARCH MONOGRAPHS (CRM)

6. David D. Barrett. *Dixie Mission: The United States Army Observer Group in Yenan*, *1944*, 1970 ($4.00)
7. John S. Service. *The Amerasia Papers: Some Problems in the History of US-China Relations*, 1971 ($6.00)
9. Jonathan Porter. *Tseng Kuo-fan's Private Bureaucracy*, 1972 ($5.00)
10. Derek J. Waller. *The Kiangsi Soviet Republic: Mao and the National Congresses of 1931 and 1934*, 1973 ($5.00)
11. T. A. Bisson. *Yenan in June 1937: Talks with the Communist Leaders*, 1973 ($5.00)
12. Gordon Bennett. *Yundong: Mass Campaigns in Chinese Communist Leadership*, 1976 ($4.50)
sp. John B. Starr and Nancy A. Dyer. *Post-Liberation Works of Mao Zedong: A Bibliography and Index*, 1976 ($7.50)
13. Philip Huang, Lynda Bell, and Kathy Walker. *Chinese Communists and Rural Society*, *1927-1934*, 1978 ($5.00)
14. Jeffrey G. Barlow. *Sun Yat-sen and the French*, *1900-1908*, 1979 ($4.00)
15. Joyce K. Kallgren, Editor. *The People's Republic of China after Thirty Years: An Overview*, 1979 ($5.00)
16. Tong-eng Wang. *Economic Policies and Price Stability in China*, 1980 ($8.00)
17. Frederic Wakeman, Jr., Editor. *Ming and Qing Historical Studies in the People's Republic of China*, 1981 ($10.00)
18. Robert E. Bedeski. *State-Building in Modern China: The Kuomintang in the Prewar Period*, 1981 ($8.00)
19. Stanley Rosen. *The Role of Sent-Down Youth in the Chinese Cultural Revolution: The Case of Guangzhou*, 1981 ($8.00)
21. James H. Cole. *The People Versus the Taipings: Bao Lisheng's "Righteous Army of Dongan,"* 1981 ($7.00)
22. Dan C. Sanford. *The Future Association of Taiwan with the People's Republic of China*, 1982 ($8.00)
23. A. James Gregor with Maria Hsia Chang and Andrew B. Zimmerman. *Ideology and Development: Sun Yat-sen and the Economic History of Taiwan*, 1982 ($8.00)
24. Pao-min Chang. *Beijing, Hanoi, and the Overseas Chinese*, 1982 ($7.00)
25. Rudolf G. Wagner. *Reenacting the Heavenly Vision: The Role of Religion in the Taiping Rebellion*, 1984 ($12.00)
26. Patricia Stranahan. *Yan'an Women and the Communist Party*, 1984 ($12.00)
sp. Lucie Cheng, Charlotte Furth, and Hon-ming Yip, Editors. *Women in China: Bibliography of Available English Language Materials*, 1984 ($12.00)
27. John N. Hart. *The Making of an Army "Old China Hand": A Memoir of Colonel David D. Barrett*, 1985 ($12.00)
28. Steven A. Leibo. *Transferring Technology to China: Prosper Giquel and the Self-strengthening Movement*, 1985 ($15.00)
29. David Bachman. *Chen Yun and the Chinese Political System*, 1985 ($15.00)
30. Maria Hsia Chang. *The Chinese Blue Shirt Society: Fascism and Developmental Nationalism*, 1985 ($15.00)
31. Robert Y. Eng. *Economic Imperialism in China: Silk Production and Exports*, *1861-1932*, 1986 ($15.00)

KOREA RESEARCH MONOGRAPHS (KRM)

2. Dai-kwon Choi, Bong Duck Chun, and William Shaw. *Traditional Korean Legal Attitudes*, 1980 ($8.00)
4. Choon-ho Park, Jae Schick Pae, and Nam-Yearl Chai. *Korean International Law*, 1982 ($8.00)
5. William Shaw. *Legal Norms in a Confucian State*, 1981 ($10.00)
6. Youngil Lim. *Government Policy and Private Enterprise: Korean Experience in Industrialization*, 1982 ($8.00)